THE WEBBS, FABIANISM AND FEMINISM

The Webbs,
Fabianism and Feminism
Fabianism and the Political Economy of Everyday Life

Edited by

PETER BEILHARZ
La Trobe University

CHRIS NYLAND
Monash University

Ashgate

Aldershot • Brookfield USA • Singapore • Sydney

Published by
Ashgate Publishing Ltd
Gower House
Croft Road
Aldershot
Hants GU11 3HR
England

Ashgate Publishing Company
Old Post Road
Brookfield
Vermont 05036
USA

British Library Cataloguing in Publication Data
The Webbs, fabianism, and feminism. - (Avebury series in
   philosophy)
   1. Webb, Beatrice, 1858-1943 2. Webb, Sidney 3. Socialism
   4. Feminism
   I. Beilharz, Peter II. Nyland, Chris

Library of Congress Catalog Card Number: 98-71957

ISBN 1 84014 307 X

Printed and bound by Athenaeum Press, Ltd.,
Gateshead, Tyne & Wear.

Contents

Acknowledgements

The authors and publishers wish to thank the following who have kindly given permission for the use of copyright material.

RKP publishers for article, Peter Beilharz, (1992), 'Fabianism' in Peter Beilharz, *Labour's Utopias - Bolshevism, Fabianism, Social Democracy, RKP, London, pp. 51 - 92 and 135 - 141.*

For article Peter Beilharz (1992), 'Fabianism and Marxism: Sociology and Political Economy', *Australian Journal of Political Science*, Volume 27, pp 137 - 146.

Industrial Relations Society of Australia for article: Chris Nyland and Di Kelly (1992), 'Beatrice Webb and the National Standard for Manual Handling', *The Journal of Industrial Relations*, Volume 34, number 2, pp 307 - 334.

Peter Groenewegen and the Centre for the Study of the History of Economic Thought, and Edward Elgar Publishing Ltd, for article, Chris Nyland and Gaby Ramia (1994), 'The Webbs and the Rights of Women' in Peter Groenewegen (ed.), *Feminism and Political Economy in Victorian England,* Edward Elgar, Aldershot, pp. 147 - 173.

Ray Jureidini (editor) *Labour and Industry,* for article, Chris Nyland, (1995), 'Beatrice Webb as Feminist', *Labour and Industry*, Volume 6, number 2, pp. 67 - 86.

We would also like to express our warm appreciation to David Freeman for reading the completed manuscript and offering a number of valuable observations.

February 1998

1 Fabianism and Feminism: The Political Economy of Everyday Life

Peter Beilharz

Fabianism has long been viewed as unfashionable, ordinary, reformist. The essays collected together in this volume do not seek to deny these kinds of characterisations so much as to revalue them.

Fashion in politics and in scholarship alike is often dangerous. Modernity continues to throw up particular fields of social problems ranging from deprivation to the lack of meaning in everyday life; these perennials need to be viewed as central, not marginal. Fashion is arguably a major issue within the social sciences today; given the connection between publishing and commodification, more and more books and papers appear confirming dominant interpretations as they are thrown off, with the attendant marginalisation of alternative views. The increasing implication of scholarship and media produces a kind of hip mainstream for which all other arguments are old hat. But there is, or ought be, more at risk in committed scholarship than this. Call us old-fashioned, but our intention in these essays is to return to older paths where style was connected to clarity, and complexity was no immediate excuse for obscurity.

The charge that Fabianism is ordinary is perhaps more interesting, though it is also clearly connected to the prominence of fads and fashions within contemporary scholarship. To say that something is 'ordinary', rather than avant-garde or exotic is obviously to denigrate, to devalue. For our part, in these essays, we seek to revalue the place of the ordinary rituals and practices of everyday life and to reappraise their significance for the social sciences. The oldest dismissive tease against Fabianism, that it is nothing more than 'gas and water socialism', too easily belittles the extraordinary significance of these basic provisions to everyday life. While fashionable arguments across the liberal arts thus arc in and around such veritable conceptual monsters as Eurocentrism, few stop to wonder at our incredible good fortune that the taps do indeed function in Melbourne or in Chicago, while various peoples in other cities and towns go without. Apparently it is all too tedious, this older insistence that human suffering is a central problem which does have some ordinary, material and remediable aspects such as those to do with housing, labour conditions or domestic technology arrangements. And then reformism is made to seem too trivial, lack lustre, too pathetically immersed in the ordinary details of everyday life to warrant the intellectual enthusiasm or political concern of the self-styled avant-garde which claims to lead scholarship forward.

It is for reasons such as these that we focus here upon the political economy of everyday life. After a remarkable revival into the 1970s, political economy lapsed again, partly because of its over-reliance on Marxism and a relative indifference towards culture, which in the meantime has been remobilised via cultural studies and has itself become a major concern in management and organization studies. Of course economy itself can be conceived as a culture, and it certainly is inconceivable outside of culture. At the same time, the further progress of global capitalist development into the nineties makes even more apparent the ongoing problems of the production and distribution of wealth. Deprivation and suffering persist in the most horrible of forms. Some of the older marxist or social democratic approaches to economics may have presumed that the goal of equality or the principled opposition to inequality were core socialist concerns, from which all else in terms of human elevation would follow. The Fabian sensibility was less inclined towards the end of inequality than towards the removal of socially constructed impediments to human development, whether social or individual. Issues such as health, education and sanitation thus became both politically urgent and, yet, preconditional rather than strictly necessary causes of possible progress. But it remains easy to sneer at Chadwick while reading Derrida.

Fabianism thus rests, still, upon premises which are unfashionably humanist. Again, this may indicate its location outside the intellectual avant-garde, which for some thirty years has become enmeshed with the trend called theoretical anti-humanism. Some of the early structuralist critique of humanism found its target in those more simplistic views that men, or men and women, were capable of anything, that men could be as gods. In some other regards, however, antihumanism has been one of those hallmark trends indicating that interest has turned away from the lives of ordinary people (like us) and become lost within textual or formalistic pretensions of the trendsetters. At the same time, most postmodern theories rest on plainly liberal or reformist premises when it comes to debates over justice, rights or cruelty. Universalism has been vastly criticized and is nevertheless still practised; for we are all still humanists, or inhabitants of a humanist culture, for which improvement remains possible if less imperative than it may earlier have seemed.

Inasmuch as feminism, too, has been caught up with philosophy and identified with poststructuralism, ordinary feminism of the kind historically tied to humanism and reformism has also been devalued. On occasion, indeed, its existence has been denied, as though feminism were or could be a monolithic tradition or form of identity politics which only the vanguard could define or defend. The consequences of these definitional slides sometimes seem uncomfortably reminiscent of those around Marxism in the seventies. In that phase, it was dogmatically asserted by scientific Marxists, not least the followers of Louis Althusser, that the only kind of real socialism was Marxism and that, by further reduction, there was only one proper Marxism, that of Althusser. Into the nineties we have been witness to apparently similar kinds of disputes in feminism about who the 'real' feminists are. Semantically speaking, it is self-evident that feminists put women first upon their political agendas and on their lists of theoretical curiosities and research projects. At the same time, varieties of feminism abound. Yet the politics of certainty has led to the denial that Fabians such as Beatrice Webb were indeed feminists. By what criteria? That they were somehow less radical than us, today? The enormous condescension of posterity has also meant the diminution of contributions like Webb's, and the consequent narrowing of the sense of feminism's richness and diversity.

Just as we seek the reaffirmation of Fabianism's value, so here do we argue for something like an ordinary feminism. Ordinary in the sense of practical, concerned with the issues which earlier reformist women and later materialist feminists were concerned, about the organisation and regulation of everyday life, domestic labour, the life of the household and of working life. Now these latter concerns are all in one sense or another sociological, or caught up with the sphere of political economy. As Naomi Black and others have argued, they are concerns which in an earlier period were central to feminism as social feminism and sociology as a social movement (Black, 1989). Now sociology has become part of the state, in effect, and the women's movements have taken up different positions in distinct parts of its terrain, from the academy to policy units within the bureaucracies. Australian feminisms have flourished in both regards, in particular as philosophy and as femocracy. Femocracy itself is arguably a variation of the ordinary reforming feminism which held up extraordinary earlier local movements like the Women's Co-operative Guild or the Fabian Women's Research Group. Only somehow the legitimacy conferred upon more recent femocracy is less often granted to ordinary feminism, the 'gas and water' feminism which we associate with activists and writers such as Beatrice Webb or Virginia Woolf. This was - to open a different issue - a middle class feminism based upon the methods of social investigation, journalist muckraking and publicity, advocacy, and sociological explanation.

This different issue - the issue of class - is both important and interesting, yet again has been marginalised from discussion. Critics and participants in these processes historically seem to have a great deal of difficulty even acknowledging the middle class impetus of the reform process, of feminism, and even of socialism. Socialists have sometimes been imagined, falsely, as uniformly proletarian in origin. After various intersections with Marxism, some feminisms seem simply to have avoided the issue of class difference or antagonism. The symmetries across the history of Marxism and feminism are sobering. Where one postulated a unitary working class actor, the other implied some kind of magical harmony among women regardless of place, time or interest. Postcolonial feminism punctured this sense of harmonism when it came to the question of the relations between women in first world and third. But if the third world is in the first, then class relations also exist at home. This is not to suggest that middle class feminism or socialism is ridiculous; to the contrary. These matters become problematical only in denial, as when middle class actors deny their origins or interests in the process of social ventriloquism. Historically speaking, both socialism and feminism have class sources in both the working and middle classes, and it is this double coincidence which has led to some great historic alliances, those which for example steered the reform process in Britain after 1945 or in Australia after 1972. Alliances, however are based on common interests, on association not on identity, and their success depends on the recognition of difference.

The residual notion that women compose something like a class against the class of men, serves to obscure the fact that women themselves belong to different classes. Again, this is not to posit insuperable antagonism between women as a fixed principle, so much as it is to indicate that alliances need to be forged across these differences. What this opens is the possibility that some middle class women (and men) might be prepared to acknowledge that their own needs are not the most pressing. This, we suggest, is the logic of the practice in cases such as Beatrice Webb's. Recognising the limits of her own kind of life, even painfully, Beatrice Webb nevertheless behaved as though there was a constituency of working class women and their families whose marginalisation in the social system was more urgent.

These matters have become more difficult to discern because of the tendency to turn Beatrice Webb into either a heroine or else a virago. The contrast between Webb's reception and that of the leading American Fabian feminist, Charlotte Perkins Gilman, is an interesting one. Gilman has become a major reference point, alongside du Bois, in sociology. Webb has been more difficult. Webb's private life, in particular, seems sometimes to be elevated over her choice to become a public actor and advocate of these urgencies. Sometimes it seems that the big question today is whether Beatrice and Sidney Webb did indeed copulate, and if so how often and with what degree of ecstasy. The idea that Beatrice might have chosen a companionate marriage with Sidney Webb, in a context of other disappointments, seems hardly to surface. Thus Carole Seymour-Jones, in her otherwise extraordinary work *Beatrice Webb - Woman of Conflict*, presents Beatrice Potter's 'choice' between Joseph Chamberlain and Sidney Webb as a split between desire and duty. In *Faust* Goethe drops that famous literary line, that perhaps we have two souls, running ever in tension with each other. Seymour-Jones seems to build an argument upon this kind of dualism, as though the patterns of human motivation were not more mixed and complicated (Seymour-Jones, 1992). Beatrice of course played with that same duality in her autobiography, apparently as a means to deal with the self that flourished and the other which remained potential. Nevertheless, we need to confront the sense that she also chose a public life, and a life of advocacy, of self development through public life rather than the pursuit of desire in the contemporary, often sexualised sense.

Why, indeed, should we have just two souls or characters? Beatrice uses the device to express her complexities, it is true. But only two? Robert Musil put it more suggestively, when in passing, in *The Man Without Qualities* he observes that 'the inhabitant of a country has at least nine characters: a professional, a national, a civic, a class, a geographic, a sexual, a conscious, an unconscious, and possibly even a private character to boot ... which is why every inhabitant of the earth also has a tenth character that is nothing else than the passive fantasy of spaces yet unfilled' (Musil, 1995: 30). Musil's early anticipation is of something more like the picture of multiplicity of identities or social roles in which we now more readily recognise ourselves. To modify the older phrase, we are *homo complex*, not *homo duplex*; the older image of split personality, body versus soul, sexuality versus spirit simply cannot capture what we are, or what a figure like Beatrice Webb was. So why should Beatrice's private expression of amorous disappointment be foregrounded to, and what does this contemporary curiosity say not about Beatrice, but about us? Why ought we refuse her choice to do good works with Sidney Webb as somehow less than honest, or authentic?

Beatrice Webb and her peers took a risk, which they may not fully have understood. They were prepared to risk the arrogance of their class, that arrogance which would claim to represent those who cannot represent themselves. Nowadays it is fashionable to rubbish representation, on the grounds that each has the right to voice. This would be charming if it were so, but the assertion confuses the conditions of the world as it 'is' and as it 'ought' to be. To assert that the marginals and outsiders must represent themselves is practically to silence them. To claim to represent others is to open processes fraught with difficulty, but for the moment we know no other way. For in the meantime it is surely more reprehensible to marginalise others by refusing to seek to represent their needs than it is to seek their own recognition, even from the outside. The issue for Fabian women like Beatrice Webb, then, was to sort out what it meant to seek reform for women - which women? and in this regard, as the logic implies, feminism cannot simply or definitionally be a matter of 'placing women first', for this would be again to elevate an abstract universal over so many differing realities. So does a politics which places poor or working class women and their families first, make for a politics which is not feminist? We do not think so, and our hope is that these essays show how Fabianism and feminism interconnect.

For the Fabians, too, knew about feminism, just as they knew about Marxism. Beatrice Webb's infamous gaffe on women's suffrage even indicates as much. Plainly her early opposition to the vote for women was a strategic and symbolic blunder. But it was not simply the manifestation of the virago's poison. Beatrice Webb also opposed 'politicalism', or the pursuit of women's suffrage as the first priority above all others. She did, by contrast, support local political activity over parliamentarism. 'Mere feminism', in her setting, was taken to be particularistic, or middle-class, a matter of privileged women seeking to extend their own privilege. In Beatrice's eyes, for better or worse, middle class women should be seeking to defend not their own interests but those of working class women. The pattern of logic may be too unilinear for us, today, but it is at the very least suggestive of a line of preference, indicating a political choice. If Beatrice Webb was slow to recognise the extraordinary significance of electoral democracy, this is also because she shared the Western period indifference towards liberal democracy and the peculiarly English caution towards modernism. After all, liberal democracy had various major opponents left and right until the period of the post-war boom. The strength, but also the weakness of the Webbs' position was to connect democracy to industrial democracy, however rendered. On this point Beatrice Webb is inconsistent; for if, as she believed, the 'democratic revolution' was central to the prospect of progress, then suffrage is also central. But Beatrice remained the product of her time, sceptical concerning parliamentary forms and liberal democracy.

Our advocacy of these other advocates is not simple minded or absolutist. We are not arguing for a simple return to Fabianism; to the contrary, its political moment has passed. But this is also part of the problem we seek to address, that those perennial social problems persist, and that a wealth of earlier responses to them has been lost in the rush after fashion. If we still remain committed to the minimization of the material sources of human suffering, then Fabianism remains one tradition at our call. This to argue for an ordinary feminism, for renewed attention to the political economy of everyday life.

This volume brings together essays written and published separately by us over the last ten years. These essays result from the pursuit of parallel paths rather than from direct collaboration between us. The authors came together accidentally, having discovered at a distance that the other was also working on Fabianism. Our disciplinary paths began, in common, in Politics, taking us through the different routes of Management and Industrial Relations, and Sociology. What we share across these disciplinary boundaries is that particular land of revisionism which values past struggles, examples and projects as ways to help address the present. Nyland's major contribution in this field has been to recover the work of reformist women and their political agendas. His papers make up the backbone of this collection. Beilharz's work has attended, in comparison, to the symbolic and theoretical aspects of rethinking socialist horizons, evaluating reformisms against the haughtier claims of the revolutionary traditions.

The volume commences with Beilharz's survey of Fabianisms from the Webbs to Shaw, Wells and Cole. Nyland and Gaby Ramia then analyse the Webbs in particular, with especial reference to the rights of women. Nyland next offers an extended analysis of Webb's feminism, after which Nyland and Mark Rix discuss the extraordinary and overlooked phenomenon of the Fabian Women's Group and Beatrice's activity within and alongside it. Nyland and Di Kelly survey Beatrice Webb and the issue of the National Standard of Manual Handling, for it is female manual labour which is so frequently occluded in other, related arguments about feminism and its interests. A coda from Beilharz closes the volume, turning full circle, perhaps, in assessing Fabianism's own claims to be taken seriously as a sociology and not only as a politics. Read together, these essays are less an attempt to stake out territory than part of a project of recovery and renewal; for our shared sense is that Fabianism remains useful, and that ordinary feminism is one of its attributes.

2 Fabianism

Peter Beilharz

Fabianism, of all socialisms, is most consistently painted grey on grey. The Fabians, and especially the Webbs played up to this; they seemed almost happy to be ridiculed as they went about their business, doing committee work, scribbling endlessly, making acquaintances and influencing people. Ironically enough, this has helped to produce the situation where Fabianism has been incredibly influential, and yet rarely taken seriously; where Fabianism has been mocked, caricatured to death, syncretised and homogenised, Fabians turned into the boy-scouts of European socialism. All Fabian cats have become apparently grey; and Beatrice and Sidney Webb, as has been remarked, have become a kind of composite personality in the history of British socialism (Britain, 1980). The Webbs could just as well be 'the Webb', for all the tendency to identify their thought. As is so often the case in the analysis of the history of ideas, however, the interest lies in differences as well as in similarities or identities. The Webbs were in some ways more alike than is often thought, in other ways more different. Their common views require analysis, but so do their differences. A similar challenge confronts us in locating and characterising the arguments of other Fabians; for just as Beatrice was not Sidney, so are there real and substantial differences between them and their rebellious nephews such as G.D.H. Cole and H.G. Wells, and avuncular Fabian figures like Bernard Shaw. Cole at different times took up the radically democratic persona of guild socialist, and then became more orthodox and party-minded with the passing of the years. Wells, for his part, became the most explicitly utopian of Fabians, whether rampaging over the achievements of the elders as a petulant young man or writing the baffling panoply of social science fiction that was his and his alone. And then, finally for our purposes, there are the similarly slippery and extraordinarily influential views of Bernard Shaw.

Sidney Webb: Harvesting the Socialist Idea

Like other socialists and especially Marxists, the Webbs were inclined to deny outright the utopian elements in their thought. They were, of course, self-styled practical people, viewing socialism as an evolutionary trend and Fabianism, effectively, as its formal culmination. Beatrice was more given to reflection on the spiritual dimension of life and of society; arguably hers is the more sophisticated attempt at social theory, and the more nuanced sense of the future. This is, at first sight, a puzzle; for although it was young Beatrice Potter who was tutored by the hard-headed Herbert Spencer, it was apparently Sidney Webb for whom the logic of social evolution was all compelling, while Beatrice remained more romantic. Yet this distinction, too, has been subject to caricature, so that Beatrice is often thought to represent the female part of their division of labour and Sidney the male. Some of the early papers of Sidney Webb show this to be a difficult dichotomy to defend. These issues can be illuminated by treating the views of Sidney and Beatrice in turn, proceeding then to the work of Cole, Wells and Shaw, the better known but less significant here for our concern, utopians fallen among Fabians.

Sidney Webb provides the first public hint of his image of socialism in his 'Historic' *Fabian Essay* of 1889. What were the utopic elements of his early thought? Webb rejects the earlier, romantic conception of the self developing individual as the ultimate goal of social Organisation. Society is the primary category, not the individual. Thus, for Webb, 'The perfect and fitting development of each individual is not necessarily the utmost and highest cultivation of his own personality, but the filling, in the best possible way, of his humble function in the great social machine.' (Webb, S. 1989, p.58) History, evolution, socialism: these were the paths surveyed by Sidney Webb in his *Fabian Essay.* Webb was part of that new climate of opinion in later Victorian England explained by Shirley Letwin in *The Pursuit of Certainty.* He drew in the air of argument popularised by Spencer, where organisms were seen to become more perfectly adapted and specialised and society itself was the larger organism (Letwin 1965, pp 328, 332, 334). Like the views of Nietzsche, these views of Spencer were widely influential, even among those who did not read at all. In England, they were shared and propagated by figures as central and as different from Spencer as G.H. Lewes (whose biography of Goethe the Webbs devoured), Leslie Stephen, who like Webb related morality to social function, and D. Ritchie, another early co-thinker of Webb.

For Webb, then, the process of social evolution followed the track viewed by Spencer, but it issued in the socialism which Spencer could not abide. Evolution itself led towards socialism for the young Sidney Webb: for him 'the Socialist philosophy of today is but the conscious and explicit assertion of principles of social Organisation which have been already in great part unconsciously adopted' (S. Webb 1989, p.58). The problem, for

Webb, was that static images had been allowed to dominate socialist, and utopian thinking. Comte, Darwin and Spencer had turned the tide intellectually; legislation and public organisation facilitated the process practically. In this context, for Webb, notions of the perfect city are not abandoned, merely restructured. Spencer's individualism was discredited by the process of social evolution itself, 'the perfect city became recognised as something more than any number of good citizens' (S. Webb 1989, p.56). For Webb the social organism need now be recognised not merely as prior but as paramount. Society came first; individuality was the result, not the premise.

Sidney Webb's early thinking about society, socialism and the future was plainly moral in motivation. As he explained to a prospective Fabienne, property brought with it the duty of stewardship. For those without private property, labour was the social duty - all people should work, in paid or unpaid work, and therefore contribute to the state (S. Webb to Burdon-Sanderson 25.11.1897, B. Webb 1978, p.110). Webb thus recognised the existence of female unpaid labour, but viewed it, as it were, as a public duty within the private sphere. Certainly the idea of duty loomed large for Webb, and this helped explain his ambivalent attitude toward Goethe. Webb used his own portrayal of the figure of Goethe in order to express his moral sensibilities to Beatrice. In 1890 he wrote to Beatrice that he had reread Carlyle's *Sartor Resartus*. Using literature as the language of love, he described Carlyle's as 'a noble book, much like you' and he found himself saying, 'Close your Byron and open your Goethe.' (S. Webb to Beatrice, 16.6.1890, B. Webb 1978, p.153) Within days he was writing again, having consumed *Dichtung und Wahrheit, Wilhelm Meister* and Lewes' Life (twice). Now Sidney made it clear that his reservations about Goethe were to do with the latter's libertarianism, his recklessness of consequence to others, especially women, his 'real selfish anarchism'. 'What, *eigentlich*, did Goethe ever *renounce*, all his life long?' Against this conception of Goethe, Webb privileged the idea of duty and social service. More than this, he saw Goethe as Beatrice saw Spencer, as the lopsided human being, the result of the too zealous pursuit of one facet of personality, the intellect. Goethe 'never did really discover what his line was', as Sidney Webb put it in his disarmingly direct prose, seeking, as he was, as much to describe his sense of self-purpose and worth as to distance himself from Goethe.

'We are not isolated units free to choose our work: but parts of a whole, the well being of which may be inimical to our fullest development or greatest effectiveness', he wrote to Beatrice (S. Webb to Beatrice, 29.6.1890, B. Webb 1978, p.158) - the words echo those in his 'Historic' essay. Webb unwittingly agreed with Max Weber that the age of the Goethean figure had passed, though he also remained sufficiently needful to threaten the cooling Beatrice that 'you need not be in the least afraid of having any Werther tragedy on your mind'. (S. Webb to Beatrice, 29.6.1890, B. Webb 1978, p.160) For Sidney would continue to serve, but lived in hope of serving in tandem: '*together we could move the world*', he pleaded with her (S. Webb to Beatrice, 30.5.1890, B. Webb 1978, p.143) The individual ought to *serve* society; even the individual-in-love was a subcomponent, whose function was constructed by the broader social purpose. Evidently these were personal and sociological maxims for Sidney Webb. The implications of these maxims were extended in Webb's 1891 *The London Programme*. Here Webb argues again that society has the higher right, before sketching a kind of gas and water version or pastoral, or a suburban edition of Trotsky's Olympia in *Literature and Revolution*. His closing chapter is entitled 'London As It Might Be'. Webb's utopia contrasted somewhat with that offered by William Morris in *News from Nowhere*. Webb's was an ideal, in his word, of dense urban communities uplifted through the collective action of municipal Organisation. The issue of municipalism is a significant one, for the Webbs were never the monomaniacal bureaucratic centralists they have sometimes been cast as. Nor were they as alien to speculation as is sometimes thought.

The London Programme, like Morris' *News from Nowhere*, makes a great deal of the centrality of water to life . The Thames is equally central to both future vistas; Webb, indeed, quotes Thales, 'all things come from water' (S. Webb 1891, p. 208). Water, for Webb, is for cleaning; drinking water ought to be as pure and as soft as from a Welsh lake. London ought to provide its citizens with free public baths, railway stations with drinking fountains and handbasins, parks should offer bathing and skating ponds. More, water should be supplied to every floor, if not tenement, and gas and hot water laid on (S. Webb 1891, p.209). Webb's London might not be white, like that of William Morris, but it will be repainted - 'Bright is the future indeed for the painter.' (S. Webb 1891, p.209) In this context Webb views Alfred Marshall himself as a visionary and romantic, with his image of London piped, heated, lit, cooled and detoxified (S. Webb 1891, p.210). Webb's own view is more comprehensive. Public libraries are effectively to replace public houses. The object is a system of urban planning in the manner of Chicago (S. Webb 1891, p.212).

In Webb's mind, this developmental trend toward socialism and municipal evolution was certain to impinge upon productive life as well as on consumption. The new London was to be a pacesetter of wages and conditions; it was to extinguish sweating, and to end the indecent spectacle of the scramble for work at the dock gates. 'With decent housing, short hours, regular work, and adequate wages the worker will at last have been placed in a position ready to take advantage of the opportunities for civilisation which life in the capital of the Empire should imply.' (S. Webb 1891, p.213) Like Spencer, the Fabians viewed civilisation as something to be used sparingly; all citizens should participate, but differentially, according to their station in life, (Wiltshire 1978, p.250) perhaps, later, according to their talents and interests. The Webbs' utopia was not one of the mass society, proletarian or other. Their view remained structured by Spencer's, even if with the collectivist twist characteristic of later Victorian thought. For the Webbs there was no essential struggle between Man and the State; with each in their place, co-operation would rule.

Co-operation was a principle which Sidney and Beatrice shared prior to their partnership. Indeed, it is striking that they both, in solitude, wrote on Marx, on political economy and on co-operation prior to the formation of the firm of Webb. Co-operation was the natural value of English socialism from Robert Owen onwards. The Fabians and those who followed them Laski, Tawney, Cole, MacDonald - viewed co-operation as an anthropological attribute. Radical social thought at the turn of the century became replete with the language of the social organism, of function and of cooperation. This came to be the basis of Fabianism's utopia: functional differentiation within a multi-class economic system. The development of Fabianism in the twentieth century then involves a shift, from municipality to state and from co-operation to central government.

Yet throughout its earliest years Fabianism's utopia is exactly the humble scenario of gas and water socialism. Clearly Sidney Webb was impressed by the humility of his claims and by the practicality of his utopia. His claims were thus both to political modesty and to sociological accuracy. In *Socialism in England* (1890) Webb rejects earlier utopias, from Plato to Comte, on the grounds of their static nature (S. Webb, 1890, p.4). Significantly, his attitude towards the forerunners is sociological and not dismissive. Plato, Campanella, More, Fourier and Owen were not merely idle dreamers but aspirant planners. Their limit was that they presented the future in images of perfectly balanced equilibrium, without taking into account the need or possibility of future organic alteration. (S. Webb 1890, p.4). Nowadays, according to Webb, now repeating the argument of his *Fabian Essay,* and owing mainly to the efforts of Comte, Darwin and Spencer, we can no longer think of the future society as an unchanging state. The social ideal from being statical has become dynamic. The necessity of constant growth and development of the social organism has become axiomatic (S. Webb 1890, p.5). In this way, for Webb, utopianism in the conventional sense has simply become anachronistic. Today we have no 'utopia'; rather we pursue the functional evolutionary *Social Organism* (S. Webb 1890, p.82). Webb's argument here parallels Kautsky's, and Marx's, in that it declares blueprints to be obsolete; science henceforth explains the autogenetical emergence of socialism. Webb sensed the parallel later, when he dated 'practical' utopianism from *The Communist Manifesto* of 1848; the point now was not to dream, but to reorganise the existing order (S. Webb 1916, p.37). The difference between Social Democracy and what Webb sometimes called by the same name was that the Germans privileged the evolution of productive forces, where the Fabians gave pride of place to functional differentiation.

By the time Webb wrote *Socialism - True and False* (1894), his views on utopianism conventionally defined were less kind or fair; partly this is so because his motivation, in this context seems to be bound up with his attempt to legitimise Fabianism now as a serious, businesslike form of socialism. Webb volunteers to discuss the romantic roots of the Fabians, born out of the Fellowship of the New Life, but here to smirk at its 'alternative', less than fully businesslike inclinations (S. Webb, 1916, p.37). Writing long before him, Webb nevertheless evokes in the mind of the modem reader the images of sandal-beating, carrot -juicing cranks later so painfully lampooned by George Orwell. The Fabian Society of course grew up and away from the fantasy world of communes and colonies; it let go, as Sidney puts it, of all faith in the recuperative qualities of spade husbandry, an apparent allusion to Robert Owen's fetish for the same inclinations (S. Webb 1916, p.3). The useful harvest, rather, was that of the socialist idea. 'Three acres and a cow' gave way to *The London Programme* just as happily as Spencerian individualism passed into empirical collectivism (S. Webb 1916, p.8).

Public administration, for Webb, then replaced 'utopianism'. The idea of the 'new beginning' in Paraguay or Peru, Mexico or Matabeleland gave way, again, to the sensible monitoring and direction of the incipient forces of industrial civilisation. Prophecy changed in form, if not in content: for the wise prophets ought henceforth to cease contemplating the project of founding utopia. The project now was not to initiate a small, local or partial community which adopted the whole faith, so much as to pursue the partial adoption of the new faith by the whole community. And this was a new faith, a faith of a scientific kind, for Sidney Webb. While

Beatrice Webb maintained a sense of faith closer to religion, even if hers was the 'religion of humanity', Sidney Webb's faith was in what he saw, or believed he saw in the evolution of English socialism. Sidney Webb's Perfect City was thus not postulated, but to him actual, a developing state of affairs characterised by municipal socialism, gas and water, pavements and town hall clocks expressing and embodying the gradual inevitability of the evolutionary process.

Yet there were also moral and philosophical well-springs for these views. Sidney's Perfect City may have seemed grey to his various critics, but its motive forces were brighter and more complex. For reasons we can only wonder about, Sidney Webb was happy to participate in the production of the image of Beatrice, the doubter, and Sidney, the wire-puller. Perhaps Sidney was more given to self-protection than Beatrice; but the result of the story is that those who read *My Apprenticeship,* or Beatrice's *Diaries* fall in love with her almost as much as Sidney himself had, while Sidney for all the world looks the clever philistine. Some early papers in the Passfield Collection cast an interesting light across this presumed emotional division of labour. What becomes clear in particular is that Sidney was also a religious thinker, and that the roots of his socialism also lay not in an ethic of efficiency - as is often thought - but in the idea of humanity. In an undated notebook young Sidney Webb wrote two essays, each running from one end of the notebook to the other. One was entitled 'The Existence of Evil'; the other, 'On Serving God'. 'The Existence of Evil' reveals a studiously rather than passionately religious Webb, discussing theodicy and the popular explanations of theodicy - Episcopalian Church of England, Calvinism. Notwithstanding all of the antinomies to be found here, Sidney concludes that 'Any religion is better than no religion.' (S. Webb, Passfield Papers VI, 1, p.34) Meodicy is interesting, for Webb, but somehow theology - even the life of the mind - is less attractive to him than to Beatrice. But for good reasons, to his mind: 'The first thing and the greatest connected with the sin and pain on earth is to do what we can to remedy it; to discover its cause is but an after amusement' (S. Webb Passfield Papers VI, 1, p. 35). 'On Serving God' is of a piece with 'The Existence of Evil'; here is Sidney Webb, spiritual but earnest, believing, but not lyrical. Webb here opens issues linking the service of God to the service of Humanity, a theme we have come to associate with Beatrice. This theme is further developed in 'The Ethics of Existence', a lecture given by Sidney to the Zetetical Society in October 1891. Here again we find themes more often associated with Beatrice's *Diaries* or her *Apprenticeship:* our lives are painful, but our daily occupations take us out of ourselves. Sidney Webb here shares this sense of anthropological pessimism, coupled with its release valve of vocational optimism. As he writes:

> The hopeful Utopian may look forward to a time when increased knowledge and increased intelligence may render injurious excesses less frequent, but within our practical ken there seems but little hope. It must be very many generations before such a change could set in the characteristics of our progress, as to prevent our urban population being universally afflicted to some slight degree with disease of the digestive organs, and with a deficient oxidation (S. Webb, Passfield Papers VI,4, p.20).

Viewed in this context, the greying gas and water socialism of *The London Programme* becomes more suggestive. For while Webb here, as elsewhere, relies on the utilitarian language of pleasure and pain, the emphasis is on pain, the image of the future is at best despondent. So although Webb rejects the arguments of nihilism and of Schopenhauer in particular, he does puzzle over the significance of the question of suicide in this context of civilisational melancholy (S. Webb, Passfield Papers VI,4, p. 37). More generally, however, he also proposes that pessimism depends largely, if not chiefly, on health: so that the necessity of social reform becomes an anthropological and civilisational issue, and not merely an instrumented fancy of aspiring administrators. S. Webb, Passfield Papers VI,4, p., p.45).

From Co-operation to Collectivism: The View of the Partnership

Sidney Webb agreed with John Stuart Mill's *Autobiography* (which he does not, however, cite) that happiness comes not of its own pursuit, but of the pursuit of something other. By 1892 the Webbs had made their own personal and historic pact to this end and by 1897 they were sharing different combinations of these and other views in *Industrial Democracy*. By 1897 the 'religion of humanity' looked somewhat less problematical a solution to the human condition than it had to Webb in his early writings. In place of the premodern, simple 'capitalist entrepreneur', they claimed socialists now faced an emergent hierarchy of specialised professionals - 'inventors, designers, chemists, engineers, buyers, managers, foremen, and what not - organised in their own professional associations', standing midway between classes (B. and S. Webb 1913, p.843). The Webbs' argument here displayed an uncanny similarity to that of Durkheim. The more developed the division of labour, the better, provided only that the professional groups themselves could bond individuals to each other and to the positively evolving order. For the moment, at least in the pages of *Industrial Democracy,* suicide had disappeared and modernity had emerged as possessing far more by way of hopes than fears, or gains than losses. Henceforth there could and ought to be not only the further development of the economic division of labour, but also its pursuit into the social order, as Durkheim had hoped in *The Division of Labour in Society,* so that there was an ever increasing differentiation between the functions of 'the three indispensable classes of Citizen-Electors, chosen Representatives and expert Civil Servants' (B. and S. Webb 1913, p.844). The civil savant, the professional expert had arrived, for the Webbs, in order to resolve Carlyle's quandary, in *Past and Present,* of the contradiction between Democracy and Sovereignty. The experts, the priests of Beatrice's 'religion of humanity' arrived like Hegel's civil service in *The Philosophy of Right,* to know and to represent the general will, or at least the best interest of society.

Here was a fundamental divide between Fabianism and Bolshevism. If the working class did not represent the general interest, then the image of the future could hardly be proletarian. It needed rather to be popular, and given the difficulties presented by the mass of 'ordinary sensual men', experts were both required and indeed necessary. But was this not then, an image of socialism constructed as a middle-class utopia? Sidney Webb discussed some of the implications in a paper entitled 'The Economic Function of the Middle Class' (1885). Here there was no extolling of the virtues of the priests of humanity. Webb proceeded, rather, in a deliberately critical way, addressing the question, are the middle classes parasitic? His argument, predicably perhaps, was that the middle class seemed to do its best to look superfluous, whereas it was in fact functionally necessary. It was indispensable in terms of management, invention and profession. In addition, it saved, and it increased culture. Yet the middle classes were careless, presuming interest-income as their right while the working class and their children expired young, and without pleasure. Sidney Webb could simply not accept this situation: interest, without adequate service rendered 'is simply - robbery' (S. Webb, Passfield Papers, VI, 20, p.32). Yet Webb at the same time added his final preFabian personal defence of private property, even though in the same breath he agreed explicitly with Marx's proposal, in *Capital,* that 'only Labour, not capital, begot money robbery' (S. Webb, Passfield Papers, VI, 20, p.37). Webb's final defence was an interesting case of sociological special pleading, revealing again the pervasive cultural influence of Herbert Spencer. Webb wrote that it was a rule of sociology, as of biology, that difference of function precedes difference of structure, therefore there must be a function for the middle class which it has so far refused to take up. Clearly the middle class did have a vocation, if not as the priests of humanity then as something administratively approximate to that task.

The middle class had thus far failed to recognise, let alone live up to its Faustian task of renunciation. Duty had failed to moderate economic interest or philosophical self-interest. Its place in the social order was functionally circumscribed, but its own autonomous sense of duty had failed to germinate. Now Webb appealed to yet another key value for late Victorian radicals, that of service. Webb explains some of his views here in a lecture on Rome, given at Hampstead in 1888 as 'a sermon in sociology'. Webb warms to the image of Rome because it offers senses of individual duty to community, city, state. Not for him the Athenian utopia of the supreme individual. For Webb, Rome with its 'supreme devotion has been a beacon light to all the successive ages, and is beyond all question our most important heritage from Rome' (S. Webb, Passfield Papers VI, 34, p.60). Rome, for Webb, is utilitarian, not indulgent, collectivist, not given to individualism. The argument then begins to parallel that in his 'Historic' *Fabian Essay:*

> One grand lesson in Sociology stands out conspicuously in Roman history and sums up the characteristics separately brought forward. If the progress of humanity is to be the ultimate end, and not merely our own personal happiness, we must have regard not only to the development of the individual but also to that of the Social Organism (S. Webb, Passfield Papers VI, 34, p.87).

There follows the exact same phrase from the *Fabian Essay,* regarding 'the perfect and fitting development of the individual', and Sidney's final return to Goethe's inadequately practised maxim: renounce, renounce, renounce (S. Webb, Passfield Papers, VI, 34, p.88f).

For Beatrice and Sidney Webb alike, then, political theory led from society to individual, and this meant that the image of the future society must be constructed not in terms of interests, but in terms of notions of community, duty and service. Socialism needs to be based on that neighbourly feeling of which local life was made up, and of that willingness to subordinate oneself to the welfare of the whole without which national existence is impossible. The individual did thus have a place in this utopia, even if he or she was often the last performer on the theoretical stage. Democracy, the Webbs explained, had as its purpose the lightening of the load of participation in productive life, setting free time and enthusiasm for culture, art and science, the pursuit of beauty, friendship, religion and wit. By 1921 they could write in *The Consumers' Co-operative Movement* that 'the final end to be served by social Organisation can be nothing but the largest possible amount of the highest possible development of individual personality' (B. and S. Webb 1921, p.481). Here they returned to some of the elements of Sidney's *London Programme,* reinforcing Ian Britain's case in his brilliant study *Fabianism and Culture* that even if the Webbs were not constantly cultural, culture was nevertheless a fundamental concern for Fabians. For the Webbs argued, in closing *The Consumer Co-operative Movement,* that culture and socialism would grow proportionately as did abundance. 'The beauty of the landscape may even come to be deemed as important as the wheatfield; the purity of the atmosphere and uninterrupted sunshine as valuable as a multiplication of factories.' More and more, they hoped, the life of the community 'will be organised, not mainly to produce goods, but to enjoy them' (B. and S. Webb 1921, pp. 483-4).

From English Utopia to Soviet Socialism

Yet while the Webbs publicly and actively spurned syndicalism and proletarian socialism, the partnership also came to be infamously seduced by the image of the Soviet experience. How did their Fabianism, this most native of socialist forms, come ultimately to look firmly eastward? Much ink has been spilled over this turn, the bulk of it simplemindedly, presuming either that reformism and Stalinism are merely statist sides of the same coin, or else that senility and depression drove the Webbs to lose their earlier, crystalline sense of vision. The explanatory challenge is in some ways more straightforward than either of these ideologically motivated responses suggests. As Brian Lee Crowley (1987) argues, for his own axe-sharpening purposes in *The Self, the Individual and the Community,* a crucial explanatory text falls between Sidney's 'Historic' essay or *The London Programme* and the mid-thirties volumes *Soviet Communism - A New Civilization.* Between the local, municipal pastoral and the hymns to Stalin falls another proximate blueprint, their 1920 *Constitution for the Socialist Commonwealth of Great Britain.* The Webbs' *Constitution* is arguably the most conspicuously utopian book in their life's work. Here again we find the proposal for a functional society, differentiated on the basis of the role accorded by the division of labour and bonded together by this interdependence and its professional corpuscles. For the Webbs the project of socialism is modernity without parasites, for parasites, those without function, are actually premodern.

The rich, those who 'live by owning', are obsolete exactly because they possess no function (B. and S. Webb 1920, p.xii). Now the Webbs take function so seriously that they introduce a differentiation between the functions of democracy. Those without economic function pose one problem. But in the society of the future there ought also to be separated realms of producers' democracy, consumers' democracy, and political democracy, the last again divided into social and political parliamentary functions. Thanks to the detail of this case, it becomes possible to set the Webbs' British utopia even more clearly apart from that of Bolshevism. For the Webbs' utopia, as sketched in the *Constitution for the Socialist Commonwealth,* is a consumers' regime, not the regime of the associated producers, and in addition theirs has elaborate political institutions of a sort, where Bolshevism, exemplified in Lenin's *State and Revolution,* has none at all. The point of similarity, however, becomes evident, that like Bolshevism this dominant variant of Fabianism does manage to imagine modernity as a cluster of social forms without truly political forms, without politics in the classical sense, so that for all their differences Lenin and the Webbs can finally agree, in principle, that the substance of politics under socialism should be administration.

Political democracy, according to the Webbs, ought optimally to be functionally desegregated into political functions - those concerning law and order, diplomacy, and defence, and social functions - those taking up issues of social welfare and rational 'housekeeping' in the manner shown by the powers of the London City Council (B. and S. Webb 1920, p.xvii). The national parliament ought to be split into two departments within the House of Commons, one to follow police functions, the other housekeeping (B. and S. Webb 1920, p.111). 'Housekeeping' seems more suggestive of Beatrice's biography than Sidney's; it also evokes the Victorian sense of differentiation between private and public spheres. As Sidney had argued elsewhere, the existing democratic machinery was essentially sound, provided that the House of Lords was stripped of its veto power. Thus modified, however, by functional desegregation, parliament could more effectively achieve its national ends. For the Webbs, politics might then become the realm of measurement and publicity; the public agenda could henceforth be set by the '*searchlight of published knowledge*' (B. and S. Webb 1920, p.196). This would be a process where, as evolutionary positivists could agree, the facts led consistently leftward, or at the very least upward, upward from above via the model of service which the Webbs proclaimed, again Durkheim-like, to be embodied in the learned professions and the civil service. Consensus could thus be reached by the cogency of accurately ascertained and authoritatively reported facts, driven home by the silent persuasiveness of public opinion. Politics would consist of a 'stream of reports' from independent and disinterested experts retained expressly for this allegedly public purpose (B. and S. Webb 1920, p.197). Beveridge was already summoned to the lobby of history.

Not only political, but also economic activity would be restructured in the world to be legislated into existence by the *Constitution for the Socialist Commonwealth.* The Webbs envisaged a complex reorganisation of industry, under which there would be three major sectors: nationalised leading sectors, municipal and local, and co-operatives (B. and S. Webb 1920, p.149). As will be seen later with further reference to Beatrice Potter's work, the Webbs always favoured consumer co-operatives; their position was adamantly against so-called associations of producers, and for the native tradition which could be traced to Robert Owen and the Rochdale pioneers. Producer organisations such as trade unions were, however, to play a major role in economic and social life for the Webbs. Indeed, for them trade unions ought to become the basis of an extensive network of professional and vocational groupings. Like Durkheim, the Webbs viewed vocational groupings or corporations as autonomous, yet functional components of the social system. Such groups were not however, to be viewed as specifically political or representative in electoral terms; for the conduct of politics, after all, the bicameral, internal or domestic and external or international parliamentary bodies already existed, exactly because functions such as those of political and economics were to be differentiated and not merged into each other. Vocational groups were thus by definition outside the state, and were explicitly not to be representative. Vocational groups would develop their own sense of purpose and civil service, developing the professional honour of the corporation, perfecting the science and art of the particular service that its members render to the community as a whole (B. and S. Webb 1920, p.149).

In terms of the traditions of social and political theory, then, we witness here an affinity not only with Hegel's conception of corporations and of the civil service as a universal class, but also a striking echo of Durkheim's own case for corporatism in *The Division of Labour in Society.* As Durkheim exhorted, 'the categorical imperative of the modem consciousness is coming to assume the following form: *equip yourself to fulfil usefully a specific function*' (Durkheim 1986, p.4). In late nineteenth century Europe, Kant's categorical imperative ceases to be an ethical maxim and becomes a systemic demand; and with this, any hope of the fully-developed personality recedes back through the pages of Goethe to the mists of the Renaissance. As Sidney had argued in his *Fabian Essay* and elsewhere, the perfect development of the individual was now no longer possible or desirable. Durkheim could well have been doing his puzzling on behalf of Sidney Webb when he asked himself the leading question, 'Is it our duty to seek to become a rounded, complete creature, a whole sufficient unto itself or, on the contrary, to be only a part of the whole, the organ of an organism?' (Durkheim 1986, p.3). Plainly Durkheim, too, had breathed in the air of Spencer's theory. The good citizen, for Webb, for Secretant and for Durkheim alike was the man who ploughed a single furrow. As Sheldon Wolin sensed in *Politics and Vision,* Durkheim lurks in this political realm, and with him, so too does Rousseau. For his own part, Wolin connects Sidney Webb to F.H. Bradley. Goethe's counsel, he reminds us, was 'strive to be a whole; and if you cannot, then join a whole'. Bradley amended this to read, 'you cannot be a whole *unless* you join a whole', for which Webb's sociological equivalent was simply that there were no individuals beyond social wholes (Wolin 1960, p.401). But if Webb and Durkheim largely shared social diagnoses, Durkheim's political prognosis was arguably closer to that of Fabian *enfant terrible* G.D.H. Cole, who although deeply influenced early by Rousseau, retained his sense of romanticism well into the twenties. For unlike the Webbs, Cole envisaged corporations or guilds as the basis not only of economic but also of specifically political Organisation, in the form of the National Guild Congress (Durkheim, 1986, p.liii; Cole, 1920). While Cole was throughout this period largely hostile towards the state, the Webbs grew more and more friendly to it. Certainly the state, and the lexicon of collectivism was part of the new century in a similar manner to the way in which, say, co-operation was a watchword of the nineteenth century. But this is not to say that the Webbs were only ever just statists: what is remarkable into the post-war period is rather the way in which the state becomes a part of almost all discourse in political and social theory. In his leading 1916 essay, *Towards Social Democracy,* Sidney had presented the Webb position accurately when he identified the two leading characteristic trends in modernity as municipalisation and co-operation (S. Webb 1916, p.18). Fabianism seems rather to have slowly accommodated its pact with the state as the missing prime mover, the massive actor and legislator necessary to deal with apparently intractable social problems, and to have done this in part, and theoretically, via the Webbs' embrace of the Soviet experience, in part, and practically, via the experience of the 1945-51 Labour Government and the Beveridge Report. Partly this was possible because, as H.G. Wells had earlier, and acutely observed, the idea of permeation led too easily to the sense that the world (and the state) was acting in the interests of Fabianism, even if the world or state did not know this in any case, Beveridge was certainly seen as a socialist and as the half-witting agent of Fabianism itself.

Were the Webbs then ever great democrats? This is probably a more interesting question to pursue than that of their statism, yet it is likely no easier to answer. The Webbs were never Stalinists, at least not in the strict sense; at most they accepted the morally compromised relativism for which Soviet socialism was well and good for the Russians who could be expected to know no better. Certainly the Webbs were personally jaded by the early thirties, both by the failure of parliamentary Labour in Britain and by the cataclysmic experience of the Great Depression; by 1923 events were already sufficient to convince them that capitalist civilisation had reached senility (B. and S. Webb 1923) The Great Depression confirmed the thesis of capitalist anarchy and collapse and at the same time reinforced the universal planomania characteristic of the times.

But what did the Webbs themselves mean by democracy? And had they not long been inclined to technocracy, whether that of Beatrice's service of humanity or Sidney's dedicated band of professional experts? Writing in *Towards Social Democracy,* Sidney defined liberty as 'the practical opportunity we have of exercising our faculties and fulfilling our desires' - and, he added, 'nothing else is worth the name of Freedom'. Co-operation, or socialism or social democracy facilitated liberty, wrote Webb (S. Webb 1916 p.7, p.14). The development of democracy meant that the typical figure of the Middle Ages, the Lord of the Manor, had given way to the characteristic personages of the nineteenth century, the improving landlord and the capitalist mill-owner, and in the twentieth had in turn given way to the elected councillor, the elementary schoolmaster, the school-doctor and the borough engineer (S. Webb 1916 p.17). Democracy was not, however, anything to do with the workplace; as Beatrice Potter had cleverly caricatured the case of her opponents in 1891, the message of socialism was surely not 'the sewers to the sewer-workers' (B. Potter 1891, p.75). Workplace democracy was neither desirable nor, when the argument came to it was it practicable. Unlike social democracy, then, or at least some variants of it, and unlike Guild Socialism democracy did most emphatically stop at the factory door for the Webbs (Wright 1978, pp.224-41). Where social democracy then sought the extension of democracy from the political sphere to the social and finally the economic, Sidney Webb's conception of the matter was that the defence of democracy involved the 'extension of representative self-government from the political to the industrial sphere, and from political to industrial and social relations' (S. Webb 1916, p.36). Democracy, for Sidney Webb, apparently only ever meant representation, along with taxation. If the 'organic' conception of human society had replaced the 'atomic', then all the parts must need whirr harmoniously. Politics was not for the average sensual type, and autonomy could not be a core human value.

In the terms of political theory, the Webbs did indeed hope for human cultivation, but not on the lines of developmental participatory democracy. Democracy seems ultimately for the Webbs to have been a mechanism or device, an instrument of mass approval or plebiscite; here they were already creatures of the twentieth century, for they were taking sides with, say, Schumpeter rather than with John Stuart Mill in viewing democracy more as means than as ends. Genuflecting before the specialists, ordinary citizens would nevertheless benefit, in the Webbs' worldview, and spiritually as well. Here Sidney Webb approvingly cited T.H. Green, along with his sense that the new atmosphere of personal obligation results, paradoxically, in an actual popular increase of individual faculties. Collectivism, for Webb, remained the mother of freedom (S. Webb 1916, p.44). Democracy, in other words, was a systemic principle for the Webbs, neither a moral imperative nor a first principle but an administrative strategy which had both its place and its limits.

This secondary or systemic status of democracy for the Webbs may help to explain its further displacement from their worldview in the thirties. For Sidney, democracy was a problem because autonomy smelled too much of careless, do-as-you-like individualism in the manner of his Goethe. For Beatrice, in this connection more complex a case, Soviet communism also filled an emotional vacuum. Barbara Caine confirms here Margaret Cole's sense that without this new enthusiasm, Beatrice would likely have joined her sisters in sharing a miserable and lonely old age. The Great War had destroyed the civilisation she had known and, as she had said herself, now posed a set of problems with which she was unable to cope (Caine 1988, pp.209-10). Her 1932 visit to the Soviet Union opened new vistas and hopes which were to become compatible with a worldview not itself based on values of participatory or developmental democracy. For Beatrice Webb the novelties of Soviet socialism were cosmetic, those of the planners and ideologues and not to be found in the practices of everyday life. By the thirties the formal organisational attributes of Soviet communism had solidified, leaving far behind the images of the proletarian utopia in Lenin's *State and Revolution* or even those of the peasant-worker *smychka* in the New Economic Policy and taking on rather a self-identity closer to that of the functional society, only now without guilds, unions, soviets or any other kind of effectively autonomous intermediary organisations.

The suggestion that there was in fact some kind of elective affinity between the Webbs' 1920 *Constitution* and Stalin's 1936 Constitution had earlier been advanced by the ever-insightful Leonard Woolf. Empirically the Webbs' *Soviet Communism* anticipated Stalin's Constitution by two years; what Woolf was onto was rather the idea that the Webbs' conversion in old age to Marxist socialism and their admiration of the Soviet system followed logically from their fundamental social philosophy, their belief in the overwhelming importance of social structure and function (Woolf 1949, p.262). Woolf's clue, itself first laid by Beatrice herself, is worth pursuing. Beatrice had confessed in her 1932 *Diary* that what attracted them in advance to Soviet Russia was that, on the one hand, it bore out their own *Constitution* and that, on the other it supplied a 'soul' to that conception of government which their *Constitution* lacked. Their personal dislike of the communist 'soul' did not prevent it from doing the job. And there was no 'd-d nonsense' here about Guild Socialism! Finally, the Religion of Humanity here came into its own (B. Webb 1985, 4, pp.279-80). As they faced the Soviet Union's self-image in the thirties, the Webbs saw a society without the functionless - neither landlord nor capitalist was there to blight the Soviet silhouette, only the local parasites, Trotskyists and wreckers. Syndicalists and hooligans had not only bitten, but also turned into dust. The Soviet social landscape seemed to resemble the land of their hopes and dreams: for here was a society with a universal bureaucratic class, an extensive degree of municipal Organisation, and a developed system of vocational groups (the by now completely integrated set up of trade unions). More, the Soviets made a functional distinction between man as citizen, man as producer, and man as consumer. and viewed leadership itself as a vocation. In the Webbs' view, this sense of functional differentiation confirmed their own: 'The USSR is a highly integrated social Organisation in which ... each individual is expected to participate in three separate capacities: as a citizen, as a producer and as a consumer.' (B. and S. Webb 1937, p.450) The uncanny similarities extended further. The Soviets were also committed, on paper, to Measurement and Publicity. The Soviet Union, for the Webbs, fitted almost exactly the requirements of their *Constitution for the Socialist Commonwealth of Great Britain,* without the benefits of the representative democratic apparatus, burdened only by what they called 'the disease of orthodoxy' (B. and S. Webb 1937, p.997; see also Crowley 1987, ch. 5). Scanning approvingly the Central Acro Hydro-

Dynamic Institute and the Campaign Against Rheumatism, they glowingly told their readers about how Research was Planned and Executed but not about the planners and researchers who were themselves executed.

Far from representing a mere lapse in judgement or the weakness or limits of the passing years, then, there is rather a striking logical consistency between the Webbs' earlier and later views on the political and social forms appropriate to the socialist future. That they misread the formal framework of Soviet social Organisation as its reality was an extraordinary blunder on the Webbs' part, but it was not theirs alone. Fellow-travelling was by no means a peculiarly Webbian phenomenon (Caute 1973). Fascism was widely viewed as the greater threat to humanity, and the Soviets as an ally against it. What is perhaps a more potentially fruitful line of inquiry to pursue here, is how it was that the Webbs were able to depart from their own espoused empirical methodology in order to fall into the trap of formalism. For even their passing critical moments in *Soviet Communism* claim to rest on their own methodological stance, elaborated earlier in their research handbook *Methods of Social Study.* Social scientists, the Webbs argued in *Soviet Communism,* were bound by their training to investigate the contemporary facts for themselves, using the generalisations of previous writers, but only as hypotheses (B. and S. Webb 1937, p.998). Sadly, when it came to the Soviet experience, the Webbs expected or claimed to expect that the physicians might heal themselves. Certainly such a view was consistent with their own theory of the professions - professionals ought to behave like this. It seems that the Webbs themselves had become hopelessly entrapped, flylike, within theoretical premises which were formalistic and based on faith and prescription rather than on empirical research. By the thirties, then, their research methodology had become diverted from the path of empirical research, and most notably from Beatrice's early path of social investigations (see Nord 1985).

Beatrice Webb: From Co-operation to Communism

Faith was more generally the realm of Beatrice Webb. Sidney, happy to be seen as the stringpuller, reinforced this sense by claiming that he had no biography, because he had 'no inside' (S. Webb in. Harrison 1987, p.55). His exaggerated attack on individualism did represent something, for his interest like de Bonald's was not in *l'homme interieur* but in *l'homme exterieur.* Beatrice, by comparison, poured her insides out in her diaries and in *My Apprenticeship.* As Royden Harrison (1987, p.35) has observed, Beatrice privately confessed that she viewed their study of the

Soviet Union as their 'last and biggest baby', an act of supererogation, a theological service performed beyond the call of duty; something fit to be ignored or criticised, but not anything which might warrant blame. In Harrison's equally paradoxical representation, Beatrice employed a Cartesian regard for the method of universal doubt together with a Rousseauesque intuition into the mysteries of the human psyche.

Even the most cursory reading of Beatrice's work is powerfully suggestive of the depth and character of her mind. Beatrice Webb inspires, where Sidney Webb explains. Beatrice's romanticism endows her sociology with a sense of insight which Sidney's published work rarely reaches. Beatrice shares with Tonnies, for example, and against Durkheim, the profound sense that the experience of modernity involves loss of community, of tradition and meaning, as well as progress and gains, and with Weber she identifies the loss of religion as a major incipient social problem in the twentieth century. But this should not be taken as a mere confirmation of the view that Sidney ought to be viewed as some kind of stand in for the unfortunate Engels in the all too typical portrait, 'Marx clever, Engels dull'. As we have seen, Sidney had a spiritual side which, though fundamental as a motivating force, he preferred publicly not to discuss. And yet, despite this hitherto unacknowledged nuance, it remains difficult to resist the sense that in one regard at least the division of labour between Beatrice and Sidney Webb did indeed resemble that between Marx and Engels. The Webbs shared obvious attractions to Comte, to Spencer, Goethe and Carlyle. Sidney signalled the way forward to the still liberal Beatrice in his '*Historic*' *Fabian Essay*. As Nord (1985, p.209) observes, this essay was designed exactly to win over the hearts and minds of well-disposed not-yet-socialists such as Beatrice herself. Sidney eventually won Beatrice's mind, and heart, or part of it; and it was this persistent sense of the spiritual and romantic which Beatrice brought with her to the Fabian union, and which gave Beatrice's work the depth of character less conspicuous in Sidney's published work.

Beatrice Webb veritably had two souls. While Sidney claimed Goethe's professional ethic - 'renounce, renounce, renounce' - Beatrice's capacity to renounce was never free of some sense of longing. Troubled as she was by self-doubt, Beatrice has an immediate fascination for those who share this attribute. As she wrote in *My Apprenticeship* - itself a Goethean title - her own life was a struggle between 'the soul that affirms' and 'the soul that denies' (B. Webb 1979). One could just as well say that it was a struggle between science and religion, for faith had taken Beatrice to social science, only to leave her there, in need of a God. As she was to confess in later life, this need became transformed, finally, into the need for a Church (Nord 1985, p.239).

Like Sidney Webb, Beatrice Potter had a sense of duty instilled into her from early years. Herbert Spencer had taught Beatrice and her wayward sisters the significance of function even at a young age. Her sense of function was reinforced by her own class location; readers of her 'private' musings fairly readily come to meet that fundamental middle-class motivation, guilt. The young Beatrice came readily upon a greater quantity of social gadflies and parasites than was likely to infest the London home of young Sidney. Indeed, it was Beatrice's need to be useful which helped to propel her into the craft of social investigation (B. Webb 1979, p.239). Beatrice yearned to belong, to be useful, to contribute, to fulfil her duty. When she speaks of her relatives in the co-operative region of Bacup, there is an element of longing mixed in with her ordinary respect for these good people (B. Webb 1979, pp.166-70). For the maturing Beatrice had acquired what she called the 'class consciousness of sin', or the 'consciousness of collective sin' which would drive her into social service and lead her to esteem the vocation of public service. While Sidney Webb had climbed into and up the Public Service, Beatrice had worked out of the private sphere and into the social and sociological margins inhabited by Charles Booth, the 'social explorers' and the socially explored.

In Beatrice's work with Booth we encounter a different research universe from that of *Soviet Communism:* statistics and participant observation are given priority, not formal attributes and authoritative hearsay. Beatrice Webb and Charles Booth had set out to refute contemporary claims that one in four Londoners lived in dire poverty, only to find the actual situation to be worse, and of course to say so. But Beatrice was no mere factgrubber, and criticised the philanthropic investigators precisely on grounds of what they did not do, the questions and problems which they were content to leave covered by masses of data (B. Webb 1979, p.214) After Booth, Beatrice embraced socialism - the facts led leftward, as it were. Characteristically, she exclaimed in her half-public inner voice: 'At last I am a Socialist!' (B. Webb, 1985, 1, 1.2.1890, p.322). Her own, pioneer work on co-operation, *The Co-operative Movement in Great Britain,* published in 1891, signalled some features of her personal transition to socialism. Shifting already towards socialism, Beatrice had begun to sketch in some attributes of her own utopia. Robert Owen was its guiding light. Like Sidney Webb, Beatrice Potter had read Carlyle, and inveighed with both against the callous cash nexus (B. Potter 1891, p.10). In this context, amidst the suffering and destitution of the nineteen century, there emerged the figure of Robert Owen. Beatrice was more taken by Owen's practice than by his theory; like Sidney Webb, she was no advocate of spade-cultivation as the harbinger of the new society. Again like Sidney, her conception of the socialist future was distinctly urban, or at least suburban. So it was the image of the mill at New Lanark which drew Beatrice Potter to Owen, not that of the enclosed rural utopia. Here was a comfortably British, not foreign doctrine, calm and legislative, neither anarchical nor murderous (B. Potter 1891, p.16) Owen's practical utopianism combined the 'socialistic legislation of the last fifty years' and the principle and practice of co-operation.

In Beatrice Potter's understanding, Robert Owen too insisted on the biological principle of functional adaptation, and applied it to the collective character of the race (B. Potter 1891, p.19). She accepted without apparent difficulty Owen's materialism, approving his sense that the good race was the product of the well-engineered environment. Owen's paternalism presented no obvious problem for Beatrice; the social betters, after all, had it as their duty to form the character of their dependants by placing them in healthy moral, and enjoyable surroundings. Politically and economically, Beatrice was convinced by Owen's insistence that the future of humanity depended on the elimination of profit. The profit-maker was to be replaced by an ideal civil servant. Yet her position was by no means simply elitist or technocratic; she quoted at length from *The Dream of John Ball,* agreeing with Morris that 'fellowship is life, and lack of fellowship is death' (B. Potter 1891, p.28). The limit of Owen's hopes, for Potter, was less in his practical image of socialism than in his sense of the strategic means appropriate to the transition. Speaking in terms anticipating Sidney Webb's later use of T.H. Green, Beatrice argued that Owen was politically premodern, for he had failed to grasp the significance of Democracy as a form of association whereby the whole body of the people acquires a collective life, an internal Will. Cobbett, by comparison, had clearer political vision, for he had understood the mind of the English Democracy, and had recognised growth as an essential element of social reformation (B. Potter 1891, p. 35).

At no stage in their apprenticeships or during their partnership did the Webbs have any time much for syndicalism. They had abhorred Lenin as a syndicalist, and had admired Stalin exactly for his allegedly advanced views on socialism as the utopia of the functional society. As early as her 1891 book Beatrice Potter had chosen explicitly to distance herself from the utopia of the associated producers. Co-operation, in her lexicon, referred to consumers in league, not producers. Association did represent a general social trend, provided only that it maintained proper functional and institutional distinctions. The 'unearned increment' of interest could and ought to be abolished, or redistributed, but only through separate organs which managed one and only one department of corporate life (B. Potter 1891, pp.70-71). Workers' self-management was a ridiculous proposition; the mines ought no more to be run by the miners than the sewers by the sewer-cleaners. Expressed in a less barbed way, her logic seems impeccable: all citizens, for example, are affected by the railways, so why should the rail system be run by the railway workers alone? Political representation ought rather, she argued, follow the parliamentary model.

Workers not only could not run their enterprises, nor ought they. Rejecting the labour theory of value and Marxism's consequent privileging of the proletariat, as good Fabians always did, Beatrice explained the principled difference using the authority of Alfred Marshall. Professor Marshall had explained that productive labour could not strictly be defined as the prerogative of the proletariat; as he argued,

> It is sometimes said that traders do not produce; that while the cabinetmaker produces furniture, the furniture-dealer merely sells what is already produced. There is no scientific foundation for this distinction. They both produce utilities. The dealer in fish helps to move on fish from where it was of comparatively little use, and the fisherman does no more (B. Potter 1891, citing Marshall's, Book 2, c.3).

People had rights as consumers, more than as producers; each part filled its function in the great social machine, no part less significant than the next, the higher no more vital than the lower. Socialism was thus characterised by the extensive evolution of good co-operatives, not bad ones, a process open-ended to the extent that there could be forged a veritable 'State within the State'. Beatrice Potter thus argued, in parallel to Sidney Webb, that the evolution of democracy and socialism amounted to the emergence of Social Democracy. Associations of producers, meantime, were actually retrogressive, literally reactionary; and here Beatrice echoed Adam Smith's barb, that they were directly opposed in their interests to the interest of the community (B. Potter 1891 p.156). Trade unions had their place, but they should recognise it, like everyone else, and stay within it. The 'Child of Promise' begot of the partnership between co-operation and trade unionism meant the defence of separate spheres: the citizens organised as consumers, the workers organised as producers (B. Potter 1891, p.193).

As elsewhere, however, the views of the Webbs on syndicalism were not as absolute or resolute as is often imagined. A significant document which warrants mention here is the 1912 pamphlet penned by the Webbs: *What Syndicalism Means: An Examination of the Origin and Motives of the Movement with an Analysis of its Proposals for the Control of Industry.* Twenty years after the publication of Beatrice Potter's first book, syndicalism had a far better press, indeed, workers' control had become a major stream in the labour movements of Western Europe. In this paper, published by the National Committee for the Prevention of Destitution as a supplement to *The Crusade,* the Webbs showed a more subtle understanding of their enemy. Syndicalism, they argued, rested not only on the rejection of capitalism or the wage system, but also on the disillusionment with democracy - and not just parliament. A class doctrine, it managed in these times to hit a nerve; syndicalism as such was 'natural' and 'pardonable' (B. and S. Webb 1912, pp.140-4). Though the Webbs did not develop this case, they evidently viewed syndicalism as the product of uneven development. The gears of the capitalist economy moved at a great rate; when meshed with artisanal labour traditions, teeth flew off. Who, in this context, could deny that syndicalism was a pardonable excess? Yet it was at the same time an obstacle, its eyes turned backwards or so far forward as to be impracticable and unconvincing. Indeed, the Webbs proposed, it was 'ethically objectionable' (B. and S. Webb 1912, p.144). It discouraged citizenship or participation in the political system, conventionally defined; and it brought about deterioration in moral character, via sabotage. In practical terms, economic activity would still remain to be organised; there would still, under syndicalism, be individuals who gave orders or who took them. And there would still need to be some kind of parliament, or General Council - so how would they differ? For even in a parliament of producers, there would still be conflicts of interest to resolve. Like Weber in his theory of bureaucracy and critique of socialism, then, the Webbs here claimed that the imagined syndicalist community would be more complicated than capitalism, not less. More, syndicalism offered a concrete step backwards in its premise that the trade union could act as an employing authority, thus destroying its utility as a trade union (an insight later forgotten when it came to the Soviet experience). Further, syndicalism worked with an over-proletarianised conception of the individual: who was to represent the non-unionised? And surely the way out was not to succumb to the ridiculous, by introducing compulsory unions and bogus unions, poets' unions and so on? (B. and S. Webb 1912, p.149-150).

What is striking here is the philosophical underpinning of the Webbs' case. For they proceed to attack the privileging of work, as such. Syndicalism offends because it identifies life and work, and this is too much even for the dedicated priests of humanity themselves;

> Important as may be material production it is not the only interest, and not even the highest or most vitally important interest of the community. We do not live to work; we work merely in order to live (B. and S. Webb 1912, p.150).

The implication is clear: all individuals have a social duty, but it is as though the obsession with duty is a personal anthropology, not a moral imperative. As they explain:

> A constitution based exclusively on wealth production seems as lopsided as a constitution based exclusively on wealth possession. Surely we shall not fight for any ideal smaller than Humanity itself; and that not only as it exists at present, but also as it may arise in the future (B. and S. Webb 1912, p.151).

We all need to work, for the Webbs, and to serve, but we also need to be free beyond work - here the argument is far closer to Kautsky than to Lenin in leisure, and in civilisation. More:

> Over and above the tribute of work that we have to pay to the world - a tribute that may be lightened by a more equitable sharing of the burden and sweetened by the sense that it is no longer aggravated by the toll levied by the idlers and parasites - there will be, in the Socialist State of the future, to which we personally look forward, all the rest of life to be lived; and lived for the first time, as far as it lies in us so to live, in the utmost liberty possible to a civilized society (B. and S. Webb 1912, p.153).

Duty, not work, emerges as the central moral view of the Webb utopia; and here, in 1912, duty is the precondition of culture.

But if there are anthropological reasons for this desire to locate and limit production and productive life to its own sphere, then there are also social factors explaining the Webb view. Beatrice had made it clear in her early study of co-operation that hers was not simply a personal or political preference for the rights of consumers over those of producers: consumers were in some ways structurally more significant than workers, in that consumption determined the conditions of production. By buying cheap or dear, consumers sent market signals which bred sweating, or decent working conditions; 'cheap is nasty' held true not only for consumers, but reached in its effects into the realm of production as well (B. Potter 1921, p.204). This is a significant thread in the Webb case, for it helps to explain the distance of the Webbs from anything like the notion that 'small is beautiful'. Small, for both Sidney and Beatrice, was sweatshop. Granted the development of industrialism, scale was a positive virtue. Size, however, was proportionate to complexity, so the Webbs had no time to entertain Lenin's fantasies about cooks governing, or each taking their turn at the administrative tasks of the day. Size was proportionate not only to complexity, but also to responsibility. In the cities, in comparison to Bacup and other small communities, 'the mill-owner, coal-owner or large iron-master is forced to assume, to some slight extent, the guardianship of his workers', compelled by state regulation and trade unions to curtail the worst excesses of formative, decentralised industrialism (B. Webb 1979, pp.335-7). The Webbs' utopia was thus not only urban or suburban rather than rural, but also urban in a modernist cast, industrial rather than artisan. Only on this basis could Beatrice hold up her hopes for the 'future religion of humanity'. As optimistically as Sidney, she viewed this as no mere vision of a 'Moral Utopia', but rather the 'Child of Promise', itself begot via the evolving principle and practice of cooperation.

By 1921 the partnership had effectively finalised its views on co-operation and the co-operative society. The tenor of *The Consumers' Co-operative Movement* was more sober than that of Beatrice Potter's own independent study, at least so far as its conclusions were concerned. By 1921 the Webbs were keen to confirm that Democracy meant Representative Democracy (B. and S. Webb 1921, p.59). Co-operatives had developed strongly into the new century, confirming their shared worldview. This trend served to reinforce their sense that co-operation was one sphere of social life, best functionally differentiated from other spheres, where trade unions and professional associations (and perhaps even the self-governing guilds which might grow out of them) would reign supreme. This theme of differentiation, division of mental and manual and separation of proper spheres of authority and capacity indicates again the perpetual motif of corporatism anticipated by Sidney Webb as early as his 1889 'Historic' *Fabian Essay*. Further along this path, Sidney had also provided Clause Four of the British Labour Party, where workers by hand or by head were offered the fruits of the socialist harvest.

By 1918 the Labour Party had become for the Webbs the active and realising agent of the Fabian utopia; and by the 1945-51 Labour Government, Fabians and radicals of all stripes, from Tawney to Cole and the Webbs, had embraced the Labour Party as the historic receptacle of their differing socialist projects. For the Webbs the party-form successfully edged out mass political forms such as syndicalism. Their capacity to embrace the party evidently aided their predisposition to the principle and practice of state power, as it encouraged their later embrace of the Soviet experience. The Webbs' apparent and passing sympathy for guild socialism, like their momentary sympathy for syndicalism, again gave way in Clause Four to the sturdier image of social differentiation. Clause Four after all spoke of the wealth of all the different producers, not of the economic fights of the industrial workers. The Webbs never finally rejected their sense of plural organisation; as they wrote in *The Consumers Co-operative Movement,* 'what is desirable in the Co-operative Commonwealth of Tomorrow is that there should be, not any one rigid structure, but all sorts and kinds of democratic Organisation, central and local, compulsory and voluntary'. Co-operatives offered the principle of decentralisation, while Political Democracy had necessarily to insist on a larger measure of the centralisation of authority and of subordination of the parts to the whole (B. and S. Webb 1921, p.181).

With specific reference to life in the socialist countryside, however, the Webbs doubted the efficacy of agricultural co-operation. Smaller scale activities such as dairies and creameries were plainly compatible with the co-operative form, but afforestation and farming would be better lent to state ownership. For if the Webbs did not agree that small was beautiful, they also chose not to prefer scale for its own sake: unlike Kautsky, they did not have a conception of an agrarian utopia that was massively industrialised and organised practically along the lines of the factory. For the Webbs the model of socialist agriculture was, like industry, to be varied and diverse. There seemed to be no reason obvious to the Webbs why peasant agriculture should not, like the individual practitioners of the professions and the arts, coexist with all possible expansion of associations of consumers in agriculture and manufacture alike (B. and S. Webb 1921, p.415). It is obvious that the Webbs envisaged no parallel British program to that of Stalin's dystopic assaults of forced industrialisation or collectivisation of agriculture. Yet despite this, the Soviet experience in agriculture as elsewhere was for them exemplary by the thirties. Somehow the images of vocational austerity and the impressions of efficiency were simply too much to resist.

The caricature of Sidney Webb's administrative hand can be detected in all this; so too can the image of the romantic aura around Beatrice's head. As has been suggested here, there was more to both of them than this. Sidney was not without his romantic motivations; his sociology, and his utopia, rested on fundamentally philosophical and ethical foundations. Beatrice also had occasion to be something less than romantic; she had a politically hard head, whether shown in her no-nonsense attitude to the idle poor in Britain or in her stance against the 1926 General Strike, or later against the wreckers and troublemakers who wilfully clogged up the works in the Soviet economic and political machine. Yet if Beatrice was hard of head, she was also needful of spirit. It was she who developed the spirited case for co-operation, and who argued for the co-operative dimension of the Webb utopia. And it was likely she, as well, who initiated the Soviet enthusiasm, with its consequent identification of the Webbs' 1920 British *Constitution* and the Stalin regime. Beatrice had responded positively to Bernard Shaw's news, on his return from the Soviet Union in 1931, that the Soviet Union had somehow taken on their own utopia. For Beatrice was deeply vulnerable to Shaw's axiom, that the Bolsheviks were people like us but who actually did what they spoke about (Caute 1973, p.78). Ironically, then, Beatrice was evidently responsible for both the romantic, co-operative dimension of the Webb utopia, and for its final, fatal ensnaring in the Soviet dystopia of the mid-thirties. She seems to have contributed to Fabianism both one of its best components, in the sense of co-operation and difference, and one of its most malignant vulnerabilities, in its sense of functionalised difference, its cult of things proto-Soviet and then pro-Soviet.

Cole and Wells: Utopias Guild and Technocratic

Certainly there is enough variation in the Webbs' views to allow contemporary responses varying from political rescue operations to outright critical rejection. The crucial point of division, here, is whether the Webbs were in fact authentic in their own identification of Fabianism with Soviet communism. The symmetry between their own hopes and the claims of Stalin is conspicuous, yet it does not immediately follow that there is an identity between these views or their utopias, nor does it follow that the historic association between the Webbs and Stalinism is sufficient to discredit their own worldview. In understanding the principle of differentiation the Webbs were in the vanguard of socialist sociology. Ultimately the adequacy of their views becomes merged with a debate still going on, whether corporatism can possibly be a strongly democratic option into the new century.

G.D.H. Cole did not use the language of corporatism, and his guild socialist utopia was vitally concerned with the issue of democracy. For Cole democracy was the primary value, not duty, and the primary thinker was not Goethe, however construed or criticised, but Rousseau. A major difference between Cole and the Webbs here was that Cole was generally cynical about categories like the state and consequently was dubious about practices such as representation. Whether implicitly or explicitly, Cole's attraction was to the idea that small was desirable if not beautiful, that simplicity and proximity were preferable to complexity and scale. In short, Cole was spiritually attuned to medievalism, for while he rejected ideas of social reversion and the blissful peasant utopia, he saw the guild as a type of Organisation which had still not exhausted its modern potentiality. Throughout the earlier decades of his life and writing Cole was concerned with the producers' case. Against the Webbs, he privileged work and production, and consequently put the case for local producers' democracy, not national consumers' democracy. His earlier views - essentially those of the period prior to the Second World War - were thus closer to Bolshevism, if we speak of Lenin's utopia in *State and Revolution,* for Cole's early utopia was basically that of syndicalism. More significantly than Lenin, however, Cole's concern with work aligned him directly to local tradition in the figure of William Morris. While the Webbs, like most other British radicals, had claimed some affinity with the firm of Morris, Cole followed a more direct line. Cole drew actively on the romantic current from Ruskin to Morris. Like Morris he saw a necessary relationship between work and aesthetics. Where the Webbs, like Kautsky, viewed work as central yet drew strong distinctions between a future of necessity and a future of freedom, locating freedom outside work, Cole wanted the future to be about freedom in work.

Like other *fin de siecle* radicals, Cole also used the language of function, but with reference to the division of social powers. In his *Self Government in Industry,* for example, Cole (1918) had argued that it was necessary to divide the functions of the state from those of trade unions. The state's realm was consumer representation; unions were to represent the producers. But what were Cole's hopes in all this? As Jack Vowles has argued in his lamentably unpublished thesis, 'From Corporatism to Workers' Control: The Formation of British Guild Socialism', the guild movement was neither always nor necessarily socialist. The Guildsmen were not only socialists, but sometimes outright medievalists, sometimes capitalists. Indeed, as Vowles (ms, p.61) observes, Ruskin could be counted as a preindustrial, agrarian syndicalist. More generally, the guilds themselves had been something less than democratic, a fact which some Guildsmen such as A. J. Penty heartily endorsed (Vowles ms, 74). So democracy was not necessarily a core value for the guild movement.

The guild movement was then turned, in part, into the guild socialist movement by the likes of Cole, who came by the Great War to advocate a functional democracy, neither a political nor a mass democracy, but a Rousseau-like utopia, adding in the corporations which Rousseau himself had rejected. Plainly syndicalism was beyond, and well after Rousseau's vision; yet Cole's attachment to syndicalism was no less limpet-like than his intellectual attachment to Rousseau. Guild socialism effectively became a kind of formal nomenclature which legitimised this half-holy marriage. What Cole could not bear, especially in the period around the First World War, was the kind of boring collectivism he associated with the Webbs. Still politically petulant, he chose to argue that the option between syndicalism and collectivism put right-thinking radicals in no bind at all.

> Forced to choose, it would be the duty and the impulse of every good man to choose Syndicalism, despite the dangers it involves. For Syndicalism at least aims high ... Syndicalism is the infirmity of noble minds: Collectivism is at best only the sordid dream of a business man with a conscience. Fortunately, we have not to choose between these two: for in the Guild idea Socialism and Syndicalism are reconciled (Cole 1918, p.122).

But was Cole's utopia a new synthesis, a new principle, or something else? Guild socialism seems in Cole's theory to work as an emblem for something new which is actually old - medieval; and to cover the commitment to something newer, but also backward-looking - syndicalism. Like Sidney Webb, Marx, and most other modern socialists, Cole argued that guild socialism was not an imagining of utopia in the clouds, but a giving of form and direction to definite tendencies already at work in society. Thus while evolution was a moving force, the process of evolution itself reached back to the guilds, and to notions of commutative justice such as the 'Just Price' (Cole 1920, p.43). Taking on the spirit rather than letter of the guilds meant arguing for a National Guild, an association of all workers by hand and brain concerned in the carrying out of a particular industry or service which would then facilitate the running of that industry or service on behalf of the whole community. Only in this way could self-government and freedom be achieved in *work* (Cole 1920, p.49). Yet this case referred not only to Rousseau, or silently to the Marx who shadows Cole's utopia. As Reckitt had wittily put it, Cole was the Bolshevik Soul with the Fabian Muzzle, but he was also more than that: he was also an English pluralist, taking up a positive stance with reference to the work of J.N. Figgis (Cole 1920, p.117) So the argument developed, in Cole's hands, that there should be all manner of guilds, for producers, for consumers, for civic service, for citizen groups, that there should be no single or central source of power, that power ought and need be pluralised.

This was why the state had no special or general claims, for Cole. Like the Webbs, and their principle of differentiation, Cole thus thought it a good organisational principle that power be dispersed, but unlike them he saw no special, sometimes even no legitimate role for the state in society. Having thus modified the work of his hero, Rousseau, by adding corporations, he also refused the very idea of a general will. It was not simply his line of objection that representation was difficult, if not impossible, that made Cole argue for democracy while the Webbs argued for Democracy. For Cole there could be no elect, no Hegelian or Webbian civil service; socialism was to be conceived as functional democracy, but with the decentred parts working in happy autonomy and not to the governing hum or clatter of the planners' office. Here, Cole's authority was not Figgis or Rousseau, but Lenin's *State and Revolution* writing in 1920, Cole does not blink an eyelid at this peculiarly diverse bunch of witnesses, united, like his varying guilds, only by their differences.

Yet above these varying guilds would still remain a National Commune or Association of Guilds, differing from the old state in that each part was functionally representative, making no claim to general representation at all (Cole 1920, p.137). Where the Webbs had their functionally differentiated principle of formal representation, Cole envisaged nothing more than a council of councils, to deliberate over the competing claims of functional groups and to perform ancillary tasks such as external relations and coercive functions. In the countryside, Cole consistently argued, collectivism was also inappropriate, and here he argued against Kautsky's views that agriculture must follow similar patterns of concentration to industry (Cole 1920, 164). But he agreed with classical Social Democracy and Bolshevism that economic power precedes political power, that labour representation of itself would change nothing. Attracted simultaneously to co-operation and to syndicalism, to evolution and revolution, Cole did indeed represent something of a puzzle, a quandary which is resolved at least momentarily by Anthony Wright's (1979) shrewd suggestion that Cole's was a bifocal vision, coupling a longer view, more rigid, with pragmatism about immediate concerns. In the longer view, Cole could afford to be romantic, looking back to the

Middle Ages, forward through the hopes of the new working class struggles after the First World War, thinking pluralistically and optimistically; in the shorter term, more and more dominant into his later years, Labour, locally and the Soviet Union internationally would loom larger. Cole thus shifted, however gradually, from a position closer to Marxism to one more akin to liberalism, with which his pluralism already showed affinities, just as his practical concerns shifted gently from social theory to social policy and his identity from that of prickly critic to practical adviser. In the lower bifocal, Cole was eventually to come far closer practically to his earlier irritants, those Webbs - and to argue, thus, that work was more like necessity, leisure more akin to freedom and so on. Guild socialism finally became, for Cole, a utopian project in the bad sense: the upper, pinkish lens eventually fell out of his vision.

Probably Wright is correct in his assessment that where the Webbs became Sovietists, Cole became a circumstantial Statist. In response to continuing economic crises, the state took on a new practical legitimacy for Cole (Wright 1979, p.154). And yet, analytically, the remnants of the superior vision also remained evident, for Cole was prepared to argue in his monumental *History of Socialist Thought* that both labourism and communism were in fact forms of evolving state capitalism. Perhaps because of his historical sense, Cole did not seem morbidly bitter about this outcome. Doubtless he had pondered Morris' epigrammatic wisdom in *A Dream of John Ball,* how it is that 'men fight and lose the battle, and the thing that they fought for comes about in spite of their defeat, and when it comes turns out not to be what they meant, and other men have to fight for what they meant under another name' (Morris 1918, pp.39-40). For he had argued, as early as 1922, that the exhaustion of guild socialism was to do with the fact that it had done its work, not least of all in influencing the Webbs' *Constitution for the Socialist Commonwealth* (G.D.H. Cole, untitled ms, *c.*1922, Box 1 B3/3/E, article 4, p.7). A similar case, as Cole later understood, could be made in defence of the terminal tradition called syndicalism. But was the bifocal not smashed, then, by the rifle butt of Stalinism? Cole had himself earlier anticipated the problem of the relationship between the Webbs' *Constitution* and the Soviet experience, the logic of his argument suggesting that guild socialism had not been integrated into Fabianism but rather had disappeared into it without trace (Cole 1932, pp.144-5). Dispositionally like Morris, a libertarian and an optimist, Cole was no more able than Morris to ignore that John Ball's dream would be lost in the long night of Stalinism and the dissolution of modern socialism into communism and statism as such.

Alongside the sober yet hopeful Cole, there stepped onto the Fabian stage two more debonair types - Bernard Shaw and H.G. Wells. Before Cole had much impact at all, Shaw and Wells were breaking into public notice as futurists, Shaw with *Man and Superman,* Wells with *Anticipations.* Shaw we will return to, for despite their dispositional differences, Michael Holroyd (1988) is right to indicate his special relationship with Sidney Webb. Wells, like Cole, was a bad boy in Fabianism's earlier history, and Wells was even badder. For while Cole clung to Rousseau, inoffensively, Wells took on the role of the modem Goethe - in the eyes of the Webbs, at least.

Wells has the reputation, unique among Fabians, of being the wilful utopian, the professional writer of utopias. As Krishan Kumar has shown, this recognition is richly deserved, for Wells was also the author of an idiosyncratic personal sociology. Sociology he viewed as the realm of utopia - and here, as Kumar (1986, p.188). suggests, the precedents are not Comte, Marx or Webb but Plato, Bacon and More. Like Shaw, Wells was to cultivate an open contempt for democracy (and Democracy) in tandem with a cult of the intellect (and intellectuals, a new class of 'Efficients'). And alongside function, and evolution, Wells forcefully draws to our attention another leading theme of the epoch - eugenics. For in Wells' vision science loomed large, and though Wells was critical of science as well it nevertheless governs his utopianism.

Symptomatically, Wells' leading statement is to be found in his A *Modern Utopia (1905)* - for it is a modernist utopia, a new utopia, Bacon advanced and extended as were guilds in Cole's utopia. Notwithstanding his fictional and sociological enthusiasm for utopia, Wells offers a similar stance to Sidney Webb's, that other people have utopias, what we have is science. Other people's utopias, for Wells, are absurd because they are based on perfect and static states. In these premodern utopias 'change and development were dammed back by invincible dams for ever'. The Modem Utopia, by comparison, is not static but kinetic - 'We build now not citadels, but ships of state' (Wells 1905, p.11). The new world, significantly, is global - this is not a utopia based in London; and this world is consequently migratory. All fixed points of identity have dissolved. Already we sense the restless figure of Faust in the margins.

Organisationally, this is a world of varied property forms, encouraged by separate associations of citizens. Eugenics emerges because it is necessary, in this world, to resort to 'a kind of social surgery' (Wells 1905 142). Duty and service are values for Wells; thus motherhood is defended as a vocation, a service to the state, supported by a kind of guaranteed minimum income system. The social system is regulated by the Samurai, a deliberate invention, a meritocratic elite. The class structure - for there are indeed classes, defined not by function but by personality - is four-fold: Poetic, Kinetic, Dull and Base, and here as elsewhere Nietzsche's Zarathustra is in the air. (Wells 1905, pp. 263, 304). All the same, the atmosphere is relentlessly modernist; so that Wells comments in passing that there 'are no more pathetic documents in the archives of art than Leonardo's memoranda' (Wells 1905, 242). Like Spencer, Wells was a Scientist, and proud of it. In his eyes, Leonardo should have been one too.

Wells conspicuously enjoys the literature of utopianism, speckling his story with references to Morris, Bellamy, Bacon, and Plato. Bellamy's own pervasive influence is especially evident in Wells' 1899 novel, *When the Sleeper Wakes*. Where A *Modern Utopia* steps boldly, if offensively into the twentieth century, influenced peculiarly by the outcome of the Russo-Japanese war, *When the Sleeper Wakes* comes out of the nineteenth century cast, where the somnambulant awake in horror into a dystopic world, at least in the direct sense that the future is worse than the present or at best, it is still evil. Surpassed by the technocratic optimism of *A Modern Utopia, the Sleeper* is somewhat less central for our concerns than the 1911 work *The New Machiavelli*. In this work Wells vigorously attacks the Webbs, appearing here as Oscar and Altiora Bailey, ascribing to them various fiendishly technocratic views which actually bear uncanny resemblance to his own. The novel is a kind of thinly veiled if one-sided public shadowboxing match between Wells and the Webbs over both the politics of the Fabian Society and the issue of Wells' philandering with Amber Reeves. It was through his behaviour in incidents such as these that Wells came in the eyes of the Webbs to act the role of the libertine Goethe impulsive, unanswerable, self-indulgent, Byron-like, a cad, individualistic to the point of explosion.

In *The New Machiavelli* Wells presents images of his own utopia as well as those which he ascribes to the Webbs. Order and devotion, he says, are the very essence of his socialism, and a splendid collective vigour and happiness its end. 'We projected an ideal state, an organised state as confident and powerful as modern science, as balanced and beautiful as a body, as beneficent as sunshine, the organised state that should end muddle for ever' (Wells 1985, p.112). Wells' utopia, transmitted here through his main character, is not without its nobility: he aspires to an England uplifted, transcendent, with neither wretched poor nor wretched rich, a nation armed and ordered, trained and purposeful amidst its vales and rivers. Faust-like, he lives through a motivating symbol which represents the challenge of improvement, 'the image of an engineer building a lock in a swelling torrent - with water-pressure as his only source of power' (Wells 1985, 154). Wells, portly and short, somehow manages nevertheless to stride through these pages as the taut, lean, white-coated savant, something of a contrast to the black-leathered figure of Trotsky. It is as though Wells somehow imagined himself Prometheus, in comparison to Trotsky, who dreamed of those who would transcend Aristotle, Goethe and Marx. Beatrice Webb meantime dreamed of a leader who might 'unite the intellect of an Aristotle, a Goethe or an Einstein with the moral genius of a Buddha, a Christ or a St. Francis' (Nord 1985, p.239). Readers of *The New Machiavelli,* however, would hardly be given this impression of Beatrice Webb. For Oscar and Altiora Bailey were firm-lipped megaphones of socialists, completing each other's sentences like the nephews of Donald Duck, advocating their own hegemony as would-be Samurai. 'If they had the universe in hand, I know they would take down all the trees and put up stamped tin green shades and sunlight accumulators. Altiora thought trees hopelessly irregular and sea cliffs a great mistake' (Wells 1985, p.165), - so scoffed Wells, powerfully influencing the public image of the Webbs as two typewriters clicking as one, apparatchiks governed by three-by-five filing cards, worshippers of ascetics rather than aesthetics.

Somehow the Webbs managed to deflect all these slings and arrows, never replying in kind - for that would show them to be as humourless as Wells claimed; and after all, Wells' outrage was largely to do not with their refined but austere collectivism, so much as with their criticisms of his own personal strategies for race-breeding. While it is today less than fashionable to separate the personal and the political, Wells' personal morality is of less concern to us here than his politics. The Webbs were right to identify the libertine, libertarian philosophical underpinning of Wells' socialism - he was, for them, a kind of Goethean stalking horse. Given that the Edwardian distinction between public and private was somewhat more emphatically drawn than it is today, however, it is also fruitful in this connection to discuss Wells' private, though clearly political polemic against the Webbs. For *The New Machiavelli* was in some ways a stylised caricature of a more specifically political, but private polemic published in the dark by the Fabian Society in 1906. For the Fabian Society, too, had its internal struggles - long forgotten, or Wells-disguised - and they were not only those of fathers and sons; the Society had its own, discreetly quiet attempts at revisionism, not only from young firebrands such as Cole, but also at the hairy hand of Wells. Wells' For Members Only publication was entitled *Faults of the Fabian.* The document itself was a premature post mortem, a savage critique disguised in parts as a friendly jostling of the Old Gang. Wells' premise and conclusion was straightforward - the Fabian Society was too small, too lethargic, too poor, too much formed by its humble origins, insufficiently given to the revolutionary task which actually stood before it. The point was to change the economic basis of society, not just to alter the way people thought about it. The Fabians were too silly - too much given to the politics of the sect, to mockery and giggling, too much marked still by their bohemian roots. And they were conceited for they believed society to be advancing whether people recognised this or not. Here Wells' critique anticipated Gramsci's comment on Trotsky, that certainty is a kind of advance guarantee against defeat, as it reminds us of Bernstein's characterisation of Marxism as a Calvinism without God. The Fabians, like sprightly schoolchildren, win mock victories too easily, failing to realise that these are pyrrhic:

> But you are socialists! We chalked it on your backs when you weren't looking! ...[nothing institutional will change, PB] yet socialism will be soaking through it all, changing without a sign of change. It is quite a fantastic idea, this dream of an undisturbed surface, of an ostensibly stagnant order in the world, while really we are burrowing underground, burrowing feverishly underground - quite a novel way of getting there to the New Jerusalem (Wells, *b51*, p.9).

The Society - the Old Gang - had miraculously managed to convince themselves of the impossible, that evolution, like Marx's old burrowing mole in *The Eighteenth Brumaire,* was written into the order of things.

Wells was characteristically scathing as well as witty in his broadside. In half-humour he tells the story of the mouse who 'permeated' the cat strangely, the cat is still alive and well, or seems so, and the mouse cannot be found. With equal ease, Wells demands readers to take up their Plutarch: the problem with this man Fabius, was that he never struck at all. And strike, they should, and must: for otherwise the Society was simply kidding itself, catnapping while congratulating itself. True to form, the Fabian Society established a Committee of Inquiry to look into the matters raised by Wells' charges. The Committee, which included Shaw, Sydney Olivier, Maud Pember Reeves and both Wells and Mrs Wells, in turn produced its own document calling for the tightening of the Fabian Basis, replacing the language of political economy with that of a fullerblooded socialism. So Wells, like Cole, took his stand against the Bureaucrats in the party. For Cole, after the First World War, this was a fully authentic stance. For Wells it was more ambivalent: for he ranted and raved yet, as Kumar (1986, ch.6) says, always managed finally to defend a middle-class socialist utopia, whether that of the scientist or the shopkeeper. Shaw, for his part, would likely have agreed with the desire for fuller blood, without sharing these images of utopia. An idiosyncratic man, he needed his own.

Utopia on Another Shaw

Bernard Shaw's views on the future were partly compatible with those of his old friend, Sidney Webb, but they were also different. In some ways Shaw does not deserve a place in this analysis, for even within a deliberately open definition it can be argued that he was no social theorist. Extraordinarily influential, however, he was, and a fascinating condensation of certain themes of the age. Most strikingly, Shaw was the early advocate of Social Democracy who came to despise democracy itself, and not just Democracy but the entire field of meanings of the concept. The critique or dismissal of democracy was not his monopoly, nor Nietzsche's. Cole, for example, had argued in a public lecture in 1920 that the Soviet system was preferable to the parliamentary system; likely his error of judgement here was to do with the images emitted by those systems rather than with their formal properties or content, and he was, after all, still then something of a syndicalist. Wells, too, was a technocrat who differed from the Webbs only in believing the Soviet system to be inadequately Comtean. Shaw was instead attracted not only to Stalin but also earlier to Mussolini, to action and to the decisive, to the sense that democracy had exhausted itself, perhaps not before time.

Readers of Shaw's *Fabian Essays* would not, however, have been struck by advance warning of these later idiosyncrasies. The early Shaw stuck to his brief; his literary projects had so far been thwarted, and the tenor of his essays was not noticeably different from that of, say, Webb's own contribution to the volume. Shaw's connection to the nihilistic stream in modem culture itself emerged gradually; its exact nature remains difficult to determine, though Shaw seems to have been consistent in one thing at least - a hostility to liberal myths of democracy and progress.

In 1889 Shaw was happy to view Social Democracy as a state of affairs achieved through Democracy, whereby the whole people was gathered into the state, so that the state could be entrusted with the rent of the country, and finally the land, the capital and the Organisation of national industry (Shaw 1989, p.182). By the turn of the century his politics were more florid. He had always been, and remained an incorrigible individualist - yet, at the same time, was a collectivist in sociology. Into the new century, the intellectual salon of his mind was populated not by Marx or Morris, but by Ibsen, Nietzsche, Schopenhauer and their local Anticipations. His sense of utopia is correspondingly different from that of the Webbs, Cole and even Wells. Shaw's commitment to Nietzschean politics was suggestive rather than substantive. The central text here, *Man and Superman* (1903) is aptly subtitled *A Comedy and a Philosophy,* and true to form Shaw spends most of our time keeping us guessing. Shaw is both wit and comic, critic and eccentric. The way in which he uses 'superman', it could just as well be the 'new man' who populates the entire genre of reforming literature. The figure of Nietzsche, like that of Superman, is thus symbolic, for as Shaw argues, Nietzsche only says what Bunyan had earlier (Shaw 1909, p.xxxii). Plainly Shaw, the iconoclast, is only ever able to feel at home in the company of other iconoclasts. As he has his revolutionist, Tanner, say: 'I no longer break cucumber frames and burn gorse bushes: I shatter creeds and demolish idols'. So Nietzsche belongs here, but Shaw views him as one of the gang. Thus he later has the Devil remind the audience that Superman is as old as Prometheus, adding that the worship of the Life Force is 'the newest of old crazes' (Shaw 1909, p.137).

Bergson does not seem to be one of Shaw's gang; perhaps this is because Shaw's 'Comedy and Philosophy' precedes Bergson's *Creative Evolution,* which was first published in 1907 (Bergson was only later to lecture in London, in 1911). Yet Shaw is very clearly in the grip of vitalistic thinking. Shaw has Tanner confess to his would-be beloved, who asks why he seeks her hand, 'The Life Force. I am in the grip of the Life Force', and then turns this, too, into a joke; she replies 'I don't understand in the least: it sounds like the Life Guards.' Plainly those who engage in this kind of parody cannot resist the temptation to self-parody either, so that it becomes even more than usually difficult to determine the relationship between the views of author and characters. For Shaw evidently enjoys placing some personal words into the mouth of his revolutionary, especially when it comes to concerns about the Life Force, Creative Evolution and the New Superman in his appendix to the play, 'The Revolutionists' Handbook'. Here Tanner-Shaw's utopia is more clearly revealed to be analytical in its premises, but disturbing in its conclusions. The premises involve arguments that civilisation is corrupt, and that in this context it is hopeless to expect much of democracy - the downtrodden will never be able to change the world. The conclusions are that only some process of sexual selection will place the human race in a situation where it can rise to this hitherto empty challenge (Shaw 1909, p.190). Tanner-Shaw here praises the 'perfectionist experiment at Oneida Creek'. The logic here in some ways resembles Trotsky: race-breeding alone can achieve a utopia where, in England, there ought to be not one but various Cromwells, a Cromwell-everyman, in France a Napoleon-everyman, in Rome a Caesar-everyman, a Germany where all are Luther-Goethes (and the women apparently are perpetually pregnant if not barefoot with these heroes) (Shaw 1909, p.193).

If the Tanner-Shaw utopia is reminiscent of Carlyle's hero-worship refracted through Darwin and collectivism, it thus offers a kind of jarring sense of the clash between themes of progress and disillusion characteristic of the turn of the century. Half of Shaw's soul is with his old friend Webb; the other half with H.G. Wells, triumphantly optimistic yet cynical about the raw human materials to hand. The latter trend seems to be predominant when Tanner-Shaw anticipates the possibility that unless we are all to become supermen, the world will remain a den of dangerous animals for the accidental supermen - Shakespeares, Goethes, Shelleys ... Wellses, Shaw? (there could only ever be one of him) - who will be fated to labour stoically on. Unlike Sidney Webb, then, Shaw refuses the unqualified ideal of progress and the idea of natural evolution to socialism. Those who simply propagandise, for Shaw, are as pathetic as St Francis or St Anthony sermonising the birds and fishes. Even will is not enough: we need, rather, the will of Superman. This returns the argument again to eugenics, for the 'only fundamental and possible Socialism is the socialization of the selective breeding of Man: in other terms, of human evolution. We must eliminate the Yahoo, or his vote will wreck the commonwealth' (Shaw 1909, p.219). Yet within moments Shaw is again pulling the reader's leg, joking about a joint stock human stud farm, which might be piously disguised 'as a reformed Foundling Hospital or something of that sort' and like the Webbs cast as the Baileys, we can only laugh or remain silent. For like Wells, Shaw argues that King Demos must be bred like all other Kings (Shaw 1909, p.223).

Shaw is probably closer to the Faustian personality than the other Fabian characters surveyed here, for while each was frenetic in his or her own way, Shaw was prepared to turn this into a maxim: 'Activity is the only road to knowledge' (Shaw 1909, p.230). Tearing about, Toad-like, in motor or on bicycle was only the outer manifestation of this hostility to the contemplative life; writing about absolutely everything on the face of the earth was another. Shaw always had views on absolutely everything, but he turned his wit and insight to the writing of popular encyclopaedias only in the interwar period. In between times he wrote his 'metabiological Pentateuch', *Back to Methuselah* (1931). Shaw here repeats the argument that his inspiration is as indigenous as it is Germanic; Bunyan pre-empts Nietzsche, Cromwell anticipates Schopenhauer. But it is Darwin who attracted his real interest, if not enthusiasm. Shaw proposes, in effect, that Darwin has been massively oversold, so that every idiot is now a Darwinist. Darwinism ignores the Mind, in Shaw's eyes; Creative Evolution offers a better view of humanity, inasmuch as it argues that as the weight lifter can develop or 'put up a muscle', so can the convinced and earnest philosopher 'put up a brain'. Neo-Lamarckianism presents a superior alternative to Darwinism: as giraffes grow long necks by use, so can humans extend themselves, upwards and onwards if not to celestial heights. Shaw embraces this theory as Functional Adaptation or Creative Evolution (Shaw 1931 p.xlvii), a view at once as English and organicist as it is continental and Nietzschean. Nietzsche's place is appraised in what he himself describes as Lamarcko-Shavian Invective: 'Nietzsche, ... thinking out the great central truth of the Will to Power ... had no difficulty in concluding that the final objective of this Will was power over self, and that the seekers after power over others and material possessions were on a false scent (Shaw 1931, p.lii). Again, the argument is likely Nietzschean by coincidence, rather than in substance. What Shaw rebelled against was the Darwinians' indifference to imagination. So called natural selection explained the easy part; it said nothing of morality, purpose, intelligence, accident. Darwinism was too materialistic: it pleased Owen, and other would-be reformers of character, leaving socialists with the mistaken conclusion that in improved environment lay the road to utopia. Shaw, for his part, took sides here with Lewes, in his *Life of Goethe.* Lewes had poured scorn on the idea: how could the world be thus true to Darwin, if there were pampered idiots born into the ruling class? (Shaw 1931, p.lvi).

Yet Shaw's theoretical populism prevents him from following such ideas through. The combination of sociological simplification and iconoclasm leaves the reader unhappily puzzled. Shaw's work presents itself as a kind of moving vignette, showing signs of very many dominant and popular ideas without explaining them or their significance, let alone placing them in any broader theoretical framework. Thus, again, for example, he offers in *Back to Methuselah* a great insight - that the Edwardian reception of Marx was influenced by the reading of works such as Buckle's *History of Civilization,* thus opening the entire issue of reception of ideas, and then lapses into a bad joke about Marx's *Capital* being widely read. Consequently, it is only to the very end of the long Preface to *Methuselah* that Shaw comes cleaner regarding His Own Part in the Matter. Now he explains that his earlier attempt in *Man and Superman* to use the Don Juan theme was too baroque; *Back to Methuselah* was to make up, by bearing the legend of Creative Evolution more plainly and forcefully, shifted this time to the Garden of Eden and its futuristic variations (Shaw 1931, lxxxiv). But is this then Shaw's utopia? Is Shaw's image of the future only a more romantic turn on Wells', socialism with lolling, idyllic supermen instead of enterprising Samurai? The answer to these questions is no. For while Shaw's wilfully utopian tracts inform and amuse us, we must look further yet for glimpses of his future. Nihilist Shaw was not; but he was, in all likelihood, something of an anarchist loosely disguised as a Fabian.

We have seen that the citizen of Shaw's abstract utopia, as evident in the plays, is the figure of the superman. All citizens, implicitly, are super people: there is no herd, no separate population of inferiors or outsiders as there is in Wells' world. What then of the future as portrayed in Shaw's political encyclopaedias, such as *The Intelligent Woman's Guide to Socialism and Capitalism* (first edn, 1928) or *Everybody's Political What's What?* (1944)? No pretence can be made here to anything like a comprehensive analysis of Shaw's public-political-pedagogical works. As ever, Shaw's views on everything are everywhere. The synoptic view offered by his analytical summary to *The Intelligent Woman's Guide* is, however, instructive; imaginably many more readers of both sex read this than the dizzy excursions into nether realms that follow. Shaw states some of his views on the future here with admirable clarity: they represent a kind of synthesis between his own wild spirit and his Fabian sobriety. Distribution of social and economic goods, he proposes, is the perpetual issue confronting human beings. Though all must eat, not everybody must work: civilisation produces surplus. If everyone worked, everyone would have a good deal of leisure. But humans were especially talented in the art of contriving more highly elaborate and unequal social arrangements. The theme of leisure is significant, because although Shaw shared the period distaste for idleness or parasitism, he evidently placed great store on leisure as the realm of freedom (Shaw 1932, ch.4). Socialism represented equality of shares of goods, and leisure. Eugenics could be countenanced, in this scheme, but the human stud farm was now rejected as too dangerous; consequently humans were thrown back on natural sexual attraction as the basis for breeding. For Shaw also respected Nature. Only equalising income could have a tangible effect on breeding.

Idleness was a problem not just because the rich could be idiots, but also because they were unproductive. There were obvious exceptions - Shaw uses the cases of John Ruskin and Florence Nightingale to illustrate his claim, because Webb-like (Shaw-like?) they combined unearned incomes with lives of great public service. Anthropologically Shaw is claiming not that idleness is a vice - given his commitment to the *vita activa,* the logic of his case is that it is in fact impossible to be idle, even for rich idiots who will, given the chance, eagerly go flapper-dancing or pursue a frenzied panoply of sporting activities (Shaw 1932, ch. 18). Hence the need that all should work, under Socialism. For work is not itself a curse, any more than what we experience as 'leisure' is a release. We ought not to work at pleasure: what we need is work with some pleasure and interest in it to occupy our time and exercise muscle and mind. We ought not live to work; rather, we need to separate out work from leisure, and rest. Shaw is thus anything but the advocate of a 'leisure society'. His sense of legitimate, Faustian frenzy is that it ought to occur in work, not leisure; and yet work itself cannot be fetishised for its own sake, a view entirely consistent with his romantic view of man as imagination.

In work, however, we are made into cretins, divided, as Marx put it, by the division of labour itself, so that we are doomed to be less than fully human: we are all, now, idiots, incapable of wholeness in life or work (Shaw 1932, ch.42). Leisure does seem to take on a greater significance for Shaw than, say, Cole, however, in that 'disablement' is firmly located within the realm of production; it does not reach into the realm of leisure, so that it is important that workers should have plenty of leisure. The place of women in all of this is something less than clear, perhaps because Shaw's addressee is the educationally enthusiastic middle-class woman, she who ought always to be thinking of England. Thus he discusses women in the labour market, but says little of domestic labour, past, present or future. Yet in all this, labour and liberty nevertheless remain counterpoised, and here Shaw reintroduces the theme that civilisation is to do with surplus, and with the saving of labour: Feudalism gives you the sweeping brush, Capitalism the vacuum cleaner, Socialism ... ? Socialism gives you liberty; liberty is leisure, and leisure liberty. The logical implication is evident: labour is the realm of necessity, leisure that of freedom, so that Shaw does here seem to be taking a step in the direction of Kautsky, and towards the utopia of leisure. 'Genuine leisure is freedom to do as we please', so quoth Shaw (Shaw 1932, p.320).

It remains uncertain whether such views are the conclusions to or premises of Shaw's now middle-class, now aristocratic socialism, for he keenly argues in defence of the 'rent of ability'. What matters here is that brains are put to good use, that is, applied to the social interest, and plainly Shaw shares the sense of the Webbs that their own labours are such - perhaps not under socialism, but at least under capitalism (fascism, and sovietism). Civilisation obviously rests on its ideas people, its blueprinters witting or other, and Shaw in this connection endorses the Webbs' proposals for parliamentary modification in their *Constitution for the Socialist Commonwealth.* His enthusiasm for these political changes is muted; the problem is simply that the older Westminster system is obsolete, more akin to the sweeping brush than to the vacuum cleaner (Shaw 1932, ch.70). Government, and implicitly strong government, is necessary to the future in any case: for without its compulsion, too many might shirk the responsibilities of social service. Compulsion, however, may lead to chaos, as it will likely elicit a potentially sinister alliance of the 'useless classes' and the trade unionists (Shaw 1932, p.354). The transition to socialism, however, ought to itself be parliamentary, though we are left wondering whether parliament will be changed before, during or after the transition, for Shaw takes his distance from any too gentle interpretation of Webb's proposed 'inevitability of gradualness'. Yet amidst such forceful resolution Shaw nevertheless recoils from regulation or overregulation, for his love of liberty is not restricted to the realm of leisure (Shaw 1932, ch.76; p.377). Certainly Shaw makes it abundantly clear that he has no time for proletarian socialism or Direct Actionism, for it is actually only Poor Man's Capitalism, like Poor Man's Gout. A middle-class utopia this is, but with the ambivalence remaining between compulsion and liberty. Characteristically, this ambivalence runs also through Shaw's views on fascism - better than liberalism, but too slavish before private property, a potential utopia beyond capitalism which refuses yet to take that bull by the horns (Shaw 1932, p.447). For such remains Shaw's hope, or at least half of it; as he concludes his Appendix, 'Instead of a Bibliography',

> Socialism means equality of income or nothing [!], ... under Socialism you would not be allowed to be poor. You would be forcibly fed, clothed, lodged, taught and employed whether you liked it or not. If it were discovered that you had not character and industry enough to be worth all this trouble, you might possibly be executed in a kindly manner; but whilst you were permitted to live you would have to live well (Shaw 1932, ch.83).

Shaw was nothing if not playful, as well as frenzied; and he played, too, with revolution. 'All very serious revolutionary propositions begin as huge jokes', he wrote elsewhere, in his essay on Ibsen (Shaw 1986, p.151, 32). As readers we remain in an interpretative limbo, puzzling still over whether Shaw still means to pull our legs or plans rather to remove other strategic parts of the torso. Under the Fabian disguise, even that of the anarchist pales into erratic individualism. So it was that Shaw read even Ibsen as a way to communism via the most resolute and uncompromising

Individualism. This returns us again to the theme of democracy. As we have seen, Shaw's *Fabian Essays* viewed Social Democracy as coextensive with socialism. The Superman, however, left democracy in his shadows and Democracy a formal commitment of a more or less mechanistic kind, as encountered in *The Intelligent Woman's Guide*.

There is little further enlightenment in Shaw's *Everybody's Political What's What?* Now Shaw sides with Cromwell, Dickens, Ruskin, Carlyle, Hitler, Pilsudski, Mussolini and Stalin against parliamentary form (Shaw, 1944). The stance was continuous with his earlier sympathy with Morris, also an opponent of parliament. He rejects what he calls the 'Hitler plan', but anticipates greater things to come in 'ultra-democratic Russia'. The muddle thickens as Shaw recommends that a change from 'our system' to the Russian system would be no change at all as far as the multiplicity of governing bodies is concerned; a bit of liquidation of slackers will help, for 'What the Russians can do we can do' (Shaw 1944, p.29) Shaw evidently favours the image of corporate life, and locates the existing malaise in the party-system, as well as in adult suffrage (Shaw 1944, 35-35, 38). He again endorses the Webbs' dual parliament strategy in their *Constitution,* but goes on to suggest now that it is the Soviet system which is to socialism as perhaps the Webb *Constitution* is to capitalism. A weaker than hitherto proposed variation on the breeding argument suggests that democracy equals equality, which can best be pursued by sufficiency of means, equality of opportunity, and rational intermarriageability for everybody, with production kept in its natural order from necessities to luxuries' (Shaw 1944, p.42). The remainder of the book tells us a great deal more of Shaw's eccentricities than of his politics, unless we are to take the one for the other. Shaw concludes by discussing Great Men, himself included - 'I happen to be classed by the sect of Shavians as a Great Man myself' (Shaw 1944, p.57), reminding us of his earlier throwaway, that there was little won in having someone else praise one's work when one could do the job oneself.

Conclusions

The utopia of Bernard Shaw may be interpreted in two distinct ways (at least). Shaw's wilfully, playfully utopian writing in the plays is suggestive of a radical future, part English, with a weak Germanic wash. His more specifically political writing varies from social democratic to resolutely undemocratic. Beneath both variants lies an amateur sociology, part governed by his sense of Buckle and Marx, Lamarck and whoever else he read or heard, for which democracy was a period or phase rather than a norm (and as we have seen, Shaw all too readily took the socialist escape clause on defining democracy, viewing it as equality or liberty or something like that). Perhaps more revealing of this than his published views is the attitude he took in correspondence to Friedrich Adler. Shaw wrote:

> We must get the Socialist movement out of its old democratic grooves ... The movement had its chance; and it proved just as incapable of seizing it as the Paris Commune of 1871 (Shaw to F. Adler, 11.10.1927, Passfield Papers ll I).

Socialism had lost its moment, Shaw argued, as had the Frankfurt School; but they did not celebrate this. Shaw, for his part, wrote days later in 1927, again to Adler:

> Now we as Socialists, have nothing to do with liberty. Our message, like Mussolini's is one of discipline, of service, of ruthless refusal to acknowledge any natural right or competence. We admit no liberty whatever until the daily debt to society is paid by the day's work. Liberty belongs, not to the day's work which it is a business of a Socialist government to organise, but the day's leisure, as to which there is plenty of room for Liberal activity (Shaw to Adler, 14.10.1927, Passfield Papers ll I).

Shaw viewed democracy as part of the loss, a price to be paid for moving on; the argument is essentially syndicalist, revealing again the historic and theoretical connection between syndicalism and fascism. Cole, by comparison, viewed democracy as everything, but preferred direct democratic forms. The Webbs formalised Democracy into functionalised channels. Wells hoped for the replacement of Democracy by Science.

Cole was the closest thing to a Marxist ever to populate the lineage of Fabian celebrities. Wells was arguably unable to transcend his utopia of the angry young engineer who would be scientist. Shaw would have liked to be remembered as William Morris, the libertarian who faced by Bellamy's frightening utopia would lie on his back and kick; but he was too much given to authoritarianism. For their part, the Webbs spanned different streams across the two centuries, emerging, as Beatrice put it, from a milieu which was 'conservative by temperament and anti-democratic through social environment' (B. Webb 1948, p.361).

As we approach the new century, Cole's utopia fades into its own past. Shaw and Wells arguably offer nothing positive at all to the socialist project today. Surprisingly, the Webbs still have the most to say to us from the Fabian tradition. For they understood, on balance, that modernity was a mixed blessing, and they were able to recognise the social necessity of differentiation in our time. The limit of their utopia is that they could not see the negative effects of this trend, but rather came to idolise the finely detailed but humanly dismembering fixed social division of labour characteristic of modernity. Perhaps it could be said that if the spirit of Cole's utopia still inspires, it is the letter of the Webbs' case which remains instructive. Fabianism as a tradition will not lead to the storming of heaven any more in the future than it has in the past. There is, nevertheless, much that we can learn from the detail of its arguments and internal tensions, from the combined strengths and weaknesses of its differentiation principle and the unfulfilled hopes of its pluralist norms.

3 The Webbs and the Rights of Women

Chris Nyland and Gaby Ramia

Beatrice and Sidney Webb's contribution to the economics of gender centred primarily on the right of all women to enjoy at least a minimal standard of economic comfort and security. Throughout their lives they campaigned to ensure that those women most vulnerable to economic exploitation were provided with a means for staving off those wishing to take advantage of their vulnerability. They were enthusiastic advocates of the unionisation of women workers and the enactment of legislation designed to ensure all people were provided with at least the minimum requirements of a civilised life and which compelled employers to provide minimum standards of employment. That women should be denied their right to protection from excessive demands on the part of those who would exploit their vulnerability, simply because males were not equally protected, was a claim the Webbs considered unacceptable. The latter conviction led them to engage in a prolonged debate with theorists and activists who insisted that governments must always adopt gender neutral labour market policies. This chapter examines the contribution made by the Webbs to these issues and outlines how their ideas were transformed over the period 1887-1920.

The Webbs' initial contribution to the economics of gender was provided by Beatrice (1888a; 1888b; 1890; 1898; 1902a; 1902b; 1902c). Through the years 1887-1892 she published a series of papers on sweated labour in East London. By sweated labour the Webbs meant:

> ... no particular method of remuneration, no peculiar form of industrial organisation, but certain conditions of employment - viz. *unusually low rates of wages, excessive hours of labour, and insanitary workplaces.* When we get any one of these conditions in an extreme and exaggerated form - for instance, when we find a woman sewing neckties in her home, straining every nerve to earn only a halfpenny an hour - still more, when we see all these conditions combined ... then we say that the labour is sweated, and that the unfortunates are working under the sweating system (B. Webb 1898, pp.139-140).

In her articles and in the evidence she gave to the 1888 Committee of the House of Lords on the Sweating System, Beatrice highlighted the disastrous effect unbridled competition had on the lives of unskilled workers and especially on women. Her personal experience of East London caused her to break forever with the free market liberalism which her middle class background and the influence of Spencer had earlier led her to embrace.

> [M]y investigations into the sweated industries of East London .... convinced me that if the capitalist system was not to lead to "earnings barely sufficient to sustain existence; hours of labour such as to make the lives of the workers periods of almost ceaseless toil, hard and unlovely to the last degree; sanitary conditions injurious to the health of the persons employed and dangerous to the public" .... capitalist enterprise had to be controlled, not exceptionally or spasmodically, but universally, so as to secure to every worker prescribed minimum conditions of employment (B. Webb 1948, p.19).

Henceforth, Beatrice insisted that the "evil spirit" that was the "soul" of the sweating system she so deplored was "unrestrained competition" (B. Webb 1902b, p.66), and as a consequence she urged the need for society to strengthen and extend both trade unionism and the Factory Acts and was highly critical of social analysts who celebrated the benefits of an unregulated labour market. This was a not uncommon response amongst feminists of the last two decades of the nineteenth century. As Feurer has observed in her excellent article:

> [T]he effect of practical experience caused many activists to reexamine their position. Actual contact with working women and experience with attempts to help improve their working conditions often challenged the old ideological braces for feminists' position on protective legislation .... Activists were brought face to face with women's problems in the workplace, which led them to reexamine positions regarding state interference, the labor market, and the possibility of women's self-help (Feurer 1988, p.249).

Beatrice's strongest criticism was reserved for those who lauded the market when their praise was based only on abstract reasoning. Thus she was scathing of the "Individualists" and that "batch of excellent ladies ... eager for the Rights of Woman to work at all hours of day and night with the minimum of space and sanitation" who knew little of the workplace yet were vehement in their opposition to the notion that employers should be legally responsible for the conditions under which workers were employed (B. Webb 1890, 899). She was convinced that social policy must be based on systematic empirical investigation. Like Charles Booth with whom she worked in East London she insisted that investigators must not start with *a priori* assumptions about economic laws. Rather, they must discover, as far as possible without bias, what were the facts of the phenomenon they were seeking to explain. In presenting her evidence to the Committee on Sweating, she stressed that her knowledge of the conditions she described were the result of direct investigation and not simply of abstract theorising. When researching the garment trade, for example, she reported that in order to gather information she had amassed data on 1300 sweat shops, classified these enterprises into five basic categories of work and then disguised herself as a seamstress and obtained employment in four out of the five categories. Further, she had followed up this exercise by having her secretary undertake interviews with the employers of the establishments in which she had worked (B. Webb 1888a, p.321).

Beatrice's stress on the factual nature of her evidence and her aversion to argument based solely on abstract reasoning was replicated by Sidney when in 1891 he was asked by the Economics Section of the British Association to prepare a paper "upon the alleged differences in the wages paid to men and to women for similar work" (S. Webb 1891, p.635). Sidney reports that initially he was reluctant to take on this task, because he had no definite ideas as to why it was that women earned less than men and because the subject had seldom been discussed with any reference to the facts of modern industry. However, he decided that he would at least attempt to collect the available data. In so doing he observed that he considered his efforts as merely an attempt to provide a preliminary survey which might generate some indications of the directions in which further study might usefully proceed.

In presenting the results of his investigation Sidney divided women's work into what he believed were four non-competing groups: manual, routine mental, artistic and intellectual. In his exposition of the data, he began by providing statistics on the time wages paid to male and female manual workers in the manufacturing industries of the United States and Britain. This evidence suggested that women manufacturing employees earned from one-third to two-thirds the amount paid to men. He next presented data on piece wages in order to determine if, in comparing occupational classifications, he was in fact equating like with like. The critical difficulty in fulfilling this latter task, was discovering any significant number of instances of men and women undertaking identical work in identical conditions. He found few instances of this situation because of the sharpness of the sexual division of labour and hence found few cases of men and women competing for the same type of employment.

Sidney next turned to "routine mental work" a sphere in which, he reported, it was more common for men and women to undertake tasks of the same kind and yet receive different levels of remuneration. However, he advised that care needed to be taken in determining the prevalence of this phenomena because of the difficulty of ensuring the work undertaken was equal in terms of quantity and quality. Moreover, the situation was complicated by the fact that women tended to have higher levels of absenteeism due to illness, generally had lower qualifications and had less labour attachment.

Having presented the statistical data relating to routine mental employment, Sidney reported that he had been unable to find any substantial factual information as regards the wages of female artistic and intellectual workers. He therefore sought to determine if it was possible to extract any general conclusions from the data he had managed to accumulate. He advised tentatively that there seemed to be four primary factors which together explained women's inferior wages. The first was custom and public opinion. This was the most potent of the four and though it was founded on the other three it was greater than the sum of their parts. The three other influences were the lower standard of life maintained by women, their lower productivity (a function of their lesser strength, labour attachment and limited opportunities for training and promotion) and their lack of protective power. To counter these adverse influences, Webb urged there was need to undertake a campaign of public education to disabuse the community of the many invalid assumptions regarding women's supposed "feminine disabilities". Women must also be provided with the skills they needed to enhance their productivity, be permitted greater access to positions of public influence, be allowed greater freedom and independence and be encouraged to demand a higher standard of living.

> Summarising roughly these suggestions, it may be said that women's inferiority of remuneration for equivalent work is, where it exists, the direct or indirect result, to a very large extent, of their past subjection; and that, dependent as it now mainly is upon the influence of custom and public opinion, it might be largely removed by education and combination among women themselves. I am inclined to hope most from a gradual spread of trade unions among women workers; and that even more in the direction of an increase

in the efficiency of labour which trade unionism so often promotes, than in the improvement in its remuneration arising merely from collective bargaining (S. Webb 1891, pp.661-662).

As the foregoing quote makes clear, this was Sidney's summation of his position regarding women's wages and as a concluding statement it was meant to be his definitive comment on this question. In her discussion of Sidney's paper, Pujol (1992, p.54), has ignored this summary and has asserted that Sidney believed that women's lesser pay was simply a consequence of their productivity relative to men. For Pujol the advantage of ignoring the summary statement is that it enables her to maintain that Sidney was a purveyor of a patriarchal economics. This is an argument that is difficult to sustain if one acknowledges that he concluded women's lesser pay is a consequence of their past subjection and the influence of patriarchal ideas and customs and that he suggested wage inequality might be most effectively overcome by encouraging women to become organised.

The Webbs conviction that social analysis needed to be founded on a substantial factual foundation and their aversion to the making of generalisations purely on the basis of deduction did not mean they were vulgar empiricists but rather that they believed effective investigation requires both facts and principles. Their commitment to a methodology which emphasised both these elements was made especially clear when, shortly after their marriage in 1892, Sidney gave evidence to the Royal Commission on Labour. When providing his testimony, Sidney observed repeatedly that if the Commissioners were to obtain the knowledge they sought it was imperative that they undertake empirical and statistical studies and not confine their analysis to the use of logic, deduction and the cross-examination of witnesses. In short, they should abjure excessive reliance on abstract principles and realise that analysts must give consideration to both principles and facts (Royal Commission 1893-94, p.266).

In his evidence to the Royal Commission, Sidney also made a number of observations specific to the issue of women's position within the labour market. He repeated Beatrice's assessment that the Factory Act needed to be strengthened and extended and observed that ideally he would prefer to see a "condition of society in which the mother of a family did not work for her living at all" though he insisted he was opposed to the state prohibiting their employment (Royal Commission 1893-94, pp.259, 299-300). Sidney's assertion regarding working mothers is a reflection of the significance the Webbs placed on "married women's work" within the home as had been revealed by Beatrice when she discussed the living conditions and home life of London dock workers.

> In common with all other working men with a moderate but regular income, the permanent dock labourer is made by his wife. If she be a tidy woman and a good manager, decently versed in the rare arts of cooking and sewing, the family life is independent, even comfortable, and the children may follow in the father's footsteps or rise to better things. If she be a gossip and a bungler - worse still, a drunkard - the family sink to the low level of the East London street; and the children are probably added to the number of those who gain their livelihood by irregular work and by irregular means (B. Webb 1902a, p.25).

The Webbs were very much aware that many working class families could not survive in a world in which mothers concentrated solely on the care of their families. For this reason, by the early 1890s they were urging the need for the "endowment of motherhood", that is community payment of a wage for housework (B. Webb 1983, pp.53-54).

After the Royal Commission presented its final report, Beatrice published a scathing review of its findings in which she castigated the Commissioners for their failure to undertake detailed empirical studies of the issues they had been asked to investigate. The Commission, she asserted, had failed and had proved a "lamentable fiasco", because the overwhelming majority of the Commissioners had been content to settle for "abstract considerations" rather than systematic investigation. She acknowledged that in some instances impressive investigative work had been undertaken which produced important factual information. This included a study of women's employment. But these were rare exceptions and in the case of the investigation into women's labour the success achieved was only due to the fact that the investigators had largely ignored their terms of reference. Beatrice also castigated the Commission for the "timid acquiescence" manifest in its recommendations. She excluded from this last criticism the Minority Report submitted by the four "working-men" Commissioners. The series of recommendations advanced by these men, she observed, were useful, practical and most importantly were "put forward avowedly as parts of a systematic industrial and political policy" (B. Webb 1984, p.8). That Beatrice approved of the Minority Report is not surprising given it was in fact written for the trade unionists by Sidney Webb.

As regards women, the Minority Report observed that there appeared little hope that trade unionism alone could free the many thousands of workers in the sweated trades from the long hours and insanitary conditions they were forced to endure. Therefore, it was recommended that the Factory Act be extended in a manner which would deal effectively with these evils. It was observed that this did not require the enactment of "special legislation for women" for the needed reforms should be designed to protect male and female workers equally. The single exception the authors of the Minority Report made to this general rule was in the lead industry where it was concluded:

> Though we are loath to recommend the closing of any career to women, we are driven, by the medical evidence of their greater susceptibility to lead poisoning, to the conclusion that their employment should be absolutely prohibited (Labour Commission 1894, p.138).

The Case for the Factory Acts

Through 1895 Beatrice delivered a series of lectures to women's groups on the need for labour market reform and in support of legislation that would extent the coverage of the Factory Act. Such a Bill was introduced in 1895 and immediately generated an intense and heated discussion. The proposed reforms gained the endorsement of the trade unions, the associations of working women, the labour feminists and the female factory inspectors, amongst others. As usual, most employers objected, though even amongst the capitalists there was no unanimity. However, the employers who did come out in opposition found that they were not alone for they received active support from the "equal rights" feminists, those whom Beatrice described as the "able and devoted ladies who have usually led the cause of women's enfranchisement" (B. Webb 1896, p.3).

The equal rights feminists, as Hutchins (1915, p.121) has observed, constituted the "Right wing of the Women's Movement" a faction characterised by a tendency to place its primary emphasise on the need for women to attain the vote, by a hostility to men and by a commitment to classical liberal economics and ideology. Their involvement in the struggle for the rights of women was primarily an outcome of the discrimination experienced by the women of the middle class. The beliefs of these individuals reflected their origins in that they tended to emphasise the liberal freedoms and in particular the right of the individual to an equal chance to compete in the market place. Though aware that by the 1890s the most enthusiastic supporters of the Factory Acts were the women factory workers, these individuals urged freedom of contract on working class women and bitterly opposed the imposition of legal restrictions on the capitalist's use of female labour.

By contrast, the labour feminists drew their support primarily from the working class and from those middle-class women who found it impossible to ignore the fact that the overwhelming majority of employed women supported the extension of the Factory Acts. As with the equal rightists the labour feminists opposed male domination and patriarchal social relations. However, they differed from the former in that they emphasised the need to give priority to improving the well-being of those women in greatest material need, urged solidarity between the sexes, and tended towards a socialistic solution to women's oppression. Moreover, they believed the free market policies that equal rightists were urging upon the women of the working class were largely designed to serve the interests of middle and upper class women. The latter individuals claimed to be fighting for the rights of all women just as the men of the bourgeoisie had claimed they fought for all men when they campaigned for the "rights of man". As far as the labour feminists were concerned, however, the rightists' claims were as fraudulent as had been the claims of the men of their class. They believed this was made clear above all by the fact that the rightists opposed regulation of the labour market despite the fact that the women of the working class wanted regulation and that the free market tended to have a disastrous effect on the lives of the women of the poorest section of society. In short, the labour feminists believed the rightists opposed regulation and ignored the interests of the women of the working class because the interests of the more privileged women in society were best served by an unregulated labour market. The difference between the two groups and the fact that their interests were not merely divergent but diametrically opposed has been well captured by Hutchins.

> The middle-class woman's agitation was inevitably influenced by the ideals of her class, a class largely engaged in competitive business of one kind or another. Equality of opportunity, permission to compete with men and try their luck in open market, was what the women of this type demanded, with considerable justification, and with admirable courage. The working woman, on the other hand, the victim of that very unrestricted competition which her better off sister was demanding, before all things needed improved wages and conditions of work, for which State protection and combination with men were essential (Hutchins 1915, p.196; see also Klein 1971, p.15 and Feurer 1988).

Hutchins' assertion that the different perspective adopted by the two factions reflected the class interests of each is similar to the argument developed by M. A. (1914, 14-16) in her Fabian pamphlet *The Economic Foundations of the Women's Movement.* A recent assessment in the same vein has been advanced by Feurer:

> To labor women [the avocation of free market economics] ....
> seemed to deny the historical position of women in the labor market.
> While unregulated access to employment meant greater freedom to
> middle-class women, it condemned working women to intolerable
> conditions .... They could point to the many prosecutions of women
> dress-shop owners who violated the factory acts as evidence that
> women's interests often diverged .... The challenge from .... feminist
> opponents of protective legislation was derided and dismissed by
> female labor activists as the rantings of upper- and middle-class
> women who denied the reality of working women's conditions
> (Feurer 1988, pp.258-259).

The rightist's disdain for the opinions of working class women is indicated by their opposition to the regulation of the hours of laundresses. Despite the fact that there were virtually no men in the industry and a survey of 67,000 laundresses found 65,939 in support of regulatory legislation the *Englishwoman's Review* opposed regulation and reported that it was "incredible" that women such as Beatrice Webb would endorse a law of this nature (cited in Feurer 1988, pp.252, 256).

Right wing feminists justified their alliance with the employers on the grounds that certain aspects of the Government's reform bill applied only to women. They insisted that this form of legislation was unacceptable as it limited women's ability to compete with men for employment. Women, they insisted, should be as free as were men to determine the conditions under which they sold their labour power and this was a principle which applied equally to the women of all classes (Hutchins and Harrison 1966, pp.173-199). In reply, though they preferred equal legal protection for both sexes, labour feminists argued that simply because male workers refused to accept state protection or could not convince the community that they should be protected was no reason for denying women protection from excessive demands on the part of their employers. Their general perspective as regard the principle of sex equality versus the principle of legislative regulation was encapsulated in Beatrice's Webb's observation:

[T]here seem to be two principles which, for the last century, have competed for public approval. There is the principle of sex equality; a principle which is good in itself and results, under certain circumstances, in bettering the conditions of a woman's life. But there is another principle: the principle of legislative regulation. Under the capitalist system we now perceive that it is imperative to regulate competitive wage-earning, and that without this regulation the physical and moral state of the workers suffers indefinite deterioration. Without this protection of the standard of life of the workers, no personal freedom or personal comfort is practicable. This principle of a legal minimum standard of life is of even greater value to women that (sic) it is to men because of their weaker bargaining power (B. Webb 1978c, p.387).

Considered in abstract, the Webbs were loath to assert which of the two principles they believed was the more significant. In the case of Britain, however, they believed that the needs of those least able to defend themselves were such that "if regulation be impracticable with sex equality" they would "prefer to get regulation and do without the sex equality" (B. Webb 1978c, p.388).

As far as the Webbs were concerned those feminists who refused to give due consideration to the facts relevant to the condition of the working woman and denied them the protection they needed, purely on the grounds of an abstract principle, were guilty of the same sin as had been the members of the Labour Commission. An example of the reasoning that the Webbs found so unacceptable was Millicent Fawcett's (1892) reply to Sidney's article on women's wages. Fawcett observed that she was in almost complete agreement with Sidney but felt that he had underestimated the importance of ensuring that the professions were opened up to women. Belittling the importance of trade unionism she argued that activists and theoreticians needed to emphasise the extent to which the market would induce a trickle down effect were women able to obtain a larger share of the highest paying occupations. Fawcett's paper was unacceptable to the Webbs because no evidence was provided to support the claims advanced and because it disparaged the value of labour market regulation. The paper was also unsatisfactory because it supported the right of women to act as blacklegs, that is so long as they did not undermine the existing standard rate by offering to work for less than the terms normally demanded by men. Fawcett argued that she had always regarded it as an error, both in principle and in tactics, to advise women that they must demand the same wages when undertaking the same work as men. Given that in many occupations the oversupply of women was greater than that of men, she held it was acceptable for employers to pay their female employees less than they paid the males they hired. Moreover, it was acceptable for women to accede to these conditions even if this meant their male colleagues would be excluded and the standard wage rate for the industry subverted (Fawcett 1892, p.176).

The alliance of capital and right wing feminism that opposed the Government's 1895 amendments to the Factory Act proved of great effect. It provided the employers with allies whose arguments undermined the support of those individuals who would normally have endorsed the moral right of employees to safe working conditions. As a consequence many important clauses in the Government's Bill were defeated. The proposal relating to the working day of women laundry workers, for example, was amended in a manner which meant that the only limit placed on the employers was that they could not compel their employees to labour more than fourteen hours per day. Likewise, the provision forbidding women and young persons from cleaning machinery while it was in motion suffered the deletion of the word "woman".

Outraged at this development, Beatrice replied by issuing a pamphlet in 1896 which was highly critical of both the actions and arguments of her rightist opponents. The tract began with her observation that it was important that nothing be done to impair the growing sense of personal responsibility in women. Indeed, reformers must seek in every way to increase women's freedom. But the question at issue was how best to attain this objective.

> When we are concerned with the propertied classes - when, for instance, it is sought to open up to women higher education or the learned professions - it is easy to see that freedom is secured by abolishing restrictions. But when we come to the relations between capital and labor an entirely new set of considerations come into play. In the life of the wage-earning class, absence of regulation does not mean personal freedom. Fifty year's experience shows that Factory legislation, far from diminishing individual liberty, greatly increases the personal freedom of the workers who are subject to it. Everyone knows that the Lancashire woman weaver, whose hours of labor and conditions of work are rigidly fixed by law, enjoys, for this very reason, more personal liberty than the unregulated laundry-woman in Notting Hill. She is not only a more efficient producer, and more capable of associating with her fellows in Trade Unions, Friendly Societies, and Co-operative Stores, but an enormously more independent and self-reliant citizen. It is the law, in fact, which is the mother of freedom (B. Webb 1896, p.5).

The rightists' claim that they had only opposed the Government's reforms because the legislation was not gender neutral was challenged by Beatrice. She observed that if this was true it was curious that these individuals had seldom been active in support of protective legislation which pertained equally to both sexes. Nearly all of the clauses of the 1895 Bill, she noted, applied to both men and women yet the anti-protectionists had given no aid to ensure that at least the sex-neutral parts of the Bill were passed. This is an accusation that has been supported by Freurer's (1988) study of the two factions. She observes that the rightist feminists invariably advised that the way to attain equality between the sexes was to abolish protection for women rather than extend the laws to men. For Beatrice the implication was obvious:

> It is clear that there lurks behind the objection of inequality an inveterate scepticism as to the positive advantages of Factory legislation. Indeed, the most energetic and prominent opponents of women's Factory Acts openly avow as much. Mrs. Henry Fawcett and Miss Ada Heather-Bigg, for instance, usually speak of legal regulation as something which, whether for men or for women, decreases personal freedom, diminishes productive capacity, and handicaps the worker in the struggle for existence (B. Webb 1896, p.4).

The enthusiasm with which many of the opponents of regulation clung to the belief that a free labour market was in the interests of all women convinced Beatrice that before examining the issue of sex-specific labour legislation she needed to deal briefly with the question of protective labour law in general. To understand the need for this form of legislation, she observed, it was necessary to realise that these laws were based on a "fundamental economic fact". This fact was "the essential and permanent inequality between the individual wage-earner and the capitalist employer" (B. Webb 1896, p.5). Citing Alfred Marshall in support, she argued that unfettered individual bargaining between capitalist and worker inevitably tends to result, not in the highest wage and the best working conditions that industry can afford, but in the lowest standard on which the worker and the worker's family can survive. Because of the existence of this imbalance in the bargaining power of employers and employees, workers generally accepted that a common rule fixing the minimum conditions of employment in an occupation was not necessarily an infringement on their liberty. Within the working class, Beatrice observed, the only issue that tended to be disputed in regard to regulation was whether the best means of introducing and enforcing the common rule was trade unionism or legislation. She also observed that workers' preferred method of regulation was normally determined purely on utilitarian grounds, that is they preferred whichever method was most effective.

Having made clear her support for minimum standards which employers were compelled to heed, Beatrice turned to the question of women's labour. She began by castigating those individuals who had called upon unskilled workers to abjure state protection and rely solely on collective bargaining believing this call had been issued merely in order that the anti-protectionists might avoid the accusation that their policies left the unskilled women workers at the mercy of their employers. It was a "cruel mockery", she insisted, to preach to these workers that they should rely solely on their ability to organise, given the paucity of the emotional, temporal and economic resources they enjoyed. The Government's Bill, she observed, would have provided the women of the sweated trades with at least some of the resources they needed in order to organise. Hence, to deny them legal protection from their employers was to deny them any protection at all. As for the claim that sex-specific legislation would disadvantage women workers because it would lead them to be displaced by men, she disdainfully observed that the threat of displacement had invariably been advanced by employers and their ideologists whenever any group of workers had sought to gain legislative protection. To her mind the opponents of the Government's Bill were merely voicing the tired and discredited arguments of their class. The only difference this time was that it was the "capitalists' wives and daughters" who were the most vocal in denying women workers protection from the demands of their husbands and fathers.

Beatrice's recognition that many of the rightist feminists who had joined with the employers in opposing the Government's Bill were hostile to all forms of protective labour law did not prevent her recognising that some of these women adhered to collectivist principles. She believed that unfortunately, these latter individuals had allowed their democratic sympathies to be overborn by a fear of handicapping women in their struggle for employment. Being sympathetic with these women's fears, she sought to disabuse them of their concerns by explaining in some detail why she supported the Bill even though some of its provisions were sex-specific. She began by observing that she was heartily in favour of regulating, by law, the working conditions of both sexes. However, as there existed a great prejudice within the community against the regulation of men's working conditions it was highly unlikely that in the near future men would be able to gain the level of protection that the women in the textile industry had enjoyed for nearly forty years. Consequently, if the women in the sweated trades were to gain any protection from their employers it was unfortunately necessary that the law only apply to females.

Drawing on the empirical evidence amassed by Sidney, women members of the Fabian Society and the female factory inspectors Beatrice also observed that many of the arguments of her opponents were founded on abstract principles and assumptions unsupported by the facts. To begin with, it was simply not true that women and men within the manual trades competed actively for the same types of employment. She acknowledged there were cases where this did occur but, given the sharpness of the sexual division of labour, these instances were rare and it was important that they be viewed in their proper proportion to the whole field of industry.

> It would clearly be a calamity to the cause of women's advancement if we were to sacrifice the personal liberty and economic independence of three or four millions of wage-earning women in order to enable a few hundreds or a few thousands to supplant men in certain minor spheres of industry (Webb 1896, p.12).

The second assumption Beatrice Webb denied was the claim that placing legal restrictions on employers' utilisation of women's labour was a pure loss to women and a total gain to men. This assumption, she insisted, was simply a delusion. Experience suggested that the workers excluded from employment by the enactment of factory legislation were not the women who competed with men. Rather, they were the female casual "amateurs" who laboured part-time and undertook factory work while being partly supported by their husbands. Because these amateurs did not have to survive solely on their wages they were able to undercut the rates and conditions of women who sought to earn their living as full time employees. This was a claim which had been documented by the Labour Commission which had acknowledged it was a cause of much resentment amongst unmarried women workers. It was these amateurs, Beatrice insisted, who were excluded by legal minimum employment standards but it was not to the benefit of men but to the benefit of the woman "professional".

In conclusion, Beatrice observed, the claim that the sex specific clauses in the Factory Act restricted the employment opportunities of women rested on a misunderstanding of the effect of this legislation on the structure of industry. Drawing on empirical research undertaken by Clara

Collet she argued that the facts showed that the growth of the factory system was increasing the demand for female labour. Further, this system of production had been shown to expand in the most dramatic manner precisely in those industries where state regulation of employment had undermined the economic viability of the sweater's den and especially in those areas where men had worked at home with their wives and daughters as unpaid assistants. It was, she insisted, an;

> ...arithmetical fact that it is the factory system which provides the great market for women's labor. Those well-meaning ladies who, by resisting the extension of Factory legislation, are keeping alive the domestic workshop and the sweaters' den, are thus positively curtailing the sphere of women's employment. The "freedom" of the poor widow to work, in her own bedroom, "all the hours that God made"; and the wife's privilege to supplement a drunken husband's wages by doing work at her own fireside, are, in sober truth, being purchased at the price of the exclusion from regular factory employment of thousands of "independent women" (B. Webb 1896, p.14).

In the years through to the end of the century, Beatrice remained active in the campaign labour feminists waged to improve the situation of women in industry. Much of her effort in this regard was put into the Labour Law Association, a society formed to promote "... the dissemination of knowledge of what the Factory Acts were, how they came about, and what had been their effects, especially upon working women" (Ward 1901, p.viii). In 1899 she attended the International Congress of Women where she defended wage regulation and argued that reliance on collective bargaining alone would induce a deterioration in women's wages. These claims elicited an angry response from her opponents who accused her of acting as a front for the interests of men (Feurer 1988, p.258; Collette 1989, p.17).

In response to these attacks, in 1901 Beatrice edited a book for the Labour Law Association which she titled *The Case for the Factory Acts.* Her chapter in this work was a feminised version of the defence of wage regulation she and Sidney had developed in their 1897 volume *Industrial Democracy.* Beatrice's objective in preparing this work and her understanding of the character of her opponents she detailed in her diary at the time.

> [The work] is to be a counterblast to the persistent opposition to factory legislation on the part of the "women's rights" movement

reinforced by the employers' wives. This opposition has for the last ten years blocked all progress in the effective application of the Factory Acts to other industries. It is led by a few blatant agitators, who would not count for much if they were not backed up by many "society" women who belong to the governing clique, and by a solid opposition to further reform from vested interests (B. Webb 1948, p.205).

In her 1901 book, Beatrice again observed that the individuals who were the greatest opponents of the Factory Acts were often in ignorance of the facts associated with this form of legislation and were merely arguing on the basis of abstract principles, that is they were guilty of what today would be known as "economic rationalism". She sought afresh therefore to explain why workers and indeed the wider society could not afford to allow conditions of employment to be determined solely by the market. She also explained the manner and extent to which the costs of sweated labour were forced on to the whole community and sought to clarify the practical lessons for women that were to be learned from studying the experience of factory legislation. For Beatrice and other labour feminists this experience showed conclusively working women's need for a comprehensive labour code which would prescribe the "minimum conditions of wages, leisure, education and health, for each class of operatives, below which the community will not allow its industry to be carried on" (B. Webb 1901, p.74).

The Exclusion of Women

In 1889 Beatrice's animosity to the right wing faction of the women's movement had led her to sign an article opposing the extension of the suffrage to propertied women. This was an act she immediately regretted and subsequently retracted. Her signing of the anti-suffrage document, nevertheless, has induced a number of commentators to brand her as an "anti-feminist". Caine (1982, p.23), for example, has argued that not only was Beatrice not a feminist she was not even "particularly active" in the late nineteenth and early twentieth century "campaigns which were waged specifically to improve the situation of women". Likewise, Pujol (1992, p.84) asserts that Beatrice was "outside the ranks" of the women's movement. These assessments, however, are difficult to sustain given Beatrice's fifty years of active involvement in the struggle to improve the lives of working class women.

A more valid assessment of Beatrice's feminism and contribution to the struggle to improve the situation of women has been provided by Nolan and deserves citation in full.

> [D]espite having been branded "anti-feminist" as a result of this single incident in her career, Beatrice Webb was, throughout her life, acutely aware of the inequities suffered by the women of her time, and of the need for discussion and organized action in their behalf. She frequently made clear to her male visitors her feelings on the equality of women. Upon hearing a friend's obviously biased remarks on the unattractiveness of virtues like courage, strength, and independence in women, and on the value of the subordination of women, she reports in her Diary:
>
> > I maintained the opposite argument (from Professor Marshall), that there was an ideal of character in which strength, courage .... persistent purpose were united to a clear and far seeing intellect; that the ideal was common to the man and to the woman...
>
> Like her predecessor, J.S. Mill, who stood in the forefront of those attempting to secure equal rights for women of nineteenth-century England, Webb's efforts in behalf of her sex took the form, not only of debate, but also of action. During a heated discussion on women with the wife of Samuel Barnett .... Webb told her "that the only way in which we can convince the world of our power is to *show* it." And she did just that, spending the next several decades of her life engaged in works designed to up-grade the status of women in England (Nolan 1988, pp.212-214).

In her analysis of Beatrice's relationship with the women's movement, Caine has also asserted that Beatrice failed to recognise the extent to which male trade unionists opposed the market interests of women because of their desire to keep their wives in the home. "She was unable or unwilling to recognise the degree of male hostility to women within these movements and, when she did acknowledge it, regarded it as a sign of residual prejudice which would decline as soon as women displayed their competence and their solidarity with male workers" (Caine 1982, p.39). Caine's assertion suggests that she is unaware of the Webb's discussion of what Beatrice termed the "bad side of Trade Unionism" (B. Webb 1901, p.71) that appears in *Industrial Democracy*. Among the activities the Webbs included under this categorisation was the male unionists' attempts to exclude women from certain trades merely because they were women. The Webbs believed the extent of this exclusion was overrated by the rightist feminists noting that because of the physical demands of manual occupations the question of women's exclusion simply never arose as an issue in many industries. Nevertheless, they accepted that such practices did occur and that often the male unionists' exclusion of women was purely a product of prejudice being based only on: "a deeply-rooted conviction in the minds of the most conservative of classes, that, to use the words of a representative compositor, 'the proper place for females is their home'" (S. & B. Webb 1897, p.496).

The Webbs deplored these patriarchal attitudes and were pleased that by the turn of the century they could discern a growing feeling within organised labour in favour of the equality of the sexes. This development they put down to the fact, not that women had convinced the unionists of their competence and solidarity, but rather to the growing dissemination of socialist principles, and more importantly, the fact that the men had become increasingly aware of the futility of the policy of exclusion. Where employers were determined to introduce women into a trade, the men had found, the exclusion strategy simply was not an effective means of defending male interests. Accordingly, organised labour was gradually abandoning the strategy of exclusion and was moving towards a policy which accepted women into all trades so long as they did not act as black-legs.

The Webbs sought to encourage male trade unionists to accept women as members of their craft and union by highlighting the fact that where equal pay did exist, as in the weaving trade, there tended to exist a "real, though unobtrusive, segregation".

> In every mill we see both men and women at work, often at identical tasks. But, taking the .... trade as a whole, the great majority of the women will be found engaged on the comparatively light work paid for at the lower rates. On the other hand, a majority of the men will be found practically monopolising the heavy trade, priced at higher rates per yard, and resulting in larger weekly earnings. But there is no sex competition (S.& B. Webb 1897, p.501).

This segregation was commonly a function of the natural or acquired attributes of the sexes. In the case of the weavers it was based primarily on physical strength. A woman weaver of "exceptional strength" who was capable of undertaking the heavier tasks was free to do so. What she was not permitted was the right to "offer her services at a lower rate than has been fixed for the men. She is not, as a woman, excluded from what is generally the men's work, but she must win her way by capacity, not by underbidding" (S.&B. Webb 1897, p.501). In other words, the notion of equality between the sexes was applied both as regards what woman could rightfully demand and what could be rightfully demanded of her.

The Webbs believed occupational sex segregation was unsatisfactory if it led to certain jobs being paid a lower rate merely because the tasks involved were deemed women's work. However, in *Industrial Democracy* they argued that it was a situation which had distinct advantages. It's primary benefit was that it decreased the ability of the employer to use women to undermine the standard rate in a trade while at the same time it enhanced the ability of women to establish and enforce their own standards. It also created a relationship where "each party is bound up with the maintenance of the other's Standard Rate." Women stood to gain by ensuring that men's rates remained high because it meant employers would not be inclined to substitute men for women. On the other hand, men stood to gain by ensuring women's rates were maintained at the highest level compatible with their productivity for by so doing it decreased the likelihood that women would be used as blacklegs by the employers. The essential point was that underbidding was contained and a disastrous downward spiral in wages avoided. The need to be clear on the Webbs' position in this regard justifies the following extended citation.

> ... workers at each operation should establish and enforce definite Common Rules, binding on all who work at their operation, whether they be men or women. The occupations which demanded the strength, skill, and endurance of a trained man would ... be carried on with a relatively high Standard Rate. On the other hand, the operatives in those processes which were within the capacity of the average woman would aim at such Common Rules as to wages, hours, and other conditions of labor, as corresponded to their position, efforts, and needs. The experience of the Lancashire Cotton-weavers indicates that such a differentiation of earnings is not necessarily incompatible with the thorough maintenance of a Standard Rate, and also that it results in an almost complete industrial segregation of the sexes. Women are not engaged at the men's jobs, because the employers, having to pay them at the same high rate as the men, find the men's labor more profitable. On the other hand, the ordinary man does not offer himself for the woman's job, as it is paid for at a rate below that which he can earn elsewhere, and upon which, indeed, he could not permanently maintain himself. But there need be no rigid exclusion of exceptional individuals. If a woman proves herself capable of working as well and as profitably to the employer as a man, and is engaged at the man's Standard Rate, there is no Trade Union objection to her being admitted to

membership ... on the same terms as a man. If, on the other hand, a man is so weak that he can do nothing but the light work of the women, these may well admit him, as do the Lancashire Weavers, at what is virtually the women's rate. The key to this as to so many other positions is, in fact, a thorough application of the principle of the Standard Rate (S.& B. Webb, 1897, pp.506-507).

The Fabian Women's Group

In 1906 Beatrice decided the time had come for her to take an active part in the struggle for women's right to vote. She consequently wrote a letter to Millicent Fawcett publicly endorsing the women's suffrage movement and began taking a more active part in the Fabian Society. The Society had always given nominal support to the notion of political equality between the sexes but had treated the suffrage issue as a topic of secondary importance. Beatrice determined this was a situation which needed redressing and accordingly, in January 1907 she seconded a motion by Mrs. Pember Reeves to have political equality of the sexes made part of the Basis of the Society (Pease 1963, pp.175-176). She followed up this act in 1908 by assisting in the establishment of the Fabian Women's Group. The members of this body became highly active in the struggle for the suffrage but were distinguished by the fact that they refused to accept the sufficiency of the demand for the vote. They believed that too great an emphasis on the franchise would result in women attaining no more than had the men of the working class who had campaigned for the Reform Bill. Of the latter Wingfield-Stratford has observed: "They had roared for the Bill, the whole Bill and nothing but the Bill, and it took them a little time to discover that what they had got was - nothing but the Bill" (cited in Klein 1971, p.24). The Fabian Women's wider focus and purpose was encapsulated in the statement as to why the group was established.

> The Fabian Women's Group was formed in order to study and to strengthen the economic position of women and to bring them into line with men in the advance towards paid work for all, for the equal advantage of all. It asks for equality of opportunity for women as for men: it asserts that if half the community is to remain in a weak economic position, progress for the other half must, in the nature of things, be retarded (Fabian Women's Group 1914, p.xvi).

Beatrice explained her "change of attitude" towards the issue of female suffrage as a product of her conviction that the state was failing to give women adequate support in those areas she considered the particular province of her sex - "The rearing of children, the advancement of learning, and the promotion of spiritual life" (B. Webb 1978b, p.242). She had become convinced that the adverse consequences of this failure were so great that there was an obligation on women to claim a share in the conduct of political affairs. In 1905 she had been appointed to the Royal Commission on the Poor Laws and the Relief of Distress. As a result of this experience and of the research she and Sidney had been undertaking into local government, the Webbs had developed a much deeper understanding of the extent of destitution in Britain. They had also became aware that destitution was an especially acute problem for women.

> That poverty had a female face was evident from the tragic evidence collected by Mrs Harlow [for the Royal Commission on Poverty]. Ninety-five per cent of Outdoor Relief was given to "able-bodied" women, sixty thousand in all, who had young dependent children and yet were forced to work .... The most pitiful tales of human suffering were of those families refused relief because of "bad character": the single mother visited in January living in one room with five children, her one-month-old baby wasting away, dependent on her neighbours for a half-pennyworth of cow's milk or the occasional tin of condensed milk; by March the baby was dead, the mother evicted; or the old lady whom the Charity Organisation Society called "a vile woman - too vile to be called a woman at all", because she was alcoholic (B. Webb cited in Seymour-Jones 1992, p.275).

By 1906 the Webbs had become convinced that the elimination of destitution required social policies which would ensure that all members of the community were able to enjoy at least a minimal standard of civilised life. In other words, the demand that there must exist minimum standards had to be extended beyond the employment relationship. It had to become a demand which would "cleanse the base of society", eradicate destitution and guarantee all members of the community the right to at least a minimal standard of decency. In short, they insisted the community must establish the welfare state.

In order to induce the Liberal Ministry that was swept to office in the general election of 1906 to introduce the reforms they believed were so desperately required, the Webbs determined that it was necessary to "make an atmosphere". This must be of a character such that the nation's leaders would feel compelled to enact the appropriate legislation. The letter to Fawcett was almost certainly part of their attempt to create this milieu. In her letter Beatrice stated that she had never believed in "abstract rights" but rather regarded "life as a series of obligations - obligations of the individual to the community and of the community to the individual" (B. Webb 1978b, p.241). Considered in the abstract, she believed women had no particular obligation to engage in parliamentary politics. However, a different situation existed if their failure or inability to undertake this activity resulted in the community failing its obligations to the individual and made it impossible for women to fulfil their particular obligations. In such a situation women must demand that they be given a say in directing the life of the community. They must have the vote.

Through the years 1906-1912 the Webbs campaigned in favour of a comprehensive system of social welfare designed to eradicate destitution. In 1909 Beatrice submitted a Minority Report to the Royal Commission on Poverty, which she wrote together with Sidney. When it became clear the Government wished to avoid its obligations, they turned to the public forming the National Committee for the Prevention of Destitution which at its height was to have some 16,000 active members campaigning for a legislative program based on the Minority report.

As part of this campaign Beatrice encouraged and actively participated in the production a of a number of tracts of specific relevance to women. Caine (1982, p.43) has suggested that Beatrice did not play an active role in the Fabian Women's Group. However, as Pugh (1984, p.114) has observed, the reality was that:

> Until mid-1912 Beatrice Webb kept the [Fabian Women's] Group busy supplementing her work on trade unionism and industrial democracy by investigating women's place in the unions, the obstacles preventing their full contribution to the national economy and proposing remedial legislative measures.

In the years prior to 1914, several important publications emerged from these efforts including a book defending factory legislation, *Socialism and National Minimum* which Beatrice published together with B.L. Hutchins; a pamphlet which documented the fact that paid employment was of vital necessity to a third of the female population; another which criticised the treatment of women by the philanthropic societies; and two others which criticised Lloyd George's National Insurance Bill. Beatrice helped construct the last two tracts while at the same time preparing her own "counter-blast", *The Prevention of Destitution* which she and Sidney published in 1911.

The New Statesman

The Webb's campaign managed to win a number of significant reforms though these were far less than what they had hoped to achieve. By 1912 it was clear the steam had gone out of the welfare campaign. However, they were far from finished with the struggle for women's rights. In 1912, Sidney edited a book, *Seasonal Trades* which detailed the oppressive conditions of employment experienced by women in a number of occupations. The following year the Webbs founded *The New Statesman* as a socialist weekly and Beatrice immediately began utilising the paper as a vehicle to improve the situation of women. In November 1913 she edited and wrote an introduction to a special supplement of the paper titled, "The Awakening of Women". The contributors to the supplement included Charlotte Perkins Gilman, Christabel Pankhurst, Mrs. Pember Reeves and Millicent Fawcett. In her introduction Beatrice argued that to understand women's demand for "a place in the sun" it was necessary to be aware that their awakening was not a manifestation of "mere feminism". Rather it was part of something bigger.

> It is one of three simultaneous world-movements towards a more equal partnership among human beings in human affairs ... paralleled, on the one hand, by the International Movement of Labour ... and, on the other, by the unrest among subject-peoples struggling for freedom to develop their own peculiar civilisations (B. Webb 1913, p.iii).

These three great movements, Beatrice observed, did not always advance together. Indeed, they oft-times appeared in mutual opposition. Nevertheless, they moved in the same direction and that was towards greater equality within humanity. In the case of all three, the oppressed were compelled to struggle against those who would arrest their development and who justified their oppression on the grounds that the dominated were inferior beings. In the case of women, millions of females had been forced to become wage earners but had been denied the potential for liberation inherent in this development on the ground that they were mentally and physically inadequate.

The tragedy of the situation is that, whilst we have forced these millions of women to walk along the wage-earning road, we have not unbound their feet! By continuing to brand the woman as the social inferior of the man, unworthy of any share in the direction of the country, upon the economic development of which we have made her directly dependent; by providing for her much less technical training and higher education than for the boy; by telling her that she has slighter faculties and smaller needs, and that nothing but toil of routine character is expected from her; by barring her out .... from the more remunerative occupations .... man has made woman not merely into a wage earner, but, taken as a whole, in the world of labour, unfortunately, also into a "blackleg," insidiously undermining the wages of man himself (B. Webb 1913, p.iv).

Both the claim that the women's movement was but part of a greater crusade and that women continued to suffer oppression despite the advances they had made were key themes in Fawcett's contribution to the supplement. The latter observed that one might be inclined to say that women's awakening was the biggest event in the history of the world but for the fact "... that it certainly forms a part of a still bigger thing - the rise and progress of democracy" (Fawcett 1913, p.viii). There remained many, she observed, who continued to deny women their humanity but increasingly these reactionaries were becoming a conservative rump. They were being driven back by women who were demanding their share of political power and responsibility, their chance in education and the right to employment within all occupations. In a reversal of her earlier commitment to the free market and to unrestrained individualism Fawcett denied employers the right to employ women for less than men and observed that in industry the cause of women was being advanced by the rise of trade unionism and by the work of the factory inspectors.

Fawcett's rapprochement with the Webbs has been missed by those analysts who have examined their relationship, such as Caine (1992). How such a transformation could have occurred Beatrice explained in the paper, "Voteless Women and Social Revolution" that she published in *The New Statesman* in February 1914. She observed that despite the breadth and intensity with which the women's movement was advancing the demand for female suffrage, it was plain to all that there was no hope that Parliament would concede the demand in the immediate future. While this fact was to be lamented, she noted it also had "some counterbalancing advantages" for those who were intent on the reconstruction of society. For what the intransigence of the anti-suffrage forces was inducing was a radicalisation of the women's movement.

> British womanhood, taken as a whole, is being transformed, under our eyes, from a passively conservative into an actively revolutionary force. In the early days of the suffrage agitation social reformers felt, with some pain, that, except on the one question of votes for women (usually for propertied women only), the "Women's Rights Movement" spelt social reaction. The eminent group of women who first claimed the vote belonged exclusively to the propertied class. They had been brought up, for the most part, in the strictest sect of Philosophic Radicalism. They were opposed to factory legislation, to the "tyranny of trade unions", to any increase in the taxation of the rich, and to any development of Municipal Socialism. They reflected, in short, the vested interests and the personal prejudices of the existing order. No one in those days doubted that if votes were given to women on the same terms as to men the Crown, the Church and the peerage, as well as the landlords and the capitalists, would thereby strengthen their hold on the British Constitution and on public administration (B. Webb 1914a, p.585).

Had nineteenth century women attained the right to vote with ease, Beatrice further noted, they would almost certainly have accorded this freedom little esteem. As it was, the fact that the two major political parties had opposed female suffrage had made its attainment a burning issue to millions of women. Moreover, the fact that only the socialists had consistently, even if somewhat mechanically, supported the demand for universal suffrage had not been lost on these millions. As a consequence, almost unintentionally, the women's movement was coming to embrace the Labour Party and socialist politics. And it was doing so to an extent where the most "Right Wing" section of the women's movement, Millicent Fawcett's National Union of Women's Suffrage Societies, had formerly allied itself with the party of the left. Prophetically, Beatrice observed, that if women were granted the vote by Parliament there would be a "stampede" of these activists back into the ranks of the right. But the longer this was delayed, she observed, the less would be the "reversion to the creed of laissez-faire in social and economic questions".

> But this is not all. Among the four millions of salaried and wage-earning women - the teachers, the clerks, the factory hands - the growing intensity of sex consciousness is being fused, by close comradeship with Socialists, into the "class consciousness" of the proletariat eager not merely for political but for economic "enfranchisement". I wonder whether Liberal Ministers quite realise how the contemptuous refusal of the suffrage by a party that claims to be democratic strikes the average woman in Lancashire cotton

mills or Leicester shoe shops? The insincerities, prevarications and tyrannies of the male Cabinet Minister, the male judge and male party journalist are becoming identified in the working woman's mind with a growing revolt against the low wages and the degrading conditions of employment which seem part and parcel of an essentially masculine capitalism. The votelessness of women (sic) is, at the present moment, tantamount to a rapidly spreading Socialism from one end of Great Britain to the other (B. Webb 1914a, p.586).

The following week Beatrice continued her promotion of the cause of women by writing the introduction to the second special supplement on women to be published in *The New Statesman*. This publication focused on women in industry, was prepared by the Fabian Women's Group, and dealt with women's wages, trade unionism, the minimum wage and the need for childcare. In her introduction Beatrice castigated those individuals who continued to insist that "woman's place is the home" observing that an ever increasing proportion of the female population simply had no choice but to sell their labour power in the market. She also challenged the notion that female wage-earners have fewer needs of body and mind, criticised the fact that women were expected to undertake the labour of the home even when they worked as full time employees and denounced the fact that the woman worker had no say as regards the taxes she paid and the laws under which she was employed (B. Webb 1914b, pp.1-2).

Reflecting the fact that the Webbs were concerned with wider issues than those relating only to the workplace and to the industrial working class, Beatrice followed up this contribution in July and August 1914 by publishing a series of five papers which she collected under the general title, "Personal Rights and the Woman's Movement". These papers dealt with the relationship between individuals and between the individual and the community, the birth-rate, women's right to maternity, the right of women to free entry into all occupations and their right to equal remuneration with men (B. Webb 1914). She also published a paper on motherhood in 1914 in yet a third special supplement of *The New Statesman* that was directly related to improving the situation of women and produced a major report for the Fabian Research Department. This latter report examined the problems of developing trade union organisation amongst school teachers, an occupation which she stressed was predominantly female (B. Webb 1915).

Beatrice was clearly the major contributor from the firm of Webbs, as far as women's rights were concerned. However, with the outbreak of the First World War Sidney produced a Fabian tract, *The War and the Workers* which was a handbook of some of the immediate measures the Webbs believed needed to be undertaken to prevent unemployment and distress that paid particular attention to women's needs. As far as women were concerned he argued that special action needed to be taken to ensure there was adequate work available for those women discharged from their pre-war employment and that training schemes were established to prepare women for new forms of employment. He also argued that it was vital that steps be taken to ensure there was adequate maternity and infancy care available both for those women who were employed and for those who were not. He followed up this contribution in 1915 by assisting the Fabian's Women's Group to produce a further tract, *The War; Women; and Unemployment* which also dealt with the wide-spread distress amongst women workers caused by lack of employment, training and adequate welfare.

The War Cabinet Committee on Women in Industry

In September 1918 Beatrice was appointed to the War Cabinet Committee on Women in Industry. This body was created to "investigate and report upon the relation which should be maintained between the wages of women and men, having regard to the interests of both, as well as to the value of their work" (War Cabinet Committee 1919, p.ii). The Committee was subsequently also asked to consider the nature of a 1915 agreement that had been forged between the trade union movement and the Government. The unions believed that the essence of this agreement was that pre-war employment conditions would be maintained and that "all women who should be put to do the work hitherto done by men should receive the same pay as the men whose work they undertook" (B. Webb 1919a, p.3). The Government denied the agreement had implied any such pledge and the War Cabinet Committee was asked to comment of the validity of the two interpretations.

Beatrice did not enjoy her membership on the Committee. She and the other members considered their efforts to be largely a waste of time given it was certain their report would be ignored.

> [W]e all feel that the Committee's Report will be still-born: the War
> Pledges are ancient history and any conclusions we come to about
> the future relation between men's and women's wages will have little
> or no effect on what actually happens. Alterations of the wage
> system will depend on the relative political and industrial forces and

neither the Government nor the Trade Unions, certainly not the employers, will proceed on the lines of ideal principle (B. Webb 1978d, p.3652).

This suspicion was validated even before the Committee had completed its work when the Government appointed a more representative body charged with examining the whole industrial situation (B. Webb 1978, p.3671). Nevertheless, in characteristic fashion Beatrice not only produced a Minority Report she also had her contribution reproduced by the Fabian Society and published as a tract titled, *The Wages of Men and Women: Should They be Equal?*

Beatrice's answer to this question was a resounding yes as was her conclusion that the Government had pledged to pay women the wage rate formerly paid to men and that it had reneged on its promise. Her disagreement with those who signed the Majority Report centred on the fact that they had only considered the conditions under which women attain employment and had refused to acknowledge that the Government was actively attempting to use the women who had entered industry during the war as blacklegs in order to undermine pre-war wage rates. She objected to the Majority's decision to focus on women's problems because she believed that to do so was to assume industry is normally a male domain. If the purpose of the investigation was to advise on the relationship which should be maintained between the wages of women and men, she insisted there should be an equal focus on both sexes. Thus, in her report she assumed that her task was to examine the principles upon which wages and conditions had traditionally been determined. She also assumed that the purpose of the examination was to decide whether these principles affected men and women differently, whether any such difference was justified, given the interests of both sexes and the needs of industry, and whether any new principle was needed upon which to base the relationship between the wages of men and women (B. Webb 1919a, p.7).

In her report Beatrice argued that the existing wage structure was detrimental to the personal character and professional efficiency of both sexes. It was also inimical to the economic well-being of the nation. The exclusion of women from the better paid occupations crowded them into the lower grades where they were compelled to accept even less than the inadequate wages paid to men on the pretence that women have no family obligations and have fewer needs, less capacity and a lower level of intelligence. She denied that women constituted a separate class who could justifiably be treated differently from men and insisted the time had:

.... come for the removal of all sex exclusions; for the opening of all posts and vocations to any individuals who are qualified for the work, irrespective of sex, creed or race; and for the insistence, as minima, of the same qualifications, the same conditions of employment, and the same occupational rates, for all those accepted by the private or public employers as fit to be engaged in any particular pursuit (B. Webb 1919a, pp.71-72). The attainment of these objectives, Beatrice insisted, could not be founded on the popular formula of "Equal Pay for Equal Work". While expressing the correct ideal, this notion was so ambiguous and open to manipulation it did not constitute any principle by which the relation between the wages of men and women could be safely determined. Evidence provided to the Committee had shown that employers were utilising the fact that it was often difficult to assess what constituted equal work as a device by which they could substitute lowly paid women for men. To overcome this difficulty Beatrice advised that the principle which should govern all systems of remuneration must be clearly defined "Occupational and Standard Rates" to be prescribed for all members of the same industrial grade irrespective of sex. These rates must be set by collective bargaining between the trade unions and the employers' organisations and enforced as minima on the whole industry. Moreover, there must exist a legal National Minimum as regards rest-time, education, sanitation and subsistence which must apply equally to both sexes.

Pujol (1992, p.86) has asserted that Beatrice's Minority Report restates the position developed in *Industrial Democracy*. This assessment, however, misses two critical developments. First, Beatrice no longer accepted there was any case for protective labour law that was sex-specific. The male dominated unions now believed that these laws should apply equally to both sexes. Consequently, it was appropriate that all special provisions applying to only one sex should be amended in a manner which would ensure that men and women were protected equally.

Beatrice's attitude towards different pay rates for men and women also diverged from the position adopted in *Industrial Democracy*. In this earlier work, the Webbs had argued that men and women should be paid the same rate where they did the same job but that the notion of male and female jobs had some attractions as it reduced the tendency for women to be used as blacklegs and reserved a proportion of jobs for women. By contrast, in her 1919 Report, Beatrice rejected this notion. She now argued that the existence of a male and female occupations served only the "vested interest of the male", being merely a device for excluding women from the higher paying forms of employment. It had given rise to the notion that whatever was women's work could be paid for at a lower rate irrespective of the skill and effort required. In reply to the employers' claim that women were not as efficient as men, Beatrice replied that this generalisation was unacceptable as a basis for setting standard rates as it discriminated against those women who did have the required level of efficiency. It was imperative therefore that the notion of male and female jobs be expunged from all forms of employment.

> There is no ground whatever for any deliberately imposed exclusion or inclusion with regard to any occupation whatever of a whole class, whether marked out by sex, height, weight, colour, race or creed. Any such artificial eligibility or ineligibility by class necessarily involves unfairness to individuals. There can plainly be no warrant for any other ground of selection or exclusion, whether in manual working occupations or in the brain-working professions, in capital enterprise or in the public service, than the aptitude and fitness of each individual (B. Webb 1919a, pp.44-45).

If it happened to be the case that in an occupation the attributes of either sex were such that they gave one or the other a significant comparative advantage it was to be expected that the advantaged sex would come to numerically dominate the trade. This was not a matter of concern so long as the efficient individual was not precluded for it would help to ensure an efficient allocation of the nation's labour resources.

Overall, in her 1919 Report Beatrice adopted a much less compromising stance than she had in *Industrial Democracy*. The tone and language adopted in the Report suggests that she had become aware of the extent to which men were continuing to exclude women from the skilled occupations. However, this is certainly only part of the explanation and to understand the other critical factor it is necessary to be aware of the debate regarding the employment of women that had been undertaken through the war years. In 1914 Beatrice had observed that a paradox existed at the threshold of the debate regarding equal remuneration for men and women. Feminists who insisted on women's right to equal pay found that within the trade union movement their strongest allies were the most anti-feminist male organisations. The members of these latter bodies endorsed the demand that women should have free entry into their craft and union and must be paid at least the same rate as men. Beatrice reported that the men insisted on the last proviso because they were aware that in many trades the demand that all rates be gender neutral was a very effective means of inducing employers to exclude women. In short, they realised that if employers were compelled to pay men and women the same rate, they commonly adopted a policy of only employing men.

The great attraction that women had in the struggle for jobs, as far as employers were concerned, was the fact that they could be hired for less than men. It was for this reason that many nineteenth century free market feminists had insisted that women had the right to take work at any price and under any conditions they chose. Beatrice, of course, found this suggestion totally objectionable because of the deleterious effect unrestrained competition had on the lives of the men and women concerned and indeed on the life of the whole community. She observed that women had no more right to take employment for less than the standard rate than they had to drive on the wrong side of the road. At the same time she was aware that to assert as an absolute principle that women must always be paid the same rate as men was to fall into the trap of the male exclusionists. Accordingly, while she believed that "paying women low wages, just because they are women, is a scandal that amounts to a crime" (B. Webb, 1914c, p.526) as late as 1914 she continued to accept that in many trades it was still useful to maintain a separate female and male standard rate.

The experience of the war years, however, caused her to rethink this position. In September 1916, Sidney again discussed women's right to work and their right to equal pay in a tract he published with Freeman titled *When Peace Comes - The Way of Industrial Reconstruction*. They argued that the period of demobilisation that would follow the declaration of peace was likely to be characterised by mass discontent. Indeed, there was the gravest danger that with the end of the war on the battlefield there would erupt "spasmodic and possibly widespread industrial war" (Webb and Freeman 1916, p.12). Employers were counting on being able to secure a heavy fall in wages, when several millions of men and women were simultaneously compelled to seek employment as the army and the war industries demobilised. The coming class conflict would revolve around wages, work intensification and the fact that the employers were certain to oppose the reintroduction of those skilled jobs that had been effectively diluted by utilising partly trained women and male labourers. He reported that the Government's pledge that they would protect the rights of the skilled workers to their former jobs and pre-war employment conditions was being mocked by the employers who were stating openly that after the war there would be no return to the former industrial situation, that they would be the masters.

For Sidney, the key to minimising the intensity of the coming conflict was the creation of sufficient work to ensure that the craftsmen were not terrified by the fear of unemployment. This development was critical, for if the skilled workers came to believe their families faced destitution as a consequence of others taking their jobs (men or women), they would feel compelled to fight. Indeed, against "being thrown into a sea of unemployment all the trades will fight like tigers" (S. Webb and Freeman 1916, p.17). Further, if there was mass unemployment after the war, Sidney forecast, unemployed men will demand the Government maintain its promise that their jobs and conditions would be saved and insist that the women and the newly introduced male labourers be removed. However, if there was abundant employment the skilled workers might be concerned that these newcomers could be used to undermine the standard rate but they were much less likely to insist on their removal. Assuming the Government adopted policies which ensured there was abundant employment, left the question of how the standard rate could be maintained and the women and male labourers kept in work. To insist that these individuals be paid the same rate as the craftsmen would almost certainly lead to their exclusion given that employers had generally found the dilutees were not as productive as the men they had replaced. As this was the case it was not reasonable to expect that the women and the labourers would agree to insist on the established standard. It was necessary, therefore, that there be established a separate standard which would reflect the difference in the productivity of the two forms of labour.

> What is required is .... "the fixing of a rate for men and women which shall be in equitable proportion to any less degree of physical endurance, skill, or responsibility exacted from the women, or to any additional strain thrown on the men, and which shall neither exclude women on the one side, nor blackleg men on the other". It is this delicate adjustment that the Government will have to make, perhaps by one of the devices suggested below (*prescribing minima only*, and securing by law the rigid enforcement of the minimum rates thus fixed). Only at this price can very serious trouble be averted (S. Webb and Freeman 1916, pp.19-20).

Awareness that there were bound to be difficulties in reabsorbing men into those sections of industry which had been feminised during the war was of course shared by others. Edith Rathbone (1917), for example, agreed that many women would be ousted from paid employment after the demobilisation if they were to demand equal pay as the unions insisted. She also agreed that the employers would invariably seek to use the women they had hired during the war as blacklegs in a campaign designed to break the standard rates paid in many occupations. Like the Webbs, she suggested the solution to this dilemma was a legally enforceable wage that accepted the principle of equal pay but also accepted that where women's biology or social position gave them a disadvantage, they should be able to accept lower rates. The level of women's pay, Rathbone advised, should be "sufficiently lower than men's rates to balance, but not more than balance, the inherent disadvantages of female labour" (Rathbone 1917, p.64).

Fawcett, (1917, 1918) on the other hand, argued that it was imperative that women be paid the same rate as men in all occupations. She applauded the fact that the men's trade unions had accepted the need for equal pay and lambasted the men of her own class for failing to do likewise. She believed those who advocated the payment of a woman's rate had overstated the extent to which a productivity gap actually existed between the sexes and underestimated the debilitating influence trade union exclusionism and society's belief in women's incapacity to undertake skilled work had exerted prior to the war. Both these influences had diminished through the war years, she asserted, and to argue for separate rates for the sexes was to assist in the revitalisation of these ideas. Given free entry into the trades and the support of the trade unions and the state, she could not see any reason why the principle of equal pay for equal work would not find an almost universal acceptance (Fawcett 1918, p.4). Indeed, she concluded, if this principle was not accepted there was no possibility that male workers would accept women into the skilled trades.

> The one chance of women being received into industry by the men already employed as comrades and fellow-workers, not as enemies and blacklegs, is in their standing for the principle, equal pay for equal work, or, as it is sometimes expressed, equal pay for equal results .... I am convinced that the best chance of women preserving, after peace returns, the industrial freedom which the war has brought them lies in the earnestness and sincerity with which industrial women maintain the principle "equal pay for equal work" (Fawcett 1917, pp.4-5).

An examination of Beatrice's diary shows that she believed herself to be the only representative of "advanced thought" on the 1919 War Cabinet Committee. By this term she appears to have meant she was the only individual who sought to preserve the interests of labour. She accepted that the three legal members of the Committee represented the interests of the Government and the Chairman-Judge she considered a "reactionary about wages", a man whose decisions were influenced by his "class prejudice". The two non-lawyers, she believed, were conservatives who wanted "a philanthropic settlement of women's wages, based largely on the function of motherhood but preserving the woman the right to undercut the man" (B. Webb 1978d, pp.3652, 3670-3672). As has been shown for the Webbs, no such right existed and it appears to have been this fact, together with the clear evidence that the Government was encouraging employers to use women to undermine standard rates, that induced Beatrice to support Fawcett's position.

Caine (1982, pp.40-41) has criticised Beatrice for refusing to accept women's right to act as blacklegs in this situation. But for the Webbs there was no real choice if compelled to choose between the right of women to work at a lower rate than men, in order to enhance their ability to take the jobs of others, and the need to preserve the ability of the working class to exert some degree of control over the wage determination process. Hence, Beatrice embraced Fawcett's demand that equal pay for the sexes be treated as an absolute principle and did so irrespective of the likely effect this would have on job segregation and market demand for female labour.

4 Beatrice Webb and the New Statesman Papers

Chris Nyland

Despite the abundant evidence that Beatrice Webb was active within the women's movement over many years, her contribution has been denied by many modern equal rights feminists. Seymour-Jones (1992, p. 206), for example, has claimed that far from being a feminist, Webb in fact embraced Spencer's belief that women were at a lower level on the evolutionary scale than were men and that their mental development was inferior to that of men because their energies were channelled into their reproductive systems. Likewise, Pujol (1992, pp. 91-92) has asserted that Webb accorded women's needs little significance and relied on the benevolence of men and male-controlled institutions for the implementation of her reform proposals, while Greenburg (1987, pp. 313-314), going to the limit, has maintained that Beatrice's refusal to embrace right wing feminism was a manifestation of penis envy! The overt antagonism that appears to underlie these assessments is directed both explicitly at Webb and implicitly at the class-conscious brand of feminism she and the Fabian Society embraced. The prevalence of the antagonism reflects the fact that many modern feminists are uncomfortable with Webb's overt meddling of class and gender and sustain a much greater level of identification with the right wing of the early twentieth century women's movement than they do with the class conscious brand of feminism embraced by Fabian women. The response is understandable but none the less unacceptable for the efforts of the Fabian feminists warrant recognition. Consequently, the objective of this chapter and the next is to extend the challenge to those who deny the feminist credentials of Webb and other Fabian women by undertaking a more detailed study of the gender specific papers that Beatrice wrote and/or edited for the *New Statesman* and by providing a close examination of her relations with the Fabian Women's Group.

The Awakening of Women

The first of *The New Statesman* papers dealing specifically with the issue of gender, edited by Webb, was published as a special supplement in 1913. Titled 'The Awakening of Women', the supplement included articles by several leading feminists of the period including Charlotte Perkins Gilman, Christabel Pankhurst, Betty Balfour, B.L. Hutchins, Adelaide Anderson, Maude Pember Reeves and Millicent Fawcett. The supplement also contained a "Select Bibliography of Feminism" which focused on the condition of women and woman suffrage. In her introduction, Webb argued it was impossible to understand the significance of women's awakening unless one realised this stirring was not merely a women's issue (1913, p.iii). This observation was not meant to belittle the women's movement but rather to make the point that women's natural allies were not the powerful within society but rather the oppressed. She argued that women's demand for equality was "one of three simultaneous world-movements towards a more equal partnership among human beings in human affairs" (Webb 1913, p.iii). Their struggle was paralleled on the one side by that of the labour movement and on the other by the resistance of those subject-races who were the victims of imperialism. While insisting these three movements for equality were moving in the same direction she recognised that they did not always advance in harmony. Indeed, within all three currents there were "reactionaries" who believed the inequality against which the other groups struggled was natural and inevitable. There were feminists, for example, who thought it just to exclude the manual working class and other races from political participation. Similarly, there were men in both of the latter groups who insisted male domination of women was a kindness and a natural right of the male.

Webb's emphasis on the commonality of the struggles of the oppressed was a primary feature of her writings on women. To convince women that they shared a common interest with workers and subject races, she quoted from an antisuffrage pamphlet written by Sir Almroth Wright inserting, when doing so "only the words necessary to show how easy it is to use all the arguments in favour of the dominance of the male sex as reasons for a similar dominance of a class of property owners or a white race." (Webb 1913, p.iii).

> The failure to recognise that man [the capitalist, the white man] is the master and why he is the master lies at the root of the suffrage [labour, nationalist] movement. By disregarding man's [the capitalist's, the

white man's] superior physical force, the power of compulsion upon which all government is based is disregarded. By leaving out of account those powers of the mind in which man [the capitalist, the white man] is the superior, woman [the labourer, the coloured man] falls into the error of thinking that she [he] can really compete with him [them] and that she [he] belongs to the self-same intellectual caste. Finally, by putting out of sight man's [the capitalist's, the white man's] superior money-earning capacity the power of the purse is ignored (Wright cited by Webb 1913, p.iii. - Webb's insertions in square brackets).

Webb observed that reactionaries such as Wright inadvertently advanced the case for feminism by highlighting the truth contained in Gilman's (1913) contribution to the supplement. The latter argued that the fact that women commonly failed to match men's achievements was not a consequence of innate inferiority. Rather, it was a product of an artificially arrested development imposed upon women by men. Supporting evidence for Gilman's hypothesis, Webb insisted, was all too evident and this not least as regards women's achievements in the industrial and professional fields.

Commenting on the papers by Hutchins (1913) and Courtney (1913) Webb again highlighted the extent to which capitalism was forcing millions of women to become independent wage earners and in so doing was compelling them to undertake many tasks claimed to be beyond their capacities - a challenge being taken up by women with an increasing degree of success. While rejoicing that this development was providing women with an unprecedented level of economic independence at the same time, Webb insisted the process was tragic in many ways. The tragedy lay in the fact that while women were being forced by capitalism to walk along the wage-earning road "we have not unbound their feet". This was a tragedy not only for women but also for wage-earning men, for it led many women to become blacklegs, that is, workers who accepted wage rates lower than was the norm within a trade.

By continuing to brand the woman as the social inferior of the man, unworthy of any share in the direction of the country, upon the economic development of which we have made her directly dependent; by providing for her much less technical training and higher education than for the boy; by telling her that she has slighter faculties and smaller needs, and that nothing but toil of routine character is expected from her; by barring her out, as Mrs. W.P. Reeves points out, from the more remunerative occupations .... man has made woman not merely into a wage earner, but, taken as a whole, in the world of labour, unfortunately, also a "blackleg", insidiously undermining the wages of man himself (Webb 1913, p.iv).

Believing that capitalism was bound to continue drawing women into industry, Webb argued that it was in the interests of male wage earners to accept women as comrades and ensure they were provided with the resources they needed to compete on equal terms. Where women had acquired these resources they had shown they could match men in the most difficult of tasks and therefore had no need to blackleg in order to obtain employment. Believing that the attainment of these resources required the unionisation of women workers and legal limitations on what their employers could demand of them, Webb opposed those feminists who favoured reliance on the free market. As shown in the last chapter, one leading liberal with whom she disputed was Millicent Fawcett. Caine (1992, p.245) has argued that Fawcett's "hostility both to protective legislation and to the role of trade unions in regard to women's work remained implacable". However, Fawcett's paper in the 'The Awakening of Women' makes it clear that she moderated her position both as regards unions and protective labour legislation. She now endorsed Webb's claim that the women's movement was but a part of a greater crusade for human equality and, in a reversal of her earlier commitment to the unregulated market, denied capitalists the right to employ women for less than men and observed that in industry the cause of women was being advanced by the rise of trade unionism and by the work of the factory inspectors (Fawcett 1913, pp.viii-ix).

Voteless Women and Social Revolution

The second *New Statesman* publication that Webb contributed to the campaign to improve women's status and well-being appeared in February 1914. This paper, titled 'Voteless Women and Social Revolution', sought to explain why even the right wing feminists associated with Fawcett's National Union of Women's Suffrage, had gravitated to the left and formed an official alliance with the Labour Party (Webb 1914a). Webb's explanation for this development centred on the fact that the suffrage movement was making little headway within Parliament and that the only major parliamentary body giving substantial support to women's right to vote was the Labour Party. She lamented this lack of progress and castigated those who would deny women their rights but also noted that it was a development that had "some counterbalancing advantages". The most notable advantage was the fact that the opposition to female suffrage was making even right wing feminists aware of the inegalitarian nature of capitalist society and this awareness was leading these women to find common cause with others who suffered inequality. As a result, even those feminists who had traditionally opposed factory legislation, the "tyranny of trade unions" and increased taxation of the rich were becoming truly radicalised.

Webb recognised that once women won the vote, many of the affluent women who were fraternising with socialism would "stampede" back to the ranks of the conservative parties, which represented their class interests. However, she pointed out that the longer the conservative forces excluded women from the electoral process, the greater would be the cost they would pay. By advancing this observation, it is probable that she was seeking both to pressure the right wing political parties to moderate their opposition to woman suffrage and to encourage the Labour Party to continue its support for women's right to vote.

Women in Industry

Webb's paper on the suffrage was followed a week later by a second *New Statesman* supplement on women, which she both edited and introduced. This collection dealt specifically with women in industry and all contributors were members of the Fabian Women's Group. This organisation was a body which had as its purpose "the complete political and economic emancipation of women" and the supplement was offered "as a contribution towards the elucidation of the problems presented by the position of women in twentieth-century industry" (Webb 1914b, p.i). In her introduction, Webb began by continuing her discussion of the impact of capitalism on women's social position. She noted that the participation of women in the production of wealth is almost as universal and certainly as ancient as humanity. What was comparatively modern and confined to the capitalist nations was the existence of a female population which laboured separately from their families and received an independent wage. It was observed that in contemporary England, one-third of the females over 15 years of age earned their own livelihood independently of father and husband. Webb applauded this development but again lamented that the equality women had attained in industry was far from complete. Society continued to assume women's needs were less than those of men and paid them accordingly. Women also undertook the work of the home even if they laboured in the public sphere, were taxed without representation and were denied any direct involvement in the determination of the laws that regulated their lives (Webb 1914b, p.i).

The contributors to the industry supplement each undertook to provide data that would detail the disadvantages suffered by working women. Webb confined her introduction to "a few words" on the "features" of women's oppression she had identified. She began by denouncing the claim that women's needs were less than those of men. It was acknowledged that they consumed less but Webb insisted they did so primarily because of custom and the refusal of employers to pay women the wages they paid to men. Also denounced was the "double service" of labour that women were compelled to endure while men "roamed free" once their single shift was done.

However, Webb reserved her main contribution for the question of the working woman's right to vote. She noted that the suffrage debate commonly assumed that the woman of property was the most obvious victim of women's exclusion from the electoral process. While stating that she did not wish to belittle the political grievance of the wealthy woman, Webb insisted it was the working woman who in reality had the greater claim to the vote. The latter earned this priority because she was a direct contributor to the wealth of society, an attribute not shared by her propertied counterparts able to live a life of leisure. The priority of the working woman also stemmed from the fact that she tended to have greater personal experience of the results of government.

> As an "employed person" she finds the hours of her labour, the safety and sanitation of her workplace, and, in some cases, even the wages she receives, determined directly by the action of Parliament. As a "poor person" she lives under special legal compulsion with regard to the education of her children, the sanitation of her home, and the provision for her sickness and invalidity. As a person who is always within sight of destitution she is perpetually confronted with the Poor Law (Webb 1914b, p.ii).

In contrasting the claims of the working and propertied woman, Webb also noted that the worker generally had greater personal experience of both the realities underlying political controversies and of participation in democratic organisations. Her working life made her aware of the limits of legislation and thus of the need to stand in unity with her class. Likewise, her participation in her trade union and consumer co-operative gave her a degree of direct participation in the democratic process rare among women of wealth. As a consequence of this involvement, Webb concluded, working class women were evolving a great work and consumer centred democracy "which is .... a complement, to the political democracy established by the upper and middle class." (Webb 1914b, p.ii)

This great achievement, she insisted, proved the justice of the working woman's claim to a full share in the government of the country.

Personal Rights, Motherhood and Citizenship

Webb's use of the *New Statesman* as a vehicle to further the campaign for the rights of women, and working women in particular, continued in a series of papers she published through May to August of 1914. In May she contributed a paper to a special supplement on 'Motherhood and the State' (Webb 1914c) which criticised social Darwinism and highlighted women's need for adequate natal and aftercare services. Webb's contribution discussed 'Motherhood and Citizenship', noting that maternity and child care had become recognised as political issues of national significance. Given that women could not vote, the politicisation of maternity meant that it was men alone who decided the policies the state adopted in relation to these activities. Webb considered this situation outrageous but did not believe it alone made a case for granting women the franchise, for women were more than physical reproducers of the species. They had interests as wide as men and should have the vote because they had a right to be involved in the determination of all social issues, not only those related to reproduction.

At the same time, Webb thought the politicisation of motherhood raised an important new issue for women as citizens. It placed an onus on women to "exercise to the utmost their influence on Local Government" which was the state sphere then responsible for providing the needs of maternity. Webb insisted women must organise within this sphere to ensure all women had adequate access to the resources they needed to give birth and raise healthy children. Moreover, women should demand these resources not as welfare handouts but as a health provision that was their due as members of the human race.

Debate on the issue of maternity continued in the *New Statesman* through May and June of 1914 with the journal publishing three articles by an author who wrote under the pseudonym of "Candida" (1914a,b,c). The latter argued that women should have the right to refuse maternity and must be free of both legal and moral constraints on their ability to exercise birth control with this right being extended to the freedom to have children outside of marriage. Webb replied to Candida in a series of papers published through July and early August (Webb 1914d). Webb began with the observation that the latter seemed more concerned with the rights of the individual than with the rights of women for she pleaded for the removal of public constraints on women's freedom almost solely on the grounds "that each individual woman has a moral right to live her own life and develop her own faculties to the degree and in the direction that is agreeable or beneficial to her" (Webb 1914d, p.396).

Webb sympathised with Candida's commitment to personal rights but rejected the emphasis she placed on the needs and desires of the individual. She observed that, as was common with right wing feminists, Candida failed to give adequate consideration to the social effects of the rights she was demanding on behalf of the individual. Rather, it was simply assumed that "the individual right coincides with the social interest". This perspective was philosophic individualism carried beyond even that of Herbert Spencer who had at least acknowledged that the rights of the individual might have to be moderated if they undermined the like claims of other individuals. Indeed, Spencer acknowledged that at times it was even necessary to restrain the rights of individuals if they endangered the social interest. The extent to which social rights needed to be recognised was of course the critical issue dividing Collectivist and Individualist. However, while the differences between these two perspectives was a matter of degree rather than of absolutes, Candida's individualism was extreme in offering no concessions to society and few to other individuals. Personal freedom was absolute and the "liberties of all" were simply ignored.

Having discussed Candida's extreme individualism, Webb proceeded to examine several "personal rights" claimed by Candida and more generally by the right wing of the women's movement. In so doing she chose to discuss these rights "in the light of the three principles of personal freedom, mutual consideration, and reciprocal obligation between the individual and the social organisation" (Webb 1914d, p.397). She began by discussing birth control and the single woman's desire to have a child. Acceptance of family planning had made great advances in Britain over the previous four decades with acceptance of birth control progressing to the stage where couples discussed openly whether they would have children, and if so, when and how many. This was a development of which Webb approved, insisting that in many ways it was a gain both to the individuals concerned and to the wider society.

Given that the demand for family planning had become socially accepted, however, Webb was puzzled as to why Candida felt it necessary to plead so fervently for its public sanctioning. Webb's dilemma was accentuated by the fact that she believed there were major questions relating to birth control that remained to be settled which Candida had elected to ignore. Not the least of these was the impact family planning was likely to have on the nation's birth-rate and the quality of its children.

Webb noted that in some nations population growth was approaching zero percent, a development that endangered the existence of whole peoples. The problems associated with this danger were compounded by the fact that birth control was more often practised by the upper and middle classes than by the poor. Webb perceived this latter situation to be a matter of concern though not for genetic reasons. Rather, she was concerned because the declining birth rate was producing a situation where an increasing proportion of the nation's children were being nurtured by families without adequate economic resources.

Webb considered unacceptable Candida's failure to pay any attention to the social dimension of family planning. Likewise, she was critical of the notion that the unmarried woman's desire for a child should be considered simply a question of personal rights. As with all other issues, Webb believed it was not only the individual's interest that should be considered but also the needs of society and the "like liberty of others". For the child born out of wedlock, this meant consideration had to be accorded the child's right to a father. For society, it meant thought had to be given to the effect on the community of encouraging sexual licence. Webb's particular concern with the latter emanated from her belief that undermining the sexual norms that limited promiscuity would remove a bulwark that provided women with some respite from sexual harassment by men. Her prescriptions for all the difficulties she identified centred on the development of the "reciprocal relation between the social organisation and the individual in respect to childbearing and child-raising" (Webb 1914d, p.430). As regards family planning, she noted that in contemporary Britain this relationship existed in an incomplete, distorted and obsolete form. Society encouraged women to have children and compelled parents to maintain their offspring but did little to ensure that individuals had the means to achieve this objective. The wage system ignored the number of children in a family, while the tax authorities actually penalised families with children. Consequently, it was common for a woman to elect not to have children because she could not afford their maintenance - a lack of real choice Webb believed to be totally unacceptable. Women had a right not to have children but they should not be forced to this option by economic pressures. Society's need for healthy children, and the individual woman's right to choose whether she was to give birth, demanded that the nation accept that it had a duty to ensure women were provided with the resources they needed. This meant the provision of the means to prevent pregnancy, if this was desired, and the requirements needed to fulfil the role of mother if and when women chose to become pregnant. Only if they were guaranteed these resources would women truly enjoy the freedom Candida believed was a woman's right. To fail to consider these broader issues was to confine the full benefits of family planning to the affluent woman. In short, to focus solely on the individual was to ignore both the collective needs of the nation and the needs of the women of the working class.

As regards a woman's right to have a child out of wedlock, Webb noted that this claim was advanced primarily by women of the upper classes who could not find a suitable mate and/or by those individuals who would not accept the indignities forced upon wives by the existing marriage laws. In reply, she noted that there was no shortage of men but merely a shortage of men with wealth. What needed reforming, therefore, was not society's notion of sexual morality but rather the conventions regarding property. Similarly, oppressive marriage laws demanded a response that centred not only on the rights of the individual but also on the reform of these oppressive laws.

Webb's concern at Candida's extreme individualism was further manifested in the third and fourth of Webb's papers on personal rights. These publications dealt with women's place in the labour market, an issue not discussed by Candida but a topic that had long divided labour and right wing feminists. Webb consequently seized the opportunity which Candida's stress on individualism had provided to discuss this issue. She began by examining the question of the "right of the woman to free entry into all occupations", noting that women had a minority of the jobs in the labour market and that they were concentrated in the worst jobs available. The individualist, she noted, had an easy solution, throw all occupations open to both sexes and introduce equal pay for equal work. Webb had difficulty with this approach because she believed both the consumer and other workers had rights which were often undermined by this policy.

A factor she believed critical as regard other individuals was "... the question of the rate of remuneration and the conditions of employment, which women ought to claim or to accept" (Webb 1914d, p.494). On the question of pay, she noted, there was a paradox.

> The Feminists who insist on the right of women workers to earnings equal to those of men find their strongest allies in the most antifeminist male organisations, whose leaders see in this "principle of equality" the least invidious method of keeping women out of their particular occupations (Webb 1914d, p.525).

These reactionary males insisted on equal pay because they were aware that when employers were compelled to pay men and women the same wage rate they very often responded by refusing to hire women. It was this "hard fact", Webb noted, that had led right wing feminists in the late nineteenth century to oppose equal pay, insisting on the right of women to take work at "any price and under any conditions acceptable to themselves, without considering the convenience or interests of men". The fact that such an approach to wage bargaining was likely to drive the wages of both men and women below the subsistence level, the individualists had considered irrelevant believing that what was important was that women be free to maximise their participation in the labour market. By 1914, the most right wing individualists had abandoned their support for wage cutting and embraced the demand for equal pay. Their adoption of this policy, however, generally failed to consider its effect on the demand for female labour being advanced as an individual right that on principle had to be supported, irrespective of its consequences. Not surprisingly, this policy was greeted with glee by those men who were determined to keep women out of industry.

In her paper Webb rejected the notion that a woman could justifiably undermine the standard rate in an occupation merely to advance her personal well being. She believed the downward pressure this form of individualism placed on wages to be neither in the interests of women nor of society. At the same time she recognised why the more reactionary professional associations and unions joined with the right wing feminists in promoting the demand for equal pay. Her prescription for this difficulty was to assert that, while the individual woman could not work below the standard rate, the women employed in an occupation could collectively choose to accept a rate lower than that paid to men. Though Webb was unhappy with this solution and within five years was to abandon the notion she saw it as a necessary compromise between the need to preserve women's jobs and the need to halt a downward wage spiral. In short, the policy aimed to both contain pressure on occupational rates and counter both reactionary males and right wing feminists who urged policies not necessarily in the interests of women workers.

> [I]f we are to escape tyranny - which may be the tyranny of one class of producers over another - each class must be left (subject always to the supreme requirement that it must not derogate from its own health and efficiency) to define for itself the particular conditions of employment which seem to its own members to promote their professional efficiency, self-development, and personal happiness .... at any rate as regards the vast majority of the four million adult manual working women, we have to negative both the male Trade Unionist's claim to impose his own Standard Rate and his own working conditions on the

women doing similar work, and the abstract doctrine of the modern
middle-class feminist in favour of identity of working conditions and of
"equal remuneration for men and women" (Webb 1914d, p.526).

The Great War

The fourth of the papers Webb wrote in reply to Candida appeared on 1
August 1914. Three days later, Britain declared war on Germany. Webb
was devastated by the outbreak of the conflict, her articles in the *New
Statesman* ceased abruptly and it was not until September 1915 that she
again appeared in the journal. In the intervening period, however, she
appears to have been active, for her September contribution was a major
study of the teaching profession with special focus on the National Union
of Teachers (NUT). The study was a wide-ranging examination of
elementary and secondary schools, special subject teachers and the
Teachers Registration Council. Women's role in the NUT was a
significant portion of the report, with Webb recognising that gender was a
major cause of division among teachers. However, the study appears to
have also made her aware that there existed a more substantial divide
within the teaching profession, this being the cleavage between qualified
and unqualified teachers. The membership of the NUT consisted of
37,496 men and 53,911 women with membership rights being the same
for both sexes though restricted to certified teachers. This rule excluded
many thousands of elementary teachers from membership, including the
40,000 members of the National Union of Unqualified Teachers ninety per
cent of whom were women. Nevertheless, the female membership of the
NUT was as enthusiastic as the men to keep out their unqualified sisters -
a response deeply resented by the latter (Webb 1915).

Webb's new-found sensitivity to the divisions induced by
qualifications became manifest in the major report on the relative wages
of men and women she produced after the war. In this study she was to
argue that it was not sex but qualifications that was the major factor
dividing workers and restricting women's labour market opportunities.
While the war lasted, however, she was more concerned with ensuring
that the financing of the conflict was not thrust solely onto the working
class.

The means by which Webb sought to contribute to the wages issue
through the early war period was explained in a plea for financial support
that appeared in the *New Statesman* in October 1915. Written by Barbara
Drake for the Joint Committee of the Fabian Research Department and the
Fabian Women's Group, the report declared that trade unionists,

representatives of the British Association and the Women's Industrial Council and others had decided to undertake "an enquiry into the new position of women in industry". Of the individuals identified as participating in the study, the Webbs were placed first, a ranking that reflected the positive role they had played in promoting women's rights within the Fabian Society. That there was an urgent need for a study of how the war was transforming the industrial status of women was stressed by Drake, who noted that unfortunately history showed that the entry of women into male-dominated trades was often used by employers as an opportunity to cheapen the cost and degrade the conditions of labour. That the employers might use the great influx of women into the war industries for this purpose was, she believed, a danger that had to be recognised and countered if vast new areas of "sweating" were not to be established.

The trade unions had agreed in March 1915 to withdraw or relax their rules and customs regarding female and unskilled labour for the duration of the war. In return, the Government and the employers had given certain safeguards, the most notable of which was that women employed on munitions work would be paid at the same piece rates as the men. Drake claimed that what was in fact occurring was that women were either being employed on time rates or their work was artificially redesigned in a manner which allowed the employers to claim that because the work was so different, the old union rates were not relevant. Consequently, the pre-war union wage standards were being "thrown to the winds, while the women are employed at rates that threaten the whole position of Labour" (Drake 1915, p.13).

Drake warned that unless this position was understood and confronted it was probable that both men and women workers would awaken after the war to find themselves powerless as never before. It was imperative, therefore, that a major study be undertaken immediately:

(1) To enquire how far, and in what occupations and processes, female labour is being introduced for the first time; or is increasing; or is replacing male labour.
(2) To find out at what rates and under what conditions women are now working, and what is the cause or explanation of or justification for any differentiation between grades or sexes.
(3) To enquire how far the readjustment of processes now being made have rendered easier the introduction of female labour, and how far they are likely to secure its permanence after the war.
(4) To enquire into the rules and customs which restrict the employment of men or of women, or influence the line of demarcation

between their work, and to enquire in what way any alteration is likely
to affect them (Drake 1915, p.13).

Over the next three years, several papers dealing with the position of
women in the war industries appeared in the *New Statesman*. These
articles were published anonymously so it is not possible to state to what
extent they reflected Webb's views and in fact the next *New Statesman*
article that provides a clear insight into her ideas on gender relations did
not appear until May 1919. This latter paper, 'Women in Industry' was
also anonymous but serves the purposes of this article for it reports
accurately the minority report Webb submitted as a member of the War
Cabinet Committee on Men and Women in Industry.

The author of 'Women in Industry' noted that through the war
period arbitrators continually had to resolve difficulties associated with
the relative wages of men and women. Once the war approached a close,
this issue was passed to a War Cabinet Committee by the government. A
basic question the Committee was asked to advise upon was whether men
and women employees should be paid the same wage rate. The
Committee had six members, five of whom were government officials and
all of whom signed the majority report. Webb was the only independent
member and she chose to submit a minority report that differed markedly
from those of her colleagues. It was observed by the *New Statesman*
commentator that the critical factor distinguishing the majority and
minority reports was their perception of the place of women in industry.
Majority members of the Committee saw women as "creatures burdened
by a peculiar sex disability" (Anonymous 1919, p.157). Webb, on the
other hand, insisted that in "industry women are just workers, and that the
question of sex is, broadly speaking irrelevant" (Anonymous 1919, p.157).
The reporter observed that Webb appeared to realise fully the implications
of the issue of relative wages, whereas the Majority of the Committee only
perceived them dimly.

> The first was the principle of the market rate for labour - that is, the
> principle of having no principle at all and of leaving the relative wages
> of men and women to be determined at hazard by the varying
> circumstances and conditions of the labour-market in each particular
> trade. This the Majority and the Minority alike preferred to reject. The
> second was the principle of absolutely equal treatment, or better, of no
> discrimination between the sexes in respect of any method of wage-
> payment, whether for time spent, or by results. This was rejected by
> the Majority, and accepted by Mrs. Webb. The third was the principle
> of "equal pay for equal work", interpreted as meaning work equal in

quantity and quality at equal expense to the employer.   This was rejected by Mrs. Webb, but accepted by the Majority in name, though not by any means completely in actual fact (Anonymous 1919, p.157).

The distinction between the Majority's policy of "equal pay for equal work at equal cost to the employer" and Webb's preference for an "equal occupational rate for the job" was not mere semantics.   As the *New Statesman* reporter observed, the Majority position ignored the many difficulties inherent in the notion of equal pay for equal work at equal cost.   It ignored, in particular, the difficulty of identifying whether the cost of the employee's output was the same for both sexes.   This was a "difficulty", the reporter observed, that was ready made for those employers who wished to substitute women for men so that a lower wage could be paid.

> Even if the principle were accepted, it would be impossible in practice to ensure its application; for, when once the door is opened to inequality, it is inevitable that the customary factor of cheapness in women's labour should reassert itself, especially as women are still weakly organised and as some of the non-industrial women's societies seem more anxious to extend the area of women's employment at all costs than to protect the rates of those who are employed.   War-time experience shows that, if once deductions for lower efficiency and increased cost to the employer are admitted, it is utterly impossible to maintain any real relation of equality (Anonymous 1919, p.158).

A fourth principle also influenced the debate, that of need.   Many more men than women, it was put to the Committee, had dependants and therefore needed a wage sufficient to provide for more than their own sustenance.   The Majority responded to this observation by setting a minimum wage for women that assumed no dependants with a higher minimum accorded to men.   This policy provided yet a further opportunity for employers to use women's increased participation as a device to cut real wages across the board.   Webb, on the other hand, argued for a minimum wage that was the same for both sexes, insisting the issue of dependants should not be resolved by the wage system.   Rather, the differing needs of families should be taken care of by the state, which should pay wage supplements direct to those families with children.

Webb opposed the so-called equal pay option and a separate minimum wage for men and women largely because she recognised the great wage-cutting opportunity it provided employers.   While wishing to enhance the job opportunities of women, she maintained her belief that this must not be achieved by inducing a downward spiral in wage rates. Accordingly, she argued vehemently for equal occupational rates and no sex discrimination on entrance. She was aware that the adoption of her principle would limit the extension of the area of women's employment but, given she now believed the employers and the state to be intent on using the increased participation of women in industry as a device to cut wage rates across the board, she decided the male and female wage option was no longer viable. Webb regretted the payment of equal rates within all occupations was likely to widen the sexual demarcation of the trades but was convinced this was a cost that had to be paid if the lives of the working class were not to be decimated by wage cutting.

The *New Statesman* reporter concluded the 1919 article by predicting that the policy advocated by Webb would in the long term be accepted in British industry.

> Her report will not be acted on to-day or to-morrow; but, when we have floundered a while longer in the sea of contradictions and absurdities in which any less ambitious scheme will fling us, we shall be driven to take the whole question in hand on the lines of her present proposals (Anonymous 1919, p.158).

This prediction has been validated by time, sadly, so has Webb's belief that the policy she advocated in her Minority report would contain the dissolution of the sexual division of labour.

Webb as a Feminist

The *New Statesman* papers constitute but a portion of Webbs' contribution to the campaign waged in the early years of the twentieth century to advance the rights of women yet nevertheless are of great value for they provide a concise and detailed insight into her thought regarding gender relations. They are also important because they have never been subjected to critical analysis or played any part in the debate regarding Webb's feminism. Together, they add substantive support to the claim that she was concerned with the economic and social injustices suffered by women as a consequence of their sex and that she rejected explicitly the claim that women were the biological inferiors of men. Moreover, they show that she did not rely solely on male benevolence or on male-dominated institutions to advance women's cause and did develop an explicit analysis of the patriarchal forces at work within the capitalist economy. In short, Webb was an active campaigner who came to throw her full weight behind "the cause", that is, the struggle for sex equality. She was a socialist rather than a liberal or right wing feminist but by any acceptable definition of the term, a feminist she was. Moreover, to borrow Hamilton's 1932 observation, Webb was "a more thorough-going equalitarian than most of the Feminists of her day or ours".

5 Beatrice Webb and the Fabian Women's Group

Chris Nyland and Mark Rix

In an influential contribution to the continuing debate over Beatrice Webb's relationship to the women's movement, a point advanced by Barbara Caine (1982) to support her claim that Webb "was not particularly active" in campaigns waged specifically to improve the situation of women was that she rarely attended meetings of the Fabian Women's Group (F.W.G.) and refused to *immerse* herself within the Group or become actively involved in its research or reform projects. Indeed, Caine asserts that rather than concentrating on the position of women and giving support to the Group, Webb confined "herself to inviting members to tea and in some cases adding her name to public statements" (Caine 1982, p.36). This chapter challenges Caine's depiction of Webb's relationship to the Fabian Women's Group and argues that Beatrice in fact had a long and productive engagement with the Group. It is conceded she rarely attended meetings and did not fully immerse herself in the organisation if by this is meant she did not abandon all other interests. However, the minutes of the Group reveal that over many years she helped shape its research program, made a great many contributions to the organisation's maintenance and development and actively promoted the Group within the Fabian Society.

Fabianism and The Woman Question 1883-1908

According to Beals (1989, p.13), in the 1890s "[t]he most striking element of the Fabian social profile was the high proportion of female members (almost one-fourth), more than any of its rival socialist groups." Perhaps for this reason, the role of women within the Fabian Society was a perennial topic of internal debate. Proportional representation for women on the Executive Committee of the Society was, for example, an issue which in the early 1890s caused division between Fabian women and between Fabian women and men. The push for proportional representation came from women who believed that their presence in the Society was inadequate to ensure they had an effective voice within its forums and on its decision-making bodies. In 1891 four of the 15 members of the Executive Committee were women which was roughly in proportion to the number of women members. Nevertheless, several women and their male allies urged the adoption of a formal quota system which would ensure that a certain number of seats on the Executive Committee were reserved for women in the 1892 election. This was a proposal that was opposed not by the men of the Society but by feminist members. Emma Brooke, Alice Corthorn and Mary Lacey, in particular, "were reluctant to make sexual difference a defining political category because they judged themselves to be the intellectual equals of men; or at least they believed they could be, if given the opportunity to participate in the work of the Society without distinctions being drawn between men and women" (Beals 1989, p.61). Arising out of the debate over proportional representation and a quota for women on the Executive Committee emerged an agreement that a Fabian pamphlet would be produced that would detail the Society's position on women's suffrage and the demand that women be accorded the civil and political rights enjoyed by men. Harriot Stanton Blatch, a prominent London proponent of women's suffrage, was given responsibility for preparing the manuscript and was assisted by a team of experts who advised her on such issues as women's trade union organisation, technical education for women and girls, the impact of the Factory Acts on women's employment, and health and legal questions pertaining to women's employment (Beals 1989, p.62).

The women's tract committee faced problems symptomatic of the Fabian Society's difficulties in coming to terms with the 'Woman Question' during the 1890s. Women within the Society were very much divided over such issues as protective labour law and, while strongly supporting woman suffrage, disagreed over the tactics that should be embraced to attain this goal. As a consequence of these divisions, Blatch was unable to reach a consensus acceptable to the different shades of opinion within the Society and it was this failure that brought Webb in to the limelight. She joined the Fabian women's tract committee in 1894 as a consultant on the Factory Acts and in January 1896 delivered a lecture to the Fabian Society on how these laws protected women industrial workers which the Fabian Executive subsequently decided to publish as the women's tract. The decision to publish Webb's paper was in effect a public statement that the Society's official position on the Woman Question was that socialists do not accept that gender emancipation can or should be divorced from class emancipation, that there are antagonistic relations between women of different classes just as there are amongst men, and that protective labour laws are in the interests of the women of the working class.

Webb's paper which was published as *Women and the Factory Acts* was the only tract produced by the Fabian Society in the nineteenth century which enunciated a Fabian view on the Woman Question. In the paper, she provided compelling evidence and adduced persuasive arguments to rebut various misconceptions and delusions about the nature and effects of protective legislation. These misapprehensions included the view that any legal or legislative limitation on women's labour was tantamount to erecting a barrier to women's employment in industry; the idea that where men and women competed on equal terms in the labour market, regulation of women's hours worked to the advantage of men and against the interests of women; and the belief that, in general, protective legislation diminished the personal freedom and economic independence of women. The fact that many middle class and professional women opposed protective legislation for precisely these reasons reflects the fact that during the 1890s the women's movement was dividing into two wings. Webb belonged very much to the class conscious section of the women's movement and it was the *class-plus-gender* perspective which she advocated that became dominant in the Society in the 1890s and which was subsequently to characterise the Fabian Women's Group.

The attempts to accommodate feminist perspectives within the Fabian Society and promote the Society's position within the women's movement continued through to the end of the nineteenth century with Beatrice playing a leading role in advancing class-conscious feminism. However, the extent to which Fabian women promoted these ideas within the Society remained relatively muted through this period, the woman question not again becoming an issue of overriding significance until the early years of the new century. When the debate did revive, it was as a consequence of two important developments in the women's and socialist movements. These were the militant suffrage campaign waged by the Women's Social and Political Union (W.S.P.U.) and the growing popularity of eugenics which was then regarded by many socialists as a progressive intellectual movement. The W.S.P.U. was an organisation formed in 1903 when feminist activists led by Emmeline Pankhurst broke from the Independent Labour Party. The militant tactics that the W.S.P.U. employed to raise awareness of the women's suffrage issue and the savagery with which the state responded "acted as a catalyst for galvanizing progressive support for the civic claims of women as a disenfranchised class" (Beals 1989, p.154).

In a less dramatic way, the issues debated by the eugenics movement also helped raise questions about the place and role of women in society and it was in the language of eugenics that concerns about the effects of a declining birth rate on national health and the future of Empire were brought to public attention. In 1903 and 1904, the Fabian Society conducted a study of the English birth-rate which helped to reinvigorate the debate within the Society regarding the proper role and place for women in society. Beals (1989, p.155) observes that the study "renewed the Society's discussion of women's role in the efficient socialist community with its focus on social policies, such as the choice of a marriage partner, reproduction, and the raising of a family" and helped reinsert discussion of the needs of women back into the mainstream of the Fabian Society's internal debates.

As a consequence of these developments, in 1907 the Society elected to include a formal commitment to women's suffrage in its Basis (that is, constitution). The Society's decision to take this progressive step owed much to the persuasiveness of Maud Pember Reeves who in 1907 put a motion to the Annual Meeting which called on Fabian socialists "to embrace equal citizenship alongside the most basic socialist issues concerning the welfare of the community" (Beals 1989, p.180). The amendment was initially opposed by the so-called "Old Gang" of Sidney Webb, George Bernard Shaw, Edward Pease and Hubert Bland who worried that incorporating support for women's suffrage in the Basis would leave the Society vulnerable to the charge of political faddism. In the end, Reeves' amendment was passed partly at least because she had organized the Fabian women to vote for the motion.

Beatrice was a vocal supporter of the push to have a commitment to equal citizenship included in the Fabian Basis. She seconded Reeves' motion to this effect and by so doing publicly extended her 1906 repudiation of the 'Appeal Against Female Suffrage' which she had signed in 1899 but soon after both rejected and deeply regretted. Her 1906 public recantation had come at a time when she believed "women suffragists were being battered about rather badly, and coarse-grained men were saying coarse-grained things" (diary entry 5 November, 1906, cited in Webb 1948, p.361). Under these circumstances, she decided, "I thought I might as well give a friendly pull to get the thing out of the mud, even at the risk of getting a little spattered myself". Her support for Reeves was a first step in this direction.

The Formation of the F.W.G.

The Fabian Women's Group was formed on March 14, 1908 at a meeting hosted by Reeves and attended by Webb and a small number of other Fabian feminists. Formation of the F.W.G. was a confident assertion by these women that they had become convinced the time had come to organise as women within the Society. Caine (1982, 37) has observed that their decision to organise arose partly from the entrenched prejudices of male members many of whom she claims were emphatic that mothers must direct all their attention to child-rearing. While not denying that some leaders of the Society may have regarded child-rearing as the overriding duty of women, Caine's assessment appears to overstate the leadership's lack of support for its female membership. Contrary to this assessment, in its Annual Report of 1908 the F.W.G. Secretary advised that those who had formed the Group had "received cordial furtherance and support from the Fabian Executive and officials". The Report also observed that women members had only to claim equal opportunities within the Society and the claim would be "admitted ungrudgingly". The concern of the Group's founders rather was that the Society's support did not extend to the systematic consideration of "larger issues" - such as what equal opportunity for men and women implied, what women should demand of a future socialist society, and what practical steps women should take to realise their demands (*Fabian News*, March 1909, p.32). On these issues Fabian feminists had come to appreciate a truth the women's movement has repeatedly rediscovered through the twentieth century, that even when operating within bodies sympathetic to feminism it is necessary for women to caucus as women if their concerns are to win the attention they deserve.

What the founders of the F.W.G. saw as being the major issues Fabian feminists needed to explore was reflected in the purposes decided on by the Group at its first meeting:

a) To study and discuss women's economic independence in its relation to socialism and, having arrived at definite conclusions, to consider how they may be applied to practical work in the Socialist and Suffragist movements;

b) To make the equal citizenship of men and women a working reality in the Fabian Society;

c) To take steps as may from time to time appear advisable to assist in the Women's Emancipation Movement; especially at the present time in the agitation for obtaining the Parliamentary franchise (F.W.G. Minutes: March 14, 1908).

Out of the initial meeting of the F.W.G. came a circular which was sent to all Fabian women inviting them to attend the first formal meeting of the Group (held on April 4, 1908). The circular outlined how equal citizenship was to be made a "working reality" in the Society. First, Fabian women were to train themselves in the effective "usages of public life and the organised expression of opinion" and, second, to ensure that the representation of women on the Fabian Executive Committee was in proportion to the number of female members. Proportional representation of women on the Executive would in turn ensure that, as the circular put it, women's "distinctive mental outlook may find adequate expression in the Society's policy". The circular noted that at the time 17 out of the 21 members of the Executive were men which meant women were under-represented. To rectify this situation, 3 women were nominated by the Group "in addition to the four able women, all members of our Group, who served last year and [who were] standing for re-election". The F.W.G. minutes of May 9th report that these four were subsequently re-elected to the Executive and that two additional members of the Group nominated by the Honorary Secretary were elected.

Citizenship and Local Government

The reform effort of the F.W.G. was divided into two separate streams, Women's Citizenship and what the Group termed the "theoretical side" of their work. The object of the latter was "to seek out and explain the conditions of economic independence for women under Socialism and the steps whereby it may be gained". Here the problem was perceived to be the identification of the factors that differentiate female workers from their male counterparts and the determination of the economic implications of these differences. This 'side' of the F.W.G.'s work was further subdivided into a number of different parts and subdivisions. These covered such matters as the differences in ability amongst and between those actively involved in child rearing and those not so involved and the steps which needed to be taken to ensure that women were able "[t]o use and develop all their physical and mental capacities in productive work, whilst remaining free and fully able to exercise their special productive function of childbearing (*Fabian News*, March 1909, p.33)". Part of the strategy adopted was to have papers on these matters read and discussed at Group meetings and then to circulate them amongst members for criticisms prior to their publication in composite volumes.

Women's Citizenship was subdivided into The Parliamentary Franchise and Local Government. In the former campaign, Group members participated actively in Suffrage protests and demonstrations, always co-ordinating their activities with other Suffrage bodies but refusing to enter into exclusive bilateral arrangements with any single women's organisation. According to the Group's first Annual Report (*Fabian News*, March 1909, p.33), the successful push to have a commitment to equal citizenship included in the Fabian Basis had made the Society the "pioneer Socialist body supporting the Suffrage agitation". Through 1908, eleven Group members were jailed for taking part in militant suffrage actions, and concerted efforts were taken to improve their lot whilst imprisoned. In a concise statement of the importance the Group attached to the Suffrage, the Annual Report noted that "[i]n view of the increasing tendency in the Society to enter upon definite political action, it becomes of immediate urgency that we should lay constant stress upon the paramount importance of the Parliamentary franchise for women from the Socialist point of view".

At the April 4, 1908 meeting of the F.W.G., a letter from Webb was tabled in which she urged that the campaign for the suffrage be extended to include practical electoral work that could produce concrete and immediate results. On numerous occasions Webb made it clear that while she considered women's right to vote to be an important issue, for her the franchise was primarily a vehicle that would assist the attainment of more concrete goals. In her letter she also advised those women campaigning for the suffrage that an arena was already open to them in which they could work to achieve material electoral outcomes. Local government, she observed, was an area of electoral activity where married women at least were "confronted with no absolute sex barrier", having the right to appear on the register as parochial electors and stand as candidates. She urged Fabian feminists to take up this opportunity. That the membership of the F.W.G. needed to be encouraged to embrace this practical, though not glamorous, work was highlighted in the Annual Report which noted that in reply to a circular sent out to members of the Group in October only 6 had affirmed they had taken steps to qualify as local government electors. The Report further observed that this response indicated there was much validity in the suggestion put to the Group by Webb that the need to arouse women "to a sense of their electoral responsibilities" applied every bit as much to the Women's Group as it did to women generally.

On May 9, the Group's meeting was fully occupied in responding to Webb's call for members to become more active in local government and, according to the Secretary, the Group's attempts to awaken women to their electoral responsibilities truly began after this meeting. In 1911, the Group published a report titled *Three Years' Work of the Women's Group* which was sent to all members, subscribers and associates of the Fabian Society. *Three Years' Work* (Executive Committee F.W.G. 1911, p.3) gives a more detailed picture and clearer insight into how the Group acted on Webb's suggestion than do either the minutes or the Annual Report of 1908:

> In local government, women's citizenship is theoretically recognised, but it is imperfect, ill understood, unappreciated, and little used, whilst the evils crying out for women's intervention are enormous. She [Webb] urged us to see what we could do in this direction. In response ten of our members volunteered to make inquiries, in as many parts of London, as to agencies already at work, and Fabians and other Socialists who might help in forming local committees, or making use of existing organisations for citizenship propaganda amongst women electors; also in supporting the candidature of women for Local Bodies. A citizenship sub-committee was formed consisting of the executive of the Group, the ten volunteers, and other co-opted members.

Poor Law Reform

Collaboration between Webb and the F.W.G. was not confined to suffrage and local government issues. In 1905 she had been appointed to the Royal Commission on the Poor Law and the Relief of Distress from Unemployment and in 1909 submitted a Minority Report. Both Webb's contribution *and* the Majority Report called for the workhouse to be abolished, for local authorities to be given responsibility for the administration of the Poor Law, the establishment of a national system of labour exchanges and the payment of unemployment benefits. Notwithstanding these similarities and convergences, Radice (1984, p.172) comments that Webb's Report treated the problem of poverty and unemployment more imaginatively and comprehensively than the Majority Report. In dealing with unemployment, for example, Webb saw this issue, not as the fault of individuals, but rather as a social problem requiring social and political remedies.

Between the spring of 1909 and the summer of 1911 (when they left on their second world tour), the Webbs spent a great deal of their time promoting the reforms proposed in the Minority Report. In May, 1909 they formed the National Committee for the Promotion of the Break-Up of the Poor Law (N.C.B.P.L.) which, according to Beatrice (1948, p.422), was a "cumbrous and equivocal title which was changed in the following year to the National Committee for the Prevention of Destitution". The Webbs were convinced the F.W.G. could be a useful contributor to the national campaign and the latter enthusiastically took up the promotion of the Minority Report. Indeed, even before the campaign was launched publicly, the F.W.G. took positive steps to support the Webbs' efforts. In March 1909 the *Fabian News* announced that the Women's Group had arranged a course of five lectures on "The Poor Laws of To-day and the Proposals for Reform" to be given by Marion Phillips whose career had begun as a researcher for Beatrice. On May 18 Mrs Townshend gave a lecture to the Group on 'The Recommendations of the Poor Law Reports with reference to Motherhood and Infancy', Marion Phillips delivered a "valuable lecture" on "The Mother as Bread-winner" on November 16 and at the October 19 meeting of the Group, Dr Ethel Bentham announced she and Marion Phillips "had utilised the I.L.P. outdoor meetings in her [Bentham's] constituency for a series of lectures on the Minority Report with much success".

Seeking to consolidate the Poor Law campaign, in June 1909 Webb sent the FWG Executive Committee a letter proposing that it enter into a "special relationship" with the Secretariat of the N.C.B.P.L. This proposal, which was agreed to, was advanced by Webb because she wished the Group to watch "over the special interests of women in the campaign". However, it was reported at the July 15 meeting of the F.W.G. Executive that the N.C.B.P.L. Secretariat had informed the Group that they disputed "Mrs Webb's right to arrange with the F.W.G. for an official exchange of representatives". Nevertheless, in a spirit of compromise - and no doubt at the urging of the Webbs - the Secretariat had "personally and informally" co-opted Charlotte Wilson, the Group's Honorary Secretary, and arranged for two of its members to attend F.W.G. meetings "when invited to do so". In February 1910, the *Fabian News* carried the Fabian Women's Group Report for 1909 in which it was noted that the "Group has maintained special relations with the National Committee for the Break Up of the Poor Law, upon the secretariat of which our Secretary was co-opted". It also reported that two Group meetings had been devoted to the reports of the Commission.

In October 1910, the Executive Committee of the F.W.G. decided to invite Webb to give a lecture to the Group on, Women and the Minority Report. She agreed and requested that the Committee notify her of the points they wished her to raise in her lecture which she titled the 'Crusade against Destitution as it affects Women' with the minutes of the meeting reporting that "many questions followed". The meeting was also reported in the *Fabian News* (January 1911, p.14) where it was noted that "[s]ome special difficulties [raised in the 'Minority Report' with regard to the economic conditions and work of women] had been laid before Mrs. Webb beforehand, and she dealt with these and also answered questions on various other points".

The National Insurance Bill which was a product of the Poor Law Commission was introduced into Parliament by Lloyd George in May 1911. The Bill sought to establish a system of compulsory sickness and unemployment insurance which was to be financed by a combination of taxation, wage deductions, employer contributions and a Treasury grant. Low paid workers were greatly disadvantaged by the fact that the Bill proposed that they make contributions to their sickness and unemployment insurance out of their already meagre and inadequate wages. The Bill also contained a number of restrictions and exclusions which fell particularly hard on women a fact clearly recognised by the F.W.G. As a consequence, fully half of the Fourth Annual Report of the Executive Committee (March 21, December 31, 1911) was devoted to 'Emergency Work: National Insurance'. The report observed (*Fabian News*, February 1912, 21), that the Bill "obviously touched the economic position of women, and revealed it in so disadvantageous a light, that it gave us [the F.W.G.] a unique opportunity for Socialist propaganda, and also for taking active part in an agitation to safeguard women's interests". On May 24, 1911, the F.W.G. hosted a Conference of Women's Organisations to which nineteen societies seeking to advance the interests of women sent representatives. In response to a request from the meeting, the Group prepared an "explanatory statement" on the Bill which included a lengthy list of amendments which were "worked out by Mrs Pember Reeves, Dr Marion Phillips and Mrs C. M. Wilson, from the suggestions of Mr and Mrs Sidney Webb, together with the demands put forward by various Women's Organizations" (*Fabian News*, February 1912, p.21).

A proposal contained in the Bill which attracted particular attention from the F.W.G. was a maternity benefit intended to protect the health of mothers and new-born babies "by efficient attendance at childbirth". The benefit to be paid, however, was only thirty shillings, an amount insufficient to cover "continued attendance by a trained nurse or midwife, upon whose care the healthy recovery of the mother so often depends". The F.W.G. highlighted the fact that the benefit was completely inadequate to meet the needs of a nursing mother and bore all the marks of having been "concocted by men for a voteless and subject feminine population". At the Fabian Conference in July 1911, Dr Marion Phillips moved on behalf of the F.W.G. that this "Conference whilst cordially welcoming the introduction of a measure dealing nationally with sickness, maternity and unemployment, considers that the Bill now before Parliament needs drastic alteration" (*Fabian News*, February 1912, p.21).

The National Insurance Bill was eventually passed into law in a manner unacceptable to the Webbs and the F.W.G. In 1913, the F.W.G consequently formed a sub-committee to facilitate co-operation between the Group, other women's organisations determined to amend the Act, and with the Webbs' Fabian Research Department. Early in 1914 Beatrice chaired a meeting of the Women's Group, called to discuss how the amendments proposed by the F.W.G. could be best achieved. In her opening address she reported that the Fabian Research Department's investigations had revealed that the Approved Societies, with which many working men and women were compelled to insure under the Act, would soon face bankruptcy unless the government gave immediate relief. The main cause of this shortfall in funds was excessive illness due to pregnancy and childbirth and the fact that, in its funding calculations for national insurance, the government had not taken pregnancy into account.

Emerging out of the campaign to amend the Insurance Act, the Group took up a proposal by Webb that it prepare a special supplement for *The New Statesman* that would focus on the needs of the child. In so doing, she urged the Group to include an article which would outline maternity and child support policies it would like to see adopted by the British Government. The special supplement, titled 'Motherhood and the State' appeared on May 16, 1914 and included articles by. C.W. Saleeby, ('The Health of the Race'), Dr D. Forsyth ('The Health of Children Under School Age'), Dr Ethel Bentham ('The Need for the Baby Clinic'), Miss Margaret C. Bondfield ('The National Care of Maternity'), Dr Helen Y. Campbell ('The Scope of the Infant Clinic') and Beatrice Webb ('Motherhood and Citizenship').

As suggested in an earlier chapter, in her article Webb highlighted the inadequacies of the provision for Maternity and Infancy under the Poor Law and the National Insurance Act and called on the government to establish maternity centres and lying-in hospitals. She also insisted that the provision for maternity and infancy no longer be a matter of insurance but of Public Health and, therefore, "administered not by the Insurance Committee or Board of Guardians, but by the County and County Borough Council". She went on to link this reform to the demand for female suffrage arguing that as more links were forged between Maternity and the State, so would the exclusion of women from citizenship become more of an anomaly. As she succinctly put it (1914b, p.11): "[t]he recognition by the State of motherhood as a social service leads direct to the conception of the mother as citizen." In short, the recognition of mothers as citizens would be an important step towards the full recognition of women as citizens. At its meeting on June 3, the Group Executive accepted Mrs Pember Reeves' suggestion that Webb be asked to propose the Group's resolution dealing with Maternity Benefit at the forthcoming Fabian Conference. She agreed to do so, and in advancing the resolution made essentially the same demands as she had raised in her article for the Special Supplement. That is, she raised again the inadequacies of the provisions for maternity made by the Poor Law and Insurance Act and called for the administration of maternity and infancy provision to be passed to public health authorities.

Besides assisting Fabian women to become involved in local government and in the campaign for the reform of the Poor Law and the Insurance Act, one other area where Webb gave sustained and practical support to the F.W.G. was in relation to women's right to work. In October 1911 a Business Meeting of the F.W.G. established a Right-To-Work sub-committee whose terms of reference were "[t]o consider and inquire into any case where laws or regulations are proposed affecting the work of women; to watch and develop opportunities for women's work and to safeguard those already existing; to advocate and find methods of carrying into effect the principle of equal pay for equal work" (*Fabian News* Supplement, February 1913, p.2). The committee conducted many investigations into women's work which included inquiries into the conditions under which women laboured at the pit brow and the payment and conditions of women school cleaners and caretakers. The sub-committee also undertook an "inquiry as to the number of working women who, besides supporting themselves, are responsible either wholly or partially for the support of others" (*Fabian News*, June 1912, p.46). To this end, the help of Fabians throughout the United Kingdom was sought in an effort to ensure that the inquiry reached all parts of the country and all sections of the female workforce. In striving to promote this objective the 1912 Annual Report (*Fabian News* Supplement, February 1913, p.3) noted "Mrs Sidney Webb gave us the valuable aid of enclosing an explanatory circular to all members of the Society, with her memorandum on the Fabian Committee of Inquiry on the Control of Industries, and she also put a note in *The Crusade*". As a consequence of Webb's efforts, the Right-to-Work sub-committee also became actively involved in a joint

Fabian Society-Independent Labour Party campaign for a legal national minimum wage.

In March 1912 the Right-to-Work committee sent the Fabian Executive the following resolution:

> In view of the urgency, complexity and far-reaching importance of the minimum wage question and the extent to which the interests of working women are involved therein, this Sub-Committee of the Fabian Women's Group suggests that a special Fabian Committee be appointed to investigate the subject and to submit to the Executive the draft of a scheme for a new tract to be laid before the Society (*Fabian News* Supplement, February 1913, p.2).

A Committee was duly appointed which included several members of the Fabian Executive and a number of existing and former members of the Fabian Women's Executive and its sub-committees - including Maud Pember Reeves, Charlotte Mary Wilson and Bessie Hutchins.

The Committee met on several occasions but because of "radical" differences in opinion among the members on the question of women workers and the minimum wage it was unable to produce a tract. However, in the spring of 1912 it did convene a conference which considered the issue of whether, with reference to the difficulties associated with the sweated labour of women, a single national minimum wage was more appropriate than different minimum wages for the separate trades. The Conference was strongly of the view that men and women who did the same work should be paid the same wage but that there should be a specific minimum determined for each trade. Webb took a very active part in promoting this position within the F.W.G. and as a result was asked to put the following resolution to the mid-year National Conference of the Fabian Society: "[t]hat this Conference is of opinion that in any determination of legal minimum wages the principle as between men and women was that of equal rates of pay for equal work irrespective of sex". The resolution was carried by the Conference by a large majority (*Fabian News* Supplement, February 1913, 2).

In early December, the Fabian Women's Executive convened a conference which was dedicated to the Minimum Wage, with special attention given to the underpayment of women and the need to counter those feminists who claimed that women should be able to work for whatever wages they wished (even if this meant they would become blacklegs). The speakers included Clementina Black of the Women's Industrial Council; Susan Lawrence of the Women's Trade Union League, Lillian Harris, Women's Co-operative Guild; and Maud Pember Reeves.

Beatrice was asked to take the Chair and present a report on the proportion of women workers with dependants. She also gave the concluding address to the Conference and in so doing revealed her concern that a single national minimum wage would lead to the exclusion of women from many trades. She observed,

> ... an attempt to fix a statutory basic national minimum would result under present conditions in inequality between the wages fixed for men and for women. The experience of the women co-operators, who had votes as men had in their own movement, showed the difficulties to be overcome before a minimum on the basis of equality could be attained. The economic value of the total of women workers, taken in the lump, was less than that of the lump of men for several reasons, e.g., that there was a small proportion of women workers in the prime of life. The only safe method to obtain equal pay for equal work was by separate Boards for each trade, where the actual character of the work done could be estimated and an equal rate insisted upon and gradually obtained (*Fabian News*, February 1913, p.19).

Later in December of 1912, Webb gave a lecture to the Fabian Society titled a 'Minimum Wage and how to get it' in which she again argued that Trade Boards should be introduced into every trade which would fix pay rates for all the separate processes involved in an occupation. If this were done, she advised, it would be easier to insist on equal pay for equal work and help secure the highest rate for each process the trade was able to bear. (*Fabian News*, December 1912, p.11). To further this process, at its meeting on May 7, 1913 the Executive of the F.W.G. decided to write a pamphlet on women's wages and at the November 5 Executive Meeting the Secretary reported that the draft was complete and had been reviewed by Beatrice who had suggested that it be supplemented with articles on women and trade unions and that it be published as a F.W.G. supplement in *The New Statesman*.

The 'Special Supplement on Women in Industry' of February, 1914, consisted of an introduction by Webb, and articles by: F.W. Hubbock, 'Women's Wages'; B.L. Hutchins, 'Women in Trade Unions'; J.J. Mallon, 'The Legal Minimum Wage at Work'; and Pember Reeves and C.M. Wilson, 'A Policy for Women Workers'. In her introduction, Webb connected the issue of a minimum wage to the movement for women's economic and political emancipation by showing that women were subject to taxes, and laws which determined their conditions of work and rates of pay over which they had no control. She observed (1914a, p.ii):

In every part of that great voluntary or "industrial" democracy which is being slowly but surely evolved by the manual workers as a set-off, or, at any rate, as a complement, to the political democracy established by the upper and middle class, we find knots of active women proving, by business capacity and self-subordinating zeal, no less by persistency and fervour of idealism, the right of human beings of their sex to take their full share in the government of the country. It is in these facts that we find the justification of the demand of the Labour and Socialist Parties of all countries and all races for the complete political and economic enfranchisement of the working woman.

The War

The intimate link established between Webb and the Fabian Women's Group as a consequence of their joint efforts to reform the Poor Law, national insurance, and to promote a minimum wage and equal pay for equal work continued following the outbreak of war in August 1914. To an increasing extent, this link was mediated through the Fabian Research Department with the two bodies extending their earlier collaboration by forming a Joint Committee to inquire into industrial problems arising out of the war and women's increased participation in industry. The establishment of the Joint Committee meant in effect that, on the issues of women in trade unions and women's war-time employment in industry, the F.W.G. officially became a part of Beatrice's research network. Her continuing involvement with the Group was exemplified at the November 4th 1914 F.W.G. Executive meeting where a letter from her was read in which she offered to draft a tract on what could be done for unemployed women. The offer was accepted, Webb submitting a draft to the Executive Committee which they collectively edited and published in March 1915 as 'War, Women and Unemployment'. As Beals (1989, p.343) observes, "[t]he tract presented coverage of the major grievances of pre-war women workers: low wages, lack of acknowledgment that women workers supported dependants, under-reporting of levels of female unemployment, and dearth of health insurance and family welfare services to support women workers on the same level ... as male breadwinners".

Shortly after the release of the tract, the F.W.G. Executive Committee convened a public meeting to consider the Government's war service for women with special reference to the opening up of new industries and training. Webb chaired the meeting which was addressed by J.J. Mallon, Mrs Pember Reeves, and Miss Broadhurst. A resolution proposed by Webb read,

> That this meeting considers that means should be taken to see   that
> women are allowed full entrance to every trade that is suitable for them;
> that adequate training should be provided; and that everything possible
> should be done by means of education, trade union organization, and
> Government supervision to guarantee that women should not be used as
> blacklegs, but should receive equal pay for equal work.

In speaking to the resolution, Webb pointed out that while it was true that
more trades were opening to women every day, "[u]nfortunately, it was
only the worst paid and routine work which was given to women, the
highly skilled and mental work being reserved for men". In seconding the
resolution Mellon remarked (*Fabian News* May 1915, p.49) that the War
had opened many trades to women that had previously been closed to
them. However, workers had not been prepared for the jump in the
demand for labour occasioned by the War and, as a consequence, women
had been forced into trades before "satisfactory arrangements" regarding
wages and employment conditions could be made for them. Moreover,
the trades newly opened to women were precisely those that were not
strongly organised, and as a result, "much harm" had been done.
Nevertheless, in many of the occupations in which women were newly
employed, there had been noticeable improvement and, if women were to
"take full advantage of this unique opportunity, too much attention could
not be paid to securing efficient and proper training and to the need for
organization". In the latter half of 1915 the F.W.G. followed up this effort
by launching a series of eight lectures on 'Women and the Dislocations
and Readjustments of War Time'. Beatrice gave the first lecture (October
13) and spoke on 'How Far it is Expedient to Press for Equal Pay for
Equal Work in War Time'. Amongst the other lecturers who presented
addresses were Dr. May Thorne ('Medical Women in War Time'), Miss
Gertrude Townend ('The Nursing Profession in War Time') and Mrs
Pember Reeves ('Infantile Protection in War Time').

   1915 also saw the formation of the Joint Committee of the
Women's Group and the Fabian Research Department which was initially
created to investigate industrial problems arising out of the War. It later
turned its attention to women in industry during war time and prospects
for the future. The purpose of the 1915 investigation was to gather
information regarding women's work and trade unionism; identify new
opportunities for women; and examine the role and effects of Trades
Boards and unregistered and casual labour. The investigation effectively
melded the research activities of these two groups under the Webbs'
tutelage.   One issue with which the investigation was particularly

concerned was the extent to which men had been displaced by women as a result of the War. The Group's major contribution to this inquiry was to collect material on unorganised women's labour a process which during 1915 was slow-moving because this information was difficult to obtain. Nevertheless, over the following year significant progress was made and, by the end of 1916, the Group had at its disposal a great deal of information about the changes in women's work and conditions that had been brought about by the war.

Webb contributed little to the undertaking of this work for her level of research and political activity dropped markedly in the early war years when, as Radice (1984, p.206) notes in relation to the war, "she began to feel more and more depressed about the horror of the endless slaughter". By the end of 1915 she was on the brink of a nervous breakdown. While she chaired an F.W.G. meeting, in January 1916, at which Professor Edith Morley spoke on 'Education in War Time', it was not until the end of 1916 that she showed signs of recovery. She thereafter became more active on the Joint Committee her influence evident almost immediately. Since the beginning of 1916 the Group had been focusing its efforts on studying women's activity in the engineering trades. She convinced them that it was vitally important that greater attention be paid to ensuring the influx of new women workers into industry did not create divisions within the working class that employers and the government could exploit after the war. She insisted that if this was not to occur it was critical that these new workers be won to unionism and accordingly she urged the Group to place greater emphasis on union work. She also suggested that they begin by undertaking an inquiry into the position of women's trade unions comparing the present situation with that outlined by the Webbs in *Industrial Democracy* (1897).

Agreeing that such an inquiry would be valuable, in May 1917 the Executive Committee of the F.W.G. appointed a small sub-committee to undertake the organisation of the inquiry. It comprised members of the Group, five trade union organisers and two factory inspectors and had the power to co-opt others with special knowledge of trade union conditions. Mrs Barbara Drake chaired the sub-committee and Lillian Dawson served as secretary. The sub-committee was in effect a branch of the Trade Union Survey then being undertaken by the Joint Committee of the Women's Group and the Research Department. Accordingly, one of its first undertakings was to circulate a questionnaire to women trade unionists in order to gain a clearer picture of women's position in trade unions.

Given the considerable overlap between the work of the Trade Union sub-committee and that of the Joint Committee of the Fabian Research Department and the Women's Group, Webb proposed to Dawson that her sub-committee amalgamate with the Joint Committee. Accordingly these bodies were reconstituted as the Joint Committee of Enquiry into Women in Trade Unions. The joint committee's first act was to organise two conferences of women unionists for the first half of 1918 focussing on women as union organisers, the problems of organising women workers and the difficulties faced by female "committeemen". A third conference organised by the Joint Committee was held in November 1918 and focused on the issue of "Equal Pay for Equal Work".

By this time Webb had been appointed to the War Cabinet Committee on Women in Industry, a body formed to determine whether the government had honoured its pledge to pay women "men's wages" when they did "men's work". Upon taking up her position on this body, she concluded that the government had not honoured its pledge but failed to convince the other members of the committee that this was the case. Her diary entry of December 8, 1918 noted (MacKenzie 1984, pp.325-326) that it looked like she would be "forced to have a minority report, all by myself". She predicted that the majority report of the committee would be "stillborn" and that "[a]lterations of the wage system will depend on the relative political and industrial forces and neither the government nor the trade unions, certainly not the employers, will proceed on the lines of ideal principle".

Webb's membership of the War Cabinet Committee and the publication of her minority report rekindled the joint effort on women's wages which she and the F.W.G. had forged in the 1912-1913 campaigns for a minimum wage and equal pay for equal work. At its meeting on June 19, 1919, the Executive Committee of the F.W.G. considered the issue of equal pay for equal work and passed the following resolution which accorded with the position put by Webb in her Minority Report,

> That in view of the ambiguity of the formula 'equal pay for equal work', and its consequent interpretation by the employers as 'equal pay for equal output', or, 'equal pay for equal productive value', which claim is almost impossible to establish, and is not established, nor required to be established by the men, in order to receive the trade union rate of wages, this meeting recommends to members of the Fabian Women's Group that 'rates of pay should in every case be fixed irrespective of sex'.

The Executive Committee also decided to hold a special conference later in the year to discuss the problem of "equal pay" which, in the Committee's view was "far deeper" than the formula of "equal wage for equal work". As the Committee saw it, either women had to be excluded from industry altogether, or else they must demand as their right equal opportunities with men in all trades and professions. In either case, they could not be allowed to be used as blacklegs.

The Conference on 'The Economic Position of Women' was held on November 27 and was divided into two sections. The topic of the morning session, over which Webb presided was 'Women as Workers', and the speakers included Dr Fairfield (F.W.G.), Ellen Wilkinson (Amalgamated Union of Co-operative Employees) and Madeleine Symons (National Federation of Women Workers). In the afternoon session the central topic was 'Women as Wives and Mothers' and the list of speakers for the session included Barbara Drake and Marion Phillips. Webb's opening remarks to the Conference highlighted the fact that she and the Executive Committee of the F.W.G. held very similar positions both on the question of "equal pay for equal work" and on the need for women who had entered industry during the war to refrain from becoming blacklegs. In concluding her address, she warned that unless women demanded men's employment conditions there would be a great disaster looming ahead for them.

The conference on the economic position of women marks a turning point in the relationship between Webb and the F.W.G. Henceforth, along with other socialist feminists, she would increasingly look to the Labour Party as the most important vehicle for promoting women's social, political and economic position. With her turn to the Party, she became convinced that the Women's Group had to tailor its agenda to the reformist programmes of larger and more influential organisations. Her conviction that this was the focus which women socialists must take was reinforced by the impact the passing of the Representation of the People Act of June 1918 had on both Labour Party parliamentary representation and on feminist activism in the wider community. The Act extended suffrage to all men without qualification and ceded the vote to women over thirty years old. This was a development Beatrice considered truly outstanding but typically saw the passage of the law as an important victory not only for women and formerly disenfranchised men but also for the working class. On June 16, 1918, she included the following passage in her diary which captures her utilitarian attitude to the franchise:

I note with interest that not once in this diary have I mentioned the outstanding event of the year's home affairs - the passage of the Representation of the People Act, extending the suffrage from eight to about eighteen millions and admitting women to citizenship. This revolution has been on my consciousness the whole time, but it has not risen into expression because I have been a mere spectator. It is only the events that are vital to one's own life that get into so personal a record. I have always assumed political democracy as a necessary part of the machinery of government; I have never exerted myself to get it. It has no glamour for me. I have been, for instance, totally indifferent to my own political disenfranchisement. But I do not ignore the fact that the coming of the Labour Party as a political force has been largely occasioned by this year's extension of the franchise (Webb in MacKenzie 1984, pp.308-309).

As a consequence of the passing of the Act, the Labour Party soon became the alternative government and the women's movement began to seriously fragment. Labour's electoral prospects increased because many more workers now had the vote. At the same time the women's movement began to dissolve because with suffrage no longer able to serve as the key unifying focus the many differing and often conflicting interests within the movement became increasingly divisive. Perhaps more to the point, with suffrage removed as a unifying issue and with socialist women now able to organise within the Labour Party, much of the heat went out of the F.W.G. While the Group was not characterised by the narrowness of many other suffrage organisations its vitality was dependent on the suffrage issue to a significant degree. With the loss of this driving influence, and with its members now having an alternative home the Group began to disintegrate, becoming in a relatively short period merely a social grouping of old comrades.

Conclusion

This paper has shown Barbara Caine's assertion that Beatrice Webb was not particularly active in the campaigns waged by the Fabian Women's Group to be without substance. Webb helped to found the F.W.G., played a leading role in shaping and developing its research program, and actively promoted its interests and goals within the Fabian Society. This was surely a good deal more than Caine's (1982, p.36) belittling assessment that Webb confined "herself to inviting members to tea and in some cases adding her name to public statements".

Caine also asserts that Webb came into conflict with the women's movement because she insisted on the need to consider social problems in their entirety, rather than concentrating on the position of women. This is a charge that appears to have a degree of truth. As has been shown over the last three chapters of this volume, throughout her life Webb remained convinced that gender emancipation was but one third of a great movement towards *human* liberty. While deeply committed to advancing women's freedom and well-being, she was equally committed to the emancipation of both the working class and subordinated races. She saw all three movements as intimately intertwined and was convinced that all three needed to be advanced as part of one great unity. Given this belief, Webb could not fully immerse herself within the F.W.G. and the women's movement but instead gave where she could (to the extent she at times drove herself beyond her physical and psychological capacities). But to acknowledge that Webb was "guilty" of embracing issues other than feminism and that her encompassing perspective did at times bring her into conflict with other feminists is not to concede that she stood outside the women's movement or that her ideas were alien to the movement. Such a charge can only adhere if one accepts a very narrow conception of what constitutes the "women's movement". Caine asserts that in the context of the late nineteenth century the term is somewhat awkward and "refers not to a coherent programme or unified group of people, but rather to a number of separate campaigns intended to extend the rights and opportunities of women" (Caine 1982, p.33). Given Webb's long and active involvement in the struggle to expand the material well-being of women, and not only the women of the working class, it should be evident that she is surely encompassed within such a definition. That Caine believes this to be not the case reflects an inadequate understanding of the extent and nature of Webb's involvement with the struggle for women's emancipation. It also reflects the weighting she places on the struggle for the franchise which she identifies as the touchstone identifying who was a member of the women's movement at the turn of the century. The fact that Webb did not suffer the delusion that winning the vote would emancipate women and was convinced that the demand for the franchise was a very limited goal is surely, however, not adequate grounds for excluding her from the pantheon of women who contributed to the struggle for women's emancipation.

6 Beatrice Webb and the National Standard for Manual Handling

Chris Nyland and Diana Kelly

The support given gender specific protective labour laws by the Webbs reflects their conviction that the immediate needs of the women of the industrial working class had to be given priority where these needs conflicted with the rights of employers and the needs of more affluent women. It was held that these basic labour laws were a critical resource providing a legal foundation upon which those working women with least resources could build effective instruments of resistance to male and class oppression. As has been shown, this perspective elicited a great deal of hostility from that faction of the women's movement which saw the laws as analogous to the discriminatory barriers they faced within their own fields and who claimed gender specific labour laws which protected working class women were opposed to women's interests.

The alliance of forces opposed to the 1895 Bill to extend the Factory Acts was of great significance providing the employers with vocal and articulate allies whose involvement in the debate undermined the unity of those who would normally have supported laws designed to protect the right of employees to safe working conditions. The consequent thwarting of the Government's intention by this alliance induced Webb to warn activists struggling to improve women's employment conditions of the danger posed by this alignment of forces. Similarly, our objective is to argue that the conflict of interest within the women's movement that led many middle class women to oppose laws which restricted what employers could demand of their female employees remains an issue of concern. We examine the unfolding of a contemporary Australian situation similar to that which confronted Fabian women in the mid 1890s. In so doing, we explain why many feminists a century later have again elected to ignore the needs of the women of the industrial working class and instead ally themselves with employers seeking to revoke laws that limit the freedom of capital to exploit working women. We examine labour laws which until the 1990s limited to 16 kilograms the weight an employer could compel a female employee to lift or carry.

Beatrice was aware that the desire to achieve women's emancipation had blinded many feminists to the fact that the needs of the working class woman differed from her middle-class counterpart (Webb 1896, pp.4, 9). The narrowness of vision she believed characterised these individuals has been well captured by Creighton.

> Much of the Movement's thinking appears to have been based upon a failure to appreciate that important element of trade union philosophy which dictates that in certain circumstances the apparent rights of the individual must be subordinated to collective interests. It also reflected a confusion between a middle-class desire to assert the *right* to work in the job of one's choice, on the terms of one's choice, and what for the working class was all too often the *necessity* of accepting whatever job was available, usually on the employer's terms (Creighton 1979, p.26).

A similar point has been advanced by Draper and Lipow who also highlight the significance of class divisions within the women's movement.

> The socialist women fought for immediate economic gains for women workers, including legislative gains to protect women workers' interests - just as every militant organisation of male workers did the same. But this simple fact produced a controversy which is as lively today as when it started, one that provides a touchstone of the class difference between socialist feminism and bourgeois feminism (Draper and Lipow 1976, pp.184-185).

Draper and Lipow note that in the case of the male worker the question of protective legislation is now so accepted as to be no longer controversial. It is forgotten that there was a time when it was often argued that a minimum wage for men would become the maximum wage, thereby hurting better paid workers even if it improved the situation of the lowest paid. Draper and Lipow concede that there is a kernel of truth in such fears but conclude on balance that if the labour movement is not organised to police the way that labour laws are utilised, there is no conceivable legislation which cannot be turned against some employees.

> What is taken for granted on men workers' behalf is not accepted as a principle for women workers as well. Why? The difficulty comes not merely from employers (who are understandably reluctant to improve

working conditions for any 'special' group) but also from the bourgeois feminists. Historically speaking, the reason for this state of affairs is quite plain. The hard core of the bourgeois feminist movements has typically been the 'career women' elements, business and professional strivers above all. Protective devices for the benefit of women workers in factories help to make life more bearable for them, but they are usually irrelevant to upper-echelon women trying to get ahead in professions. Worse, they may introduce restrictions which get in the way. At the very least, the 'pure' feminists demonstrate their social purity by rejecting the idea that the women's question has something to do with class issues. Protective legislation for *women* workers is, abstractly considered, a form of 'sex discrimination' - just as legislation for men workers is a form of 'class legislation' and was long denounced as such. The bourgeois feminists are better served by making feminine equality as abstract an issue as possible, above all abstracted from the social struggle of classes (Draper and Lipow 1976, pp.185-186).

Beatrice Webb and the women of the Fabian Women's Group were primarily of the middle-class but were able to lay aside their own interests where these conflicted with the interests of women whose class position rendered them much more vulnerable than themselves. While supporting equality of the sexes, they opposed the notion that increased gender equality could justifiably be bought at the cost of increased class inequality. They did not deny that in some instances the likelihood of women obtaining employment was constrained by sex-specific labour laws but insisted this was a problem inherent in any form of general regulation.   "Either way there must be hard cases, and individual grievances. The question is whether, taking the whole population and all considerations into account, the evils will be greater under regulation or under free competition" (Webb 1896, p.4).

As Draper and Lipow observe, Webb's point is as valid today as it was in the 1890s. Protective laws can limit women's access to certain occupations and often have been utilised by employers and male workers in a manner that is discriminatory. At the same time, they have provided a great many working women with a degree of protection that has contributed to their health and safety. Further, by limiting the powers of the employer these laws have often diminished the class inequality that characterises the employment relationship. In this duality, lies the fundamental difficulty that must be faced by democrats who would reform this area of labour law. The reformer who wishes to eliminate any tendency these laws may have to restrict women's market freedom but who does not wish to reduce the protection enjoyed by women workers must find a solution that simultaneously resolves these issues.

Webb's British and Australian Descendants

In suggesting that a similar situation to that faced by Webb exists in contemporary Australia we do not wish to push the analogy too far for there are important differences between the situation in Britain in the 1890s and that which exists in contemporary Australia. One critical difference is that at present there exists very little appreciation within the women's movement that many female industrial workers are advantaged by legislation that protects their health and safety. While this situation is not unlike that which exists in the United States and Britain, at least in those nations both supporters and opponents of special labour laws for women were active in the debate prior to the relevant legislation being amended. For example, when Britain's Equal Opportunities Commission (EOC) urged in 1979 that sex-specific labour laws be abolished, the Trade Union Congress *and* sections of the women's movement opposed this. The most notable of the feminists who resisted the Commission's proposal were associated with the Rights for Women Unit of the National Council for Civil Liberties. From the early 1970s these women mounted a continuing campaign of resistance both to the Confederation of British Industry and that faction of the women's movement opposed to special protection for female industrial workers. Together with the Trade Union Congress, the feminists of the Women's Rights Unit argued passionately for the preservation of the protection provided to women by traditional labour laws (Coote 1975; Coussins 1979, p.5). The essence of the feminists' response is well captured by Coyle,

> The EOC is *right* in its appraisal of the existing legislation as inadequate and unworkable; but is *wrong*, in its conclusion and recommendations, to argue that the solution lies in removing the legislation altogether. The EOC considers that without protective legislation women will be freer to choose whether or not to work the night shift, seemingly unaware that it will mean *employers* will be freer to *force* women to do so. Further, the EOC does not recognize the inadequacy of the Health and Safety Legislation which is supposed to make good any gaps left by the departure of protective laws, *and* seems to be ignoring the fact that women enter the labour market on weak, unorganized and unequal terms. At least protective legislation recognizes the vulnerability of female labour and should be kept, not in its present protective/paternalistic form but as part of a progressive

move to minimize socially undesirable hours for everyone (Coyle 1980, p.1).

The British feminists opposed to the EOC's "reforms" insisted that any changes to the law must enhance both equality of opportunity and the protection of employees. More specifically, they advocated the extension of the legislation to men and the democratisation of the means by which relevant laws are applied in the workplace. The latter objective was to be achieved by enhancing the right of employees to participate directly in the governance of these laws. What was not acceptable was the trading of gender equality for increased class inequality. Indeed, the feminists of the Rights for Women Unit insisted that such proposals did not constitute an exercise in equality but rather merely amounted to a reduction in the rights of women workers (National Council for Civil Liberties 1986, p.1).

> It should be the EOC's aim to achieve equality for women without deterioration of their working conditions, instead of equalising 'down' ... If the EOC's recommendations were implemented, women would simply be equally vulnerable with men to the pressures of working long and unsociable hours to gain a decent wage. It is an insult to women for the EOC to campaign on their behalf for such a spurious kind of equality (Coussins 1979, p.9).

> NCCL believes that ... any changes to the protective laws in order to achieve equality should be in the direction of a "levelling up" and not a "levelling down" of working conditions (National Council for Civil Liberties 1986, p.5).

Whereas the British trade unions received substantial support from scholars and feminists when questioning the wisdom of abolishing laws which protect women from exploitation by their employers, a similar development has not occurred in Australia. Two rare exceptions are Thornton (1990) and Bacchi (1990), both of whom have castigated the notion that "equalising down" promotes equality. Bacchi notes that for as long as we use a conception of equality which abstracts people from their particular circumstances, it will look as if we are faced with impossible political choices — such as, how do we justify increasing equality of opportunity between men and women if this means that we must simultaneously increase class inequality? She insists that what we need do to resolve this difficulty is to challenge the meaning assigned to the term "equality". In particular, we need to ensure that the context and manner in which this term is used is appropriate. By so doing we can determine both whether its use has real meaning and content, and whether we face impossible choices or real and meaningful alternatives. Thus, the protection debate should not simply focus on whether men and women are the same or different in their essence and whether the law should reflect this sameness or difference. Rather, it should seek to determine the processes that convert sex characteristics into disadvantages. If one applies this perspective to protective weight lifting limits for women, for example, then what will be centred upon is that element in our socio-economic system which makes it necessary for workers to have to lift heavy weights. This factor, of course, is that the pursuit of profit drives the capitalist enterprise to pursue greater efficiency even where this means pushing the demands upon workers beyond the point where they conflict with human capacities. From this perspective, the choice facing reformers ceases to be equality of the sexes versus class equality. Rather, the question is, are we willing to pay the economic price that would be required to create a situation where sex-specific strength differences between men and women become irrelevant in the workplace?

That this is the real choice facing those who wish to assist women to obtain greater formal access to manual occupations, tends to be hidden by those who would accept increased class inequality as the price that must be paid. Such individuals prefer a discourse which makes it appear we are faced with a choice which requires us to make a trade-off between two forms of equality, when the reality is that we must choose between greater material well-being or greater democracy. The solution to the problem of how to resolve simultaneously the difficulties faced by the democrat who wishes to enhance women's access to manual occupations, without increasing class inequality, requires that safety standards be such that they are able to encompass sex-specific characteristics. If policies based on this premise were to be adopted, the protective labour law debate would be able to break free of whether the state should treat women the same or differently to men. Thus, as Bacchi suggests, were we to be offered a programme of extending the 16 kilogram standard to all workers, both male and female, we would not need to choose between protection and discrimination. Rather, we would have to decide whether we are willing to pay the economic price of creating a work environment where the demands an employer can legally make of an employee are within the capacities of both sexes (Bacchi 1990, pp142-143).

In asserting that Australian contributors to the debate on sex-specific labour legislation have paid inadequate attention to the protective aspect of these laws, it is not suggested that Bacchi is the only theorist to have considered this issue. Rather, as with the individuals with whom Webb struggled in the 1890s, it is a question of emphasis. Australian intellectuals who have participated in this debate have tended to minimise the significance of the protective aspects of special labour laws for women by stressing the limited coverage of this form of legislation, the extent to which its enforcement has been effective and by dismissing the importance of biological differences between the sexes. At the same time they have concentrated great effort on emphasising the discriminatory aspect of the relevant labour regulations.

Largely because of the consequent lack of balance in the Australian debate, it has become common even for those of the left to place quotation marks around the word protective. This is meant to indicate that they believe sex-specific labour laws have little if any protective value and that they are in reality merely instruments of discrimination. This situation has created an environment where it has become relatively easy for those opposed to providing women with special forms of legal protection from their employers to campaign successfully for the repeal of this form of legislation. Indeed, the imbalance in the Australian debate has created an intellectual environment where it is possible for the state to abolish protective laws and for democrats to welcome such an act even in the face of opposition from the women most likely to be affected adversely by this form of labour market deregulation. For example, protective statutes relating to manual handling by women in shops and factories were repealed in Victoria, in 1988 and New South Wales in 1991 despite overt resistance by the two union bodies that represented the women formerly covered by the protective standards.

The next section of this chapter will focus on how the alliance of forces which campaigned within Australia in favour of the abolition of special forms of legal protection for women employees managed to achieve the abolition of the sex-specific weight limits formerly extant in most states and territories. This provides a case study which can clarify our understanding of the thinking of those diverse forces taking part in the anti-protective labour laws campaign.

The National Standard for Manual Handling

Traditionally, there has not existed a prescribed Australia-wide standard which specified the maximum weight an employer could compel an adult female employee to lift or carry. Each state set its own rules in this regard. However, there was a high degree of uniformity in that, with the exception of Western Australia, an employer could not legally instruct a female factory or shop employee to lift or carry more than 16 kilograms without assistance or without some form of mechanical aid. There was no corresponding stipulation in relation to men. This situation began to be transformed in the late 1980s. Beginning with Victoria, the states and territories gradually replaced the old weight stipulations with "gender-free" standards. The standards adopted were those proposed by the National Occupational Health and Safety Commission (Worksafe), though in 1988 Victoria pre-empted Worksafe with an all but identical standard. The weight provisions stipulated in the National Standard are presented below.

> For lifting, lowering or carrying loads:
>
> (a) in seated work, it is advisable not to lift loads in excess of 4.5 kg;
>
> (b) some evidence shows that the risk of back injury increases significantly with objects above the range of 16-20 kg, therefore, from the standing position, it is advisable to keep the load below or within this range;
>
> (c) as weight increases from 16 kg up to 55 kg, the percentage of healthy adults who can safely lift, lower or carry the weight decreases. Therefore, more care is required for weights above 16 kg and up to 55 kg in the assessment process. Mechanical assistance and/or team lifting arrangements should be provided to reduce the risk of injury associated with these heavier weights;
>
> (d) generally, no person should be required to lift, lower or carry loads above 55 kg, unless mechanical assistance or team lifting arrangements are provided to lower the risk of injury (Worksafe 1990, p.35).

These standards are significantly higher than the maximum weight an employer could legally instruct a woman employee to lift or carry under the old labour laws. These so - called "gender neutral" standards also differ from the old limits in that, as can be seen from the language in which they are couched, they are much less prescriptive. Indeed Worksafe makes it clear that the standards are merely guidelines, with their appreciation only relevant where "workable". The process by which Worksafe came to advocate "equalising down" in the level of protection enjoyed by women industrial and shop workers is highly instructive of the character of the alliance seeking to abolish much of the sex-specific labour legislation in Australia.

Since its establishment in 1984 Worksafe has been striving to eliminate the discriminatory content in Australia's labour laws. This activity was given high priority because the Commonwealth Sex Discrimination Act of 1984 included a provision which overrode all state laws. This was perceived as including labour regulations relating to women in the various states' factory acts. Following the enactment of the Federal legislation, the states were given a grace period of three years to amend any offending laws. After this time, state governments could retain their former provisions only if they gained an annual exemption from the Federal Human Rights and Equal Opportunities Commission.

One form of activity which Worksafe took up as an area of particular importance when seeking to eliminate inequality, was manual handling. This issue became an area of concern for three reasons. First, a great number of injuries are associated with manual handling, a fact not always appreciated by individuals employed in sedentary occupations who commonly assume that in modern industry the physical demands of manual occupations are such that they seldom place excessive demands on the capacities of employees. A second factor causing Worksafe to emphasise manual handling in the 1980s was that the Australian Council of Trade Unions published a statement on manual handling in 1984. This was perceived as providing a foundation for negotiations between employers and unions. The unions' 1984 statement focused equally on the need to eliminate the discriminatory dimension of the existing law and the need to preserve the protection these laws accorded employees.. The statement, then, continued the tradition advocated by the Webbs and the socialist feminist movement. Its means of dealing with protection and discrimination simultaneously was to insist that the 16 kilogram standard be extended to men. The duality of this emphasis is captured in clause 1 and 5.

1. The ACTU recognises that the manual lifting of heavy and awkward loads is responsible for a great number of injuries and long term health problems amongst Australian workers. These include:

   - abdominal hernias;
   - aggravation of circulatory and respiratory disease;
   - back injuries;
   - fatigue, leading to accidents, and injuries arising from sudden exertion.

   Back pain resulting from musculo-skeletal damage is considered to be the number one occupational injury in Australia, and is the greatest single cause of work time lost through injury.

   5. Affiliates should seek to apply the 16 kg weight lifting limit to *all* their members over 18 years of age regardless of sex, and should seek to remove clauses from awards or determination which make provision

for protecting one sex only (ACTU-VTHC Occupational Health and Safety Unit, 1984).

The third factor which led Worksafe to be particularly concerned with the existing manual handling legislation was the case of *Najdovska and Ors v. Australian Iron and Steel in 1985*. In this case the Court found that Australian Iron and Steel had earlier used Section 36 of the New South Wales Factories, *Shops and Industries Act* as a screening device in a manner which was both cavalier and discriminatory towards women. Section 36 of the Act covered women who worked in the delineated areas of the private sector and from 1983 covered women employed by the Crown. As regards manual handling it stated "No person employed in a factory shall be allowed or required to lift or carry by hand a greater mass than ... in the case of females over eighteen years of age - 16 kilograms" (cited in Anti-Discrimination Board 1984, p.10). The 1 million dollar compensation payment to the thirty-six women involved in this case ensured it obtained wide publicity and encouraged employers to insist that the state and federal governments take steps to amend legislation which would allow such developments.

The means adopted by Worksafe to deal with the problems associated with manual handling was to develop a "National Standard and General Code of Practice on Safe Manual Handling". This Code aimed to promote the occupational health and safety of workers by specifying the most effective actions to be taken by employers and employees in situations where manual handling occurs. Following the declaration of the Code, Worksafe hoped that relevant State and Territory authorities would consider its implementation "in line with the requirements of their respective legislative and regulatory mechanisms" (Worksafe Australia 1986, p.3).

In December 1986 as part of the process of formulating the National Standard, a discussion paper was issued by Worksafe. This draft document was written by a working party which was tripartite in character but which also included individuals associated with relevant interest groups. A reading of this discussion paper indicated to many observers that at least some members of the working party saw their membership as primarily an opportunity for removing discriminatory aspects from the old regulations. Those individuals who reached this conclusion did so partly because the document's review of the legislative provisions then in force concentrated almost totally on their discriminatory element. That these statutes had provided many women in low skilled and low paid jobs with a degree of legal protection was only acknowledged briefly. Indeed, the only attention that the review accorded the protective capacity of the old regulations was to note that: "[t]he existing provisions have given some protection to women in certain areas of work where alternative limitations on loads are enforced, e.g. the limits on packing boxes used in supermarkets. The anomalies have also served a useful function in prompting some understanding of the need for effective measures to control manual handling injury" (Worksafe 1986, p.15).

The review's scant consideration of the protective dimension is surprising given that one of the members of the working party, Chloe Refshauge, had overseen the drafting of a major report for the New South Wales Anti-Discrimination Board (1984, pp.14-16). In this report it was acknowledged that these regulations had often played a vital role in enabling women employees to win compensation claims for manual handling injuries. The working party, therefore, certainly had access to such knowledge. A more accurate description of the function and protective utility provided by the 16 kilogram standard has been offered by Burvill when commenting on Section 36 of the New South Wales Factories, Shops and Industries Act:

> To a limited extent, Section 36 does provide some degree of protection against injury from the lifting of heavy loads. It provides a standard that can be used by unions to ensure that safety conditions are established and maintained in work places and it provides a basis for women to claim compensation where it can be established that the injury occurred as a result of the breach of Section 36. An additional benefit is that the statutory limit on lifting has resulted in the reduction of loads to be handled in some industries. In the retail industry, for example, cartons have been broken down to units within the 16 kilo limit so that *all* workers within supermarkets, both male and female, reap the benefits (Burvill 1985, p.27).

The reason the prescribed 16 kilogram standard was so important in compensation cases was because it fixed a limit beyond which employers could not claim contributory negligence on the part of an injured employee. If the weight that the employer instructed a woman worker to lift was beyond 16 kilograms, an employer could not claim that the individual contributed to any subsequent injury and was thus only entitled to diminished compensation.

The emphasis on equality of opportunity in the 1986 document was also reflected in the changes to the established weight provisions recommended by the working party. The new weight standards that were advocated are presented in Table 1. With the exception of the representatives from the Confederation of Australian Industry, the members of the working party supported the policy put forward by the Australian Council of Trade Unions for the extension of the 16 kilogram standard to all workers male and female.

Table 1   Action levels under the conditions of an ideal lift

Actions	
1. Up to and including 16 kg	No special action required. (CAI and NT prefer UK HSC actions for level 1.
2. Above 16-25 Kg	No unaided lifting, emphasis on work practices (CAI and NT prefer UK HSC actions for level 2.
3. Above 25-34 kg	No unaided lifting, job redesign preferred. (CAI and NT prefer UK HSC actions for level 3.
4. Above 34 kg	Mechanical handling systems must be provided. (CAI and NT prefer UK HSC actions for level 4).

The Confederation of Australian Industry and the Northern Territory prefer United Kingdom Health and Safety Commission actions for all four levels.
Source: Worksafe, (1986, p.50).

The response to the draft document by employee and employer peak organisations was predictable. The Executive of the Australian Council of Trade Unions approved the draft code at its meeting of March 17th 1987 passing the following motion.

> The ACTU Executive supports the approach adopted by the National Occupational Health and Safety Commission in its Manual Handling Discussion Paper and endorses the Draft Code of Practice, especially its objective of minimising risks associated with manual handling through the re-design of work processes, its coverage of all aspects of manual handling injury management, the action levels concept and the non-discriminatory approach it takes (Australian Council of Trade Unions 1987).

Employer organisations, on the other hand, denounced the draft vehemently. They were particularly critical of the suggestion that the 16 kilogram standard should be extended to men (Wills 1987; New South Wales Employers' Federation 1987a, 1987b, 1987c; Howie 1988). Speaking for the Business Council of Australia, the Chairman of its Task

Force on Deregulation, Dean Wills, claimed the working party had advocated the generalisation of the 16 kilogram standard because it had been diverted from its proper role by individuals who had a political agenda more concerned with equality of opportunity than the establishment of safe working conditions. Wills also expressed doubt that there existed the degree of discrimination in manual employment claimed by the working party.

> Chapters 2 and 3 of the Paper concentrate very heavily on sex discrimination aspects which are not strictly speaking germane to the safe manual handling question. The Code is, therefore, distorted to take account of supposed discriminatory aspects of existing safe manual handling practices and legislation whereby maximum loads lifted by women are lower than those for men. It is, of course, a fact, recognised here and overseas, that on average men are capable of safely lifting heavier loads than women. The report concedes that differences do exist between men as a group and women as a group according to the types of manual activity but that there is considerable overlap. It is not discriminatory to recognise that in regulation any more than it is discriminatory to recognise categories such as young, old or other groupings whose average handling strength is differentiated. The paper is therefore inconsistent in that, whilst it proposes no discrimination in lifting limits on account of sex, it does propose special provisions on account of youth. The arguments used for non-discriminatory individual treatment if they prevail should apply to all categories (Wills 1987, p.11; see also Employers' Federation of New South Wales 1987, p.2).

Employers were also critical of the working party's failure to provide any costing of the proposed extension of the 16 kilogram standard suggesting that the cost of this action "would run into at least tens of millions of dollars". Consequently, they demanded that the Commonwealth Government make some attempt to price the reform before it was advanced any further. This demand was acceded to by the Commonwealth Minister for Industry, Technology and Commerce who instructed the Cabinet's Business Regulation Review Unit to undertake a costing of the proposals advocated by the working party. The Unit's subsequent report was highly critical of the suggestion that the 16 kilogram standard be extended to males, estimating the cost to be approximately nine billion dollars. Given this cost, the Unit insisted that the reform be abandoned. Indeed, in a burst of deregulatory enthusiasm, the Unit went on to suggest that the state should reduce rather than extend its attempts to regulate the sale of employees' labour-power. Further, when doing so governments should not only retreat from protecting women but should act likewise in relation to children. The Unit recommended that "State regulations which prevent full participation in the workforce by women and juniors be withdrawn and be replaced by management practices targeted more specifically towards the protection of the small number of individuals actually at risk." (Business Regulation Review Unit 1987, p.17).

The Unit's free market perspective was endorsed by employer organisations. Wills of the Business Council claimed the proposed reform was objectionable not only because of the cost involved but also because it was inherently interventionist and hence a hindrance to the flexibility of the enterprise. If the state had to become involved in the management of safe manual handling, he insisted, it should develop a non-interventionist strategy which should be based on broad guidelines. The interpretation and application would be left to those in the workplace rather than to state regulators. Wills' advice to the Federal Government and the working party was very explicit:

> If the Government feels the need to involve itself in this area it should:
>
> - go back to the drawing board to produce and [sic] approach that is less interventionist and that will allow Australian industry to deliver goods and services more competitively at home and in foreign markets;
>
> - avoid at all costs another detailed Code possibly supported by another body of regulators
>
> - produce a series of flexible non-prescriptive guidelines which would encourage safe handling without discouraging commonsense on-the-spot solutions to handling problems in the workplace (Wills 1987, p.8).

While the employers were critical of the program of reform suggested by Worksafe's working party, they also appear to have appreciated that what they termed the "mixed agenda" of some the members of this body created a rare opportunity. In short, the employers' actions suggest that they realised that the degree of emphasis the draft Code placed on enhancing women's formal access to manual occupations provided a historic chance for employers to increase the control they could legally exercise over female employees. A clear indication of this awareness is apparent in that, following his criticism of the working party's emphasis on the discrimination issue, Wills immediately raised the question of whether the law relating to manual handling should recognise the existence of differing categories of workers. New guidelines could be introduced, he suggested enticingly, that broadened the range of what was considered reasonable manual handling activity (Wills 1987, pp.11-12).

Wills' suggestion offered an alternative means of dealing with the discrimination issue to that proposed by the working party. Rather than equalising up, women's access to manual occupations could be enhanced by abolishing the old limits on the employers' freedom and replacing them with a new set of lifting limits which would apply to both men and women. What the Business Council's was proposing was that the working party should reject the policy advocated by the Australian Council of Trade Unions and feminists such as Bacchi. The ACTU and Bacchi had sought to deal simultaneously with discrimination and the safety implications of the inequality between employer and employee. In short, it was being suggested by the Business Council that the working party treat women in a manner that was abstracted from their class position and that the traditional forms of protection be replaced by broad, less clear and less enforceable norms which would apply to all workers.

The employers' response left those on the working party who hoped to eliminate the discriminatory aspects of the old laws in a difficult position. That this was the case suggestion is a presumption based on a number of factors. First, this body had access to clear statements from those trade unions whose members were most likely to be affected by the abolition of the 16 kilogram standard that they were decidedly opposed to any such proposal. In these statements the unions insisted that if it was not possible to grant their preferred option of extending the 16 kilogram standard to men, at the very least the old standard should be retained for those employees who traditionally enjoyed this form of protection (Shop Distributive and Allied Employees Association 1987, p.2; Federated Miscellaneous Workers Union of Australia 1987).

The second factor underpinning the assumption that the working party would have been discomfited by the Business Council's proposal is the fact that the working party was aware of the possible consequences of abolishing the old regulations without replacing them with statutes that were equally firm. In 1984 the New South Wales Anti-Discrimination Board report that had been supervised by Refshauge had specified the probable consequences of repeal without replacement.

> Superficially the repeal of the mass limit would remove the discriminatory content. Its repeal, however, is also likely to have the following effects -

- Handling units may increase in mass and both men and women may be required to lift heavier loads, thus worsening working conditions.

- Women working for employers under the Factories, Shops and Industries Act would be required to lift more than 16 kg.

- In cases of injury from manual handling, the protection afforded by section 36 is removed and the argument of contributory negligence can be made against the injured employee.

- Its repeal may detract from the inadequate protection of all employees in all workplaces against the risk of injury incurred in manual handling (Anti-Discrimination Board 1984, p.84).

The third issue which may have caused the working party concern when responding to the employers' proposal was that there were insufficient technically trained people in Australia able to undertake occupational risk assessment. This point was stressed in 1988 by the ergonomics consultant Alan Howie in relation to the Victorian Code of Manual Handling.

> Certainly the knowledge, skills and experience required to sensibly fulfil the requirements of the legislation are not readily available. There are probably less than 200 professionals in Victoria who can sensibly advise on solutions to unacceptable work situations. Tools to assist others such as software packages are only in an early stage of development. Even training for acquisition of basic skills in areas such as ergonomics [sic] and task re-design is almost unobtainable. This bodes ill for the level of back injury claims and for their economic impact. It is also useful to remember that more than 400 years ago, Elizabeth I pointed out that a law which was impossible to obey was likely to bring disrepute on any Government which introduced it (Howie 1988, p.6).

In a review of British sex-specific labour laws, Lewis and Davies (1991) observed that if reformers committed to improving the position of all women were faced with a choice between accepting either the retention of protective labour legislation or a formal equality of opportunity which ignored the class position of the women involved, they would be in an impossible situation. As with the Webbs, these scholars recognised that this impossibility stems from the duality inherent in protective labour laws. "Policies built on a premise of difference and of protection offer some amelioration for women at the bottom of the heap ... [while] policies built on a premise of equality (whether in the older guise of 'fair field and no favour' or in the modern one of 'equal opportunities') offer some improvement for women at the top of the heap" (Lewis and Davies 1991, pp.22-23). To choose one or the other of these options, they argue, is to abandon those women not favoured. As posed by Lewis and Davies, the claim that this is an impossible choice has some validity. In relation to the manual handling standard, however, these were not the alternatives faced by those on the working party and by Worksafe. Rather, what had to be chosen were the means and sources by which the desired reform was to be paid. There were two alternatives. The working party could have advised that Australians of all classes pay the economic and political costs involved in the trade unions' proposal, or conversely, it could have chosen to have industrial women workers pay for the reform by compelling them to accept a weakening in the level of protection they enjoyed. Faced with this situation, the Webbs and those feminists with whom they were aligned would have rejected the employers' suggestion. The hostility such a response would have elicited from the employers would undoubtedly have made it necessary for reformers to seek alternative means to continue the campaign for the elimination of both discrimination and unsafe practices in the workplace. Given the price demanded by capital, however, the Webbs and their socialist feminists contemporaries would have been convinced there could be no justification for endorsing the policy advocated by the employers.

Unfortunately, this was not the decision made by the working party and Worksafe. These bodies had to confront an effective alliance of employers, free market economists and the members of a narrowly focused, predominantly middle-class women's movement, the overwhelming majority of whom perceived the protective laws merely as a device for the perpetuation of discrimination and patriarchy. When faced by this united front, Worksafe chose to over-ride the objections of the labour organisations that represented the women most likely to be adversely effected by the abolition of the traditional forms of protection. Thus the unions' demand that the 16 kilogram statutory limit be extended to both male and female employees was rejected. The old standard was replaced by a vague regulation, the most stringent stipulation of which states, "generally, no person should be required to lift, lower or carry loads above 55 kg".

Some Alliance Justifications

The gradual adoption of Worksafe's National Standard for Manual Handling by Australian state and federal governments, removed a significant element in the defences of those women who labour in factories and shops. Given that the alliance which worked successfully to achieve this objective intends to carry its deregulatory campaign into other employment areas, it is important that analysts in all nations become more involved in debating sex-specific labour laws than they have in the recent past. In short, theorists must return to the tradition advocated by Fabian and other socialist feminists who advised that the arguments and assumptions of all participants in the protection debate must be analysed critically before any 'reforms' of this nature are undertaken. Accepting this advice, the rest of this paper will examine some of the claims advanced by those who supported the abolition of the weight lifting limits.

The first assertion to be considered is that which claims that a broad based, non-prescriptive code of practice is a more effective means of protecting the health and safety of women employees than were the old statutory limits. The difficulty with this claim is that it is merely an assertion not based on empirical evidence and that the years since this approach was embraced have seen a significant increase in the incidence of workplace injury. How effective the old laws were at protecting women employees does not appear to have been seriously assessed by Worksafe prior to the publication of its National Standard. No systematic attempt was undertaken, for example, to compare the statistical data relating to the health and safety and labour market segmentation records of women in factories and shops, in what may be termed 16 kilogram states, with the situation in Western Australia where no such regulation existed. This failure to test the protective capacity of the old laws prior to their abolition must be considered unacceptable.

That Worksafe's code of practice will be a more effective defender of women's health and safety must also be open to doubt given the vagueness of much of its terminology and that its application only applies where deemed "workable". This term, together with its many qualifiers, endangers women in that it ensures Worksafe's recommended standards lack the precision of the 16 kilogram standard. In Victoria, officials of the Shop Distributive and Allied Employees Association have reported that they have found it all but impossible to enforce the 1988 code of practice as a consequence of the "so far as is practicable" clause and its riders. The union also reports that employers have shown a marked disinclination to engage in the consultation recommended by that State's "gender neutral" manual handling law. Further, union's workplace safety representatives have greater difficulty in applying the legislation's code of practice than with the former 16 kilogram standard.

The shop assistants' experience replicates that found in other industries. Hopkins and Parnell (1984), for example, have demonstrated that in the coal mining industry this kind of escape clause has inhibited the enforcement of health and safety standards. Likewise, Braithwaite and Grabosky (1985), in their study of the enforcement of health and safety law concluded that vague guidelines, rather than specific standards, make enforcement of regulations much more difficult.

> Obtaining convictions under general clauses is bound to be more difficult than prosecuting the same conduct under specific standards. Moreover, the average Australian factories inspector and the average factory manager are not technically competent to assess what is an unsafe level of exposure ... without the guidance of a standard (Braithwaite and Grabosky 1985, p.36).

The 16 kilogram standard was a far from satisfactory instrument for protecting women workers. Nevertheless, it did place a substantive, easily understood restriction on the demands that employers could make of their female employees which could be more easily enforced and defended than the vague guidelines offered in Worksafe's National Standard. It was for this reason above all that Australian employers, as with their counterparts in the United States and Britain, were so enthusiastic to support the repeal of the sex-specific standards. Employers do not like this form of legislation because as the British feminist Coyle (1980, p.9) has observed: "Despite all the shortcomings of ... protective legislation it represents a gigantic concession wrought from capital".

Coyle's observation brings us to the second issue we wish to discuss which is Worksafe's apparent presumption that there exists a Robenesque unity of interest between capital and labour in the area of health and safety. This is reflected in the fact that the National Standard fails to recommend that any specific steps be taken to ensure that the resolution of health and safety disputes between employers and employees is recognised institutionally. Indeed, the final draft of the National Standard fails to offer any advice as to how the guidelines it recommends are to be enforced once the old statutory regulations are abolished. Occupational health and safety is an industrial relations issue emanating from a relationship that is inherently conflictual. It needs to be perceived as such if the interests of workers are not to be undermined. As Creighton and Gunningham (1985, p.4) have noted, any analysis of occupational health and safety which ignores or attempts to distort the reality of class relations at work cannot carry conviction. This is true of all employment situations but is especially so in the case of unskilled and semi-skilled workers. Employees in industries like retailing, for example, have a greater need for such laws than have skilled workers such as nurses and those with trade qualifications. This is because the weak market power of shop assistants renders them so much more vulnerable than their highly skilled counterparts. Webb stressed this point when she observed that where women employees have little market power it is critical that there exist legal standards which establish absolute limits on any possible downward spiral in working conditions.

> The real enemies of the working woman are not the men, who always insist on higher wages, but the "amateurs" of her own sex. So long as there are women, married or unmarried, eager and able to take work home, and do it in the intervals of another profession, domestic service, we shall never disentangle ourselves from that vicious circle in which low wages lead to bad work, and bad work compels low wages. The one practical remedy for this disastrous competition is the extension of Factory legislation, with its strict limitation of women's hours, to all manufacturing work wherever carried on (Webb 1896, p.12).

Very few of the women activists who participated in the alliance which campaigned to abolish the protective labour laws gave any thought as to how women employees were meant to offset the undermining of their anti-employer defences that would result from weakening the level of legal protection they enjoyed. Some anti-protectionists did recognise that a difficulty existed and consequently argued that women must "organise to ensure that regulatory strategies reflect and respond to the needs and experiences of women" (O'Donnell and Hall 1988, p.116). A similar acknowledgment of the enhanced role that must be played by unions, when sex-specific labour laws are abolished, was advanced by Wentworth (1979, p.64).

The problem with the trade union prescription is that while it might be applicable to some sectors of the female labour force, it offers little to those many women who cannot be organised effectively for whatever reason. Such arguments are similar to those advocated by the Webb's middle-class opponents of the late nineteenth century. Of these individuals Creighton has observed that they seldom had any conception of the difficulty involved in effectively unionising the female manual labour force. Moreover, they also evinced no comprehension of the demands of manual employment and the vulnerability of women workers whose sector of the labour market is characterised by very high levels of unemployment.

Unionization was, and remains, the most effective way to combat exploitation of women workers, but it was unrealistic to think of it as an adequate alternative to legislative protection at that time. Women were notoriously difficult to organize into effective trade unions, and were in general in far too weak a position, in both social and economic terms, for voluntary action to be of more than marginal relevance (Creighton 1979, p.26).

Beatrice Webb (1896, p.9) observed that it is "cruel mockery to preach Trade Unionism, and Trade Unionism alone" to unskilled women workers while denying them legal protection from the demands of their employers. In the case of the new manual handling standard, to suggest that women should compensate for their loss of legal protection by joining trade unions is a particularly ironic exercise. This is because, despite trade union demands that they should do so, Worksafe failed even to recognise the existence of unions as institutions which should be involved in the maintenance and enforcement of the new standards. Gunningham has noted there appears to be only two effective strategies for ensuring that management adopts a conscientious, rigorous approach to health and safety. One is for more vigorous and effective enforcement of statutory standards; the second is for a form of worker participation, which involves granting direct rights and powers to worker representatives. The first model has to some extent been followed in the United States under the Occupational Safety and Health Act 1970. The second has been embraced most fully in Scandinavia and in certain other European countries (Gunningham 1985, p.40).

The working party that compiled the 1986 draft manual handling code advised there was a need to maintain the voluntary institutional defences of women employees. Indeed, while seeking to enhance the legal protection of workers by extending the 16 kilogram standard to both men and women, they sought to strengthen the ability of workers to defend themselves. They did so by proposing that employees and their health and safety representatives be given both the right and the power to play an active and effective role in the development and enforcement of safe methods of manual handling. The working party also recognised explicitly the conflictual nature of workplace health and safety. This is indicated by their suggestion that where trade unions exist in the workplace they should play an integral part in the management of this aspect of the employment relationship.

This Code should be implemented by management in consultation with employees. Where unions exist in a particular workplace, they should be included in consultations. Where they exist, occupational health and safety committees or representatives should review *all* existing processes involving manual handling, and advise on systematic programs of job and workplace redesign; such a review shall include the potential to use mechanical aids wherever possible, and the interpretation and application of action levels for forces, and abatement factors. The introduction of changes in the workplace or job design should only occur following full consultation with employees through established consultative processes (Worksafe 1986, p.44).

While some European employers might permit workers and their representatives to play an effective role in occupational health and safety, as Gunningham suggests, Australian employers have not welcomed the suggestion that local employees do likewise. Representatives from both industry and umbrella employer associations have stated that they do not accept that safety representatives or unionists should be provided with enforceable rights or powers in the area of health and safety. Derek Buckland (1985), a spokesman for the Metal Trades Industry Association and an employer representative with Worksafe and Ken Crompton (1985) of the Victorian Chamber of Manufacturers, for example, have both made it clear that their organisations believe that at most employee representatives should only have the right to be consulted on health and safety issues. As far as these employers are concerned, health and safety should not be an issue for negotiation and employee safety or union representatives should not have any powers of enforcement. They believe that workers have a right to be on safety committees which play a consultative role but nothing more. Commenting on the effectiveness of the form of worker involvement in health and safety advocated by the employers, Gunningham has observed:

> This version of worker participation is unlikely to bring about the degree of safety that workers require. Denied any effective decision-making power beyond the right to be 'consulted', their contribution to workplace safety must inevitably be limited. So long as managers and workers agree on what is to be done, no difficulties arise, but in the event of disagreement, worker participation in the Robens style is little more than a sham. ... In these circumstances, voluntary agreements and 'consultation' are unlikely to bring about the degree of safety that workers require (Gunningham 1985, p.47).

Despite the fact that the working party was aware that employees require institutional defences, a consultative role is all that Worksafe recommends be given to workers' health and safety representatives. In its

National Standard, the working party's recommendations were not accepted and the employers were apparently conceded what they wanted. The new standard and code of practice makes no mention of trade unions whatsoever. Nor is it recommended that safety committees or safety representatives be provided with any powers or rights of enforcement. Individual state governments can introduce legislation to make this possible but it certainly is not urged explicitly by Worksafe. All this body recommends is:

> The National Standard for Manual Handling ... requires assessment and control of manual handling tasks to be carried out by employers in consultation with employee(s) who are required to carry out the tasks and their representative(s) on health and safety issues (Worksafe 1990, p.18).

> Consultation involves the sharing of information and exchange of views between managers, workers and/or their representative(s) on health and safety issues. It includes the opportunity to contribute to decision making in a timely fashion to resolve manual handling risk(s) (Worksafe 1990, p.11).

Moreover, consultation need not even be conducted on a formal basis but can be undertaken by "informal processes" if the employer and the employee so "choose".

The third and final issue to be considered in this section is the assumption, embraced enthusiastically by many members of the anti-protection alliance, that men and women do not differ as groups in any significant manner relevant to manual handling. In its discussion of the design principles that the employer should heed when selecting equipment and furniture for the workplace, the National Standard observes that employers need to be aware of the "enormous range of physical dimensions, for example height and reach" to be found in the workforce (Worksafe 1990, p.19). It is also suggested that is desirable that employers design activities and tasks to suit the abilities of the widest possible range of individuals so as to avoid discrimination against particular groups. However, no "groups" are identified by those offering this advice. In the case of women engaged in manual handling this lack of specificity constitutes a hazard. It fails to draw to the attention of employers the fact that there is a need to ensure that innate differences between male and female workers, as groups as well as individuals, are sufficiently catered for within the workplace. Moreover, it implicitly informs employers that the sex of those instructed to undertake manual handling tasks is not an issue to which they need pay any attention.

That employers would agree they need to make no special efforts to cater for the physical needs and capacities of their female employees is understandable, given their desire to maximise their freedom as regards the use of the latter's labour-power. Why advocates of women's rights should support this hypothesis is less obvious. However, it is probably explained by two primary phenomena. First, many of these individuals have no personal experience of what it means to be a manual employee. This is true not only of the professionals and white collar workers active in the women's movement, but also of an increasing number of trade union officials. Second, many who believe or claim to believe that innate differences between the sexes do not affect in any way the respective capacities of men and women to undertake manual labour. Such individuals dismiss out of hand Beatrice Webb's claim that one element that has contributed to the character of the sexual division of labour is the biological differences between the sexes.

> In many cases the physical strength or endurance required, or the exposure involved, puts the work absolutely out of the power of the average woman. ... Hence, where women can really perform a given task with anything like the efficiency of a man, they have, owing to their lower standard of expenditure, a far better chance than the man of getting work. The men, in short, enjoy what may be called a "rent" of superior strength and endurance (Webb 1896, p.11).

The reality is that women have on average two-thirds of the muscular strength of equally trained men and this example of sexual dimorphism is not merely a product of culture (Bishop *et al* 1987). The two-thirds rule is, of course, only an average figure relating to the whole body. Female strength capacity can range from 35% to 85% of that available to equally trained men depending on what part of the body is being considered. Celentano and Noy, for example, report that:

1) overall total body strength of women was about 63.5% of that of men, with a range of 35-86%;

2) static strength in the upper extremities of women was 59.5% of men, with a range of 47-79%;

3) static strength in the lower extremities of women was 71.9% of men, with a range of 57-86%;

4) static trunk strength of women was 63.8% of men, with a range of 37-70%;

5) dynamic strength characteristics (primarily muscle strength measurements involving lifting, lowering, pulling, and pushing; these values are median percentage values) of women were 68.8% of men, with a range of 59-84% (Celentano and Noy 1981, p.5).

Celentano and Noy (1981, p.6) also sought to determine the degree of overlap in the respective muscular capacities of men and women. The existence of an overlap is important in the protective labour laws debate because the fact that some women are stronger physically than some men is often utilised as a justification for dismissing the relevance of the differential in strength capacities that exists between the sexes. However, the extent of this overlap is often overstated by the anti-protectionists who commonly fudge the issue by merely describing it as "considerable". In reality, as Celentano and Noy have shown, the overlap is not of great magnitude. Indeed, as Table 3 shows, many 5th percentile values for males exceed the 95th percentile values for females for the same measurement variable.

Table 2 Comparison of Cable Tension Strength Values Obtained From Men and Women

VARIABLE	SEX	MEAN	S.D.	5%ile	95%ile
Shoulder Flexion	F	22.6	3.8	16.3	28.9
	M	50.1	11.4	31.3	68.9
Elbow Flexion	F	25.2	4.8	17.3	33.1
	M	57.2	11.6	38.1	76.3
Hip Flexion	F	50.9	11.9	31.3	70.5
	M	62.6	16.3	35.7	89.5
Knee Extension	F	58.8	15.2	33.7	83.9
	M	102.8	25.7	60.4	145.3
Trunk Flexion	F	33.8	8.8	19.3	48.3
	M	90.9	24.3	50.8	131.0
Grip Strength	F	26.4	3.8	20.1	32.7
	M	50.4	8.8	35.9	64.9

Strength values are reported in kiloponds. Grip Strength was measured with the Smedley hand dynamometer.
Source: Celentano and Noy, 1981, p.6.

The results obtained by Celentano and Noy, though replicated by others, have been challenged by a number of the individuals opposed to protective labour laws. These critics have noted such factors as the small number of subjects commonly studied in such research. However, the critics have not come forward with research data of their own which invalidates these results. Nor did the working party which established the National Standard commission new research to test their validity. This last omission was perpetrated despite the fact that physical strength is a significant factor influencing safe manual handling and inadequate physical strength is much more often a problem for women engaged in manual occupations than it is for men (Magora 1970; Eldred 1975; Chaffin 1974, 1978; Celentano, Nottrodt and Saunders 1984). Moreover, as Denning has observed the issue is not simply one of muscular strength.

> The problem is not just that the average man has bigger muscles than the average woman. Women and men do not use their arms and legs in the same way because their muscle systems are distributed differently. The strength differences between the sexes are most apparent when individuals are lifting, lowering or carrying heavy objects. The anatomy of the female pelvis is different from that of the male; this makes it especially difficult for women to lift things from a stooped position. Because her whole pelvic architecture is designed to be more flexible to allow for child birth, a woman is at greater risk from strains of the joint between the lower spine and the pelvic girdle (the sacro-iliac joint) (Denning 1985, p.14).

Health and safety specialists have attempted to highlight the danger to female manual employees of ignoring the work implications of the natural differences between the sexes. The ergonomist Joan Ward, for example, argued that with the increased participation of females in the labour force it was imperative that this factor be heeded. Her concern related in particular to the weights women might have to lift when engaged in manual handling.

> This [biological difference between the sexes] has particular importance for manual handling tasks (lifting, carrying, pushing, pulling, etc.) in industry, and the back injuries and pain that are associated with such tasks. ... in the United Kingdom, a new organization, the Back Pain Association, has been set up to give advice on the prevention of back pain which, it calculates, causes 56,000 workers daily to be off sick. Their advice is concentrated on *how* to lift and carry, etc. - it does not advise *how much* should be lifted or handled. It is obviously important, however, as women will be playing an increasing part in the industrial labour force and will thus be increasingly at risk of injury, that the question of "how much" shall be handled is crucial. The difference in strength capacities between men and women is therefore of importance (Ward 1978, p.595).

Finally, no statistical study of the respective vulnerability of men and women in manual handling occupations appears to have been undertaken in Australia prior to Worksafe publishing its national standard. This is despite the fact that at the International Occupational Health and Safety Convention, held in Victoria in 1988, the key international speaker, Tore Larsson, informed the trade union, employer and government delegates that Swedish statistical studies were suggesting that relative to men women in occupations involving "dynamic muscular work" were experiencing a disproportionate number of injuries and illnesses (Larsson 1988; Malker and Zamore 1987). Larsson stated that the Swedish research has indicated that women tend to suffer many more injuries when undertaking heavy manual work than do men. He also informed the Victorian conference that this evidence had led Swedish health and safety researchers to conclude that for women physically demanding jobs "are even more damaging to their health than they would be to the health of their husbands". He advised that the Swedes were now convinced that the cavalier approach their society in the 1960s took towards the health and safety implications of the biological differences between the sexes is going to produce major health problems over the next decade. "There is a great risk that a large proportion of this generation of female, industrial workers will constitute a heavy burden on the medical and social system in the next 5-10 years. But I think that the problem is confined to women in industry - and is not really a problem for those that sit in offices" (Larsson 1988, p.24).

Conclusion

In 1911, Hutchins and Harrison pleaded with the middle-class women then struggling to advance the interests of their sex, not to confuse their own situation with that of female employees in factories and shops. They warned that to treat the situation of the female industrial worker as in no significant way different from her professional counterpart is not only theoretically inadequate, it amounts to a subordination of the needs of the female industrial worker to those of the employers and the female members of the labour aristocracy employed in sedentary occupations.

> It was true that the woman with her living to earn had her grievance in being restricted to the one overcrowded profession or teaching; it was equally true that the well-off woman of leisure had hers in being denied an outlet for her energies, or restricted to the uninspiring and mediocre ideals of her own class; numbers of intelligent but half-educated girls

have rightly enough recoiled from spending their best years in idleness or in unavailing efforts at "doing good" a la Lady Bountiful. The mistake that some of them have made is in transferring their own grievance to a class whose troubles are little known and less understood by them; in supposing that while they pined to spend themselves in some "intolerable toil of thought", Mary Brown or Jane Smith should also pine to spend herself in fourteen hours a day washing or ironing (Hutchins and Harrison 1966, p.184).

In introducing the National Standard for Manual Handling, Worksafe and the anti-protectionist alliance elected to ignore this plea. They did so when they chose to reject the policy advocated by the Australian Council of Trade Unions, the women workers they represented and feminists such feminists as Bacchi. Worksafe et al and elected instead to accept that women industrial workers should be the ones who would have to pay the required price for the formal enhancement of women's right of access to manual occupations. The price of this 'reform' was the undermining of the legal protection these workers received from the state. This was an undermining introduced by professionals who will not be expected to undertake manual labour. Indeed, Worksafe did not even bother to survey women employees in factories and shops to determine whether these individuals wished to have the 16 kilogram limit repealed. This was despite the fact that their trade union representatives were bitterly opposed to this proposal. In short, the decision to abandon the legal protection enjoyed by women industrial workers was made by employers and professionals in the face of clear opposition from the workers' organisations most directly involved and without any substantial attempt to ascertain the opinions of the women most likely to be affected.

The introduction of the National Standard for Manual Handling is a classic example of those middle-class policies against which the Webbs struggled in the late nineteenth century. What this experience suggests is that claims by individuals who would reform protective labour legislation, that they wish only to eliminate the sexist elements in these laws and would never countenance the undermining of the well-being of their working class counterparts to attain this objective, must be met with at least some degree of scepticism. Labour and women studies analysts need to return to the tradition pioneered by the Webb and the Fabian Women's Group. In other words, the arguments of all participants in the debate over sex-specific labour laws must be analysed rigorously. If this is not done those who remove protection from women workers will have to share some of the responsibility for any undermining of their health and safety that may result.

7 Fabianism and Marxism: Sociology and Political Economy

Peter Beilharz

Those committed to the history of ideas have long viewed Bolshevism as a particular form of Marxism which came, after 1917, to dominate socialist movements around the world. Analysts such as Wright (1986) make this point when they insist on speaking of socialisms, plural, as a normal condition or fact. Social democracy in Germany is one repressed tradition; Fabianism is another (Beilharz 1991). In this paper I endeavour to disinter Fabianism via political economy. For just as socialisms have been compulsorily homogenised into authorised genera, so has Fabianism been compacted and subjected to caricature. Those new to the field-or not so new-could be forgiven for thinking that the Fabians were a sect, whereas they were in fact a circle. One need only think of its leading figures-the Webbs, Cole, Shaw, Wells-to realise how different Fabianism's thinkers are. The focus in this paper is on the Webbs, and this raises another question, regarding the reception of their thought. The Webbs themselves have been caricatured to intellectual death, portrayed variously as heartless administrators, philistines, liberal Stalinists-'two typewriters clicking as one' - and so on. The lack of neat union between leading Fabian thinkers is nowhere more evident than here, for this image of the Webbs was largely fuelled by Wells' own personally vindictive book of 1911 *The New Machiavelli* (Wells 1985). More, the reception of Fabianism as an intellectual tradition is complicated by its own historical transformation across the period, say, from 1890 to 1950. The difficult and frequently ignored fact of the matter is that Fabianism begins as a municipal and local tradition, yet it finally liquidates into the Beveridge Plan and the Attlee Government (Fabian Society, 1942/3). Fabianism becomes an administrative tradition, but it is not always as narrow a tradition as Crowley (1987) suggests. As earlier writers like McBriar (1962 pp.149-55) have argued, there is a vague reliance of Fabianism on utilitarianism, but with all the ambiguity that the term actually connotes.

In the case of the Webbs, the emphasis is on the qualified view of John Stuart Mill-better Socrates dissatisfied than a pig satisfied rather than on the calculus of Jeremy Bentham. In different terms, as Britain (1982) indicates in the title of his leading study, there is no substantive contradiction in the apparently oxymoronic juxtaposition of the words *Fabianism and Culture*. As those who read the texts themselves discover, Beatrice Webb's sociology in *My Apprenticeship* is both cultural and romantic, while certain unpublished documents in the Passfield Papers make it clear that even Sidney Webb's motivation to reform was in the first place religious, rather than instrumental or administrative in nature (Webb n.d.).

Lifting the Calumnies

Beyond these specific problems of interpretation there are the larger problems of the construction of English sociology itself. It is one issue that the Fabians themselves have been cast as elitist social engineers and theoretical blueprinters whose visions were mechanical, where, say, Morris's in *News From Nowhere* were still and idyllic. A more serious problem with specific reference to native political economy is that like other local traditions, Fabianism has been cast as insignificant because unscientific. This charge rests essentially upon a trick of definition, that which finds its Marxist origin in the section of *The Communist Manifesto* where Marx and Engels implicitly establish a qualitative chasm between socialisms utopian and scientific - theirs, and ours as it were. The argument of Marx and Engels here both denies their own, vital utopian impulse and at the same time fetishises their monopoly claim to scientificity.

Throughout the 1950s Fabianism evidently declined. The major thinkers had died, or aged. The key text of the fifties was Crosland's *The Future of Socialism,* an important work which nevertheless in some ways paved the path for the boyishly technocratic enthusiasms which were to follow, with Wilson. But into the sixties, leading younger radicals were prepared already to deny their own, local traditions and to lay the practical preconditions of the strategy of theoretical importation for which *New Left Review* later became justly famous. Having informed the English that they had no real social theorists to speak of, Anderson extended the judgment to Fabianism as a warped and obsolete political tradition.

> No more poisoned legacy could have been left the working-class movement. Complacent confusion of influence with power, bovine

> admiration for bureaucracy, ill-concealed contempt for equality, bottomless philistinism-all the characteristic narrowness of the Webbs and their associates became imprinted on the dominant ideology of the Labour Party (Anderson 1965, p.37).

Anderson's views of the condition of English sociology have been ably contested, among others by Collini (1978) and Goldman (1987). His views of the Fabians have been less dexterously tackled by critics, perhaps because of the overwhelmingly administrative tenor of much twentieth century English sociology (Abrams 1968). Yet those who read Carlyle cannot help but be struck by the borrowings taken by Marx and Engels, which now return to us in the Marxisant synthesis of another capable but marginalised social critic, Jeremy Seabrook; and those who read Titmuss, for example, or T.H. Marshall, cannot but be struck by the theoretical presence of motifs from Mauss and Maine in their thinking.

There is, in short, a rich ethnic legacy here, and this in both, related fields of sociology and socialism alike. Foxwell made this point well and clearly some time before Anderson's intervention, in his Introduction to Menger's *The Right to the Whole Produce of Labour*. Foxwell's marginal précis, that useful convention designed to aid the Victorian reader, itself already flags the message: 'Undeserved neglect of the English socialists'. Foxwell elaborates:

> It must be evident from this brief survey of the writings of six principal English socialists [Godwin, Charles Hall, William Thompson, Gray, Hodgskin and Bray], that the body of doctrine they advanced was of such a character as to deserve the serious attention of all who were concerned with social philosophy (Menger 1889).

As Menger observed, this 'almost complete ignorance of English and French Socialism, especially of the older period, has contributed not a little to the disproportionate esteem which the writings of Marx and Rodbertus now enjoy in Germany' (Menger 1889, p.cxv; Claeys 1987).

Sociology and Political Economy

Early sociology, notwithstanding its obsession with organism and evolution, also took unto itself concern with the traditional concerns of philosophy. What was the good society? What was the good citizen? The retrospectively astonishing fact about its orientation, however, is that sociology tended, from the beginning, to subsume the political category of citizenship to the economic category of productivity. The hegemony of political economy within sociology here is striking, for arguments about citizenship in terms of civic virtue now gave way to claims about those who did and those who did not contribute to the material common wealth. The good citizen was he who had his shoulder to the wheel of national economic life, or who piloted the juggernaut from above. One key figure here was Colquhoun, who published with his *Treatise on the Wealth, Power and Resources of the British Empire* (1814) a celebrated table which claimed to demonstrate which citizens were really productive and which were not (Menger 1889, p.xlii). Thus there emerged the theoretical distinction between productive and unproductive labour which, in different forms, has plagued sociology ever since. Fabians and Marxists (and others) henceforth took to their respective theoretical barricades armed with different definitions of real producers and superfluous parasites.

Menger and Foxwell were among those able to recognise the significance of this shift. Menger's own study is a significant work in the history of ideas, only it is weak, ironically, in its explanation of the contribution of Marx. Menger credits especial significance to Godwin and to William Thompson; Marx, according to Menger, actually plundered Thompson (Menger 1889, p.101). Marxism, however, becomes dominant into the twentieth century under the star of the October Revolution, Marxism turned then into catechism, Dialectical and Historical Materialism, forces and relations of production and even more significant in socialist pedagogy, blackboarded theorems concerning the extraction of hours of unpaid labour from workers (Macintyre 1980; Marxist Study Courses 1934). Menger had suggested that there were two main labour responses to capitalism in terms of political economy some argued for the right to labour, or subsistence, while others argued for the right to the whole produce of labour. The labour theory of value supplanted physiocracy as a new, one-factor explanation of the production of wealth. Here there is a direct connection between classical political economy and Marx. For the Marx of the *1859 Preface* (1970) the key to the anatomy of civil society is not to be found in civil society but elsewhere-in political economy. Political economy became the skeleton key to the understanding of society, and, within it, the labour theory of value was the inner secret of the capitalist accumulation process. The class of the momentarily meek, which would inherit the earth, was that engaged in real, material, productive labour.

Marx described his theory as scientific, in the German sense of *Wissenschaft*, the connotations of which were closer to those of the systematicity aspired to by Hegel's *Logic* than to the positivism of Comte or English empiricism. Yet part of Marx's appeal to English speakers was very plainly this claim to scientificity. Marxism was true, therefore useful. The millenarian element in the labour movement often read this as 'true, therefore inevitable' when it came to making sense of the more apocalyptic claims of Marx in the penultimate chapter of *Capital* Volume One. The Fabians, in this scenario, would have to be wrong, for they were not armed with science. They did not subscribe to the labour theory of value. They associated work in general with productivity, rather than factory labour in particular. But too frequently the critical sense is also given that the Fabians must surely have been simply ignorant of the labour theory of value, for if they had known it they would surely have believed it, as it was true. Little wonder that the Fabians were rarely taken seriously by more scientific minds - they were not only philistines, they were also idiots.

Fabian Political Economy

The situation, in fact, is rather different. That the Fabians were not philistines has been amply demonstrated by Britain (1982). When it comes to political economy the fact is that the Fabians knew Marxism, and rejected the labour theory of value. That Cole knew Marx has never seriously been in doubt (Cole 1934; Wright 1979). But this in itself is little help, for Cole was also the most conspicuously Marxiant of Fabians. Cole, like most significant English socialists, was heavily influenced by Ruskin. Ruskin was also, however, an influence on the Webbs, not least of all because he anticipates the argument that, contrary to the claims of Marxism, consumption actually determines production, because consumers determine or at least influence production through exercising choice. Ruskin thus opens up the issue of cheap as shoddy, shoddy consumer demand legitimating sweatshop conditions, a theme which then resurfaces in the work of the Webbs (Thompson 1988, p.164).

I have argued elsewhere that the dominant motifs in the sociology of the Webbs are not those of Spencer or of Bentham, so much as those of Durkheim (Beilharz 1991, chap.3). Their attachment to socialism was firmer than that of Weber, but they also possess some affinities with Weber's marginalism. Their flavour, however, is of course English, and finds its political economic inspiration in the stream that runs from Ruskin to Alfred Marshall. Yet they did know Marx. The story is told of Shaw that his early London habits included reading Wagner and *Capital* together in the British Museum - at the same time. Whether this usage is contrived or not, the Webbs, true to character, each took on the task of reading Marx with single-minded earnestness. Documents held in the Passfield Papers at the London School of Economics make it clear that Sidney and Beatrice both read and analysed Marx (Potter 1886; Webb 1886). This is especially evident in Beatrice's case, for her notes show that she understood even the notoriously difficult opening of *Capital,* the argument about commodities which generations of readers have avoided, preferring rather to shift directly onto the concrete sociology of the factory which is the core of Marx's great work.

Beatrice Potter spelled out the implications of Fabian political economy in her 1891 book, *The Co-operative Movement in Great Britain* (Potter 1920). Here she drew directly on Marshall's *Principles of Economics,* having already considered and rejected Marx's own particular political economy. She quoted with approval from Marshall:

> It is sometimes said that traders do not produce; that while the cabinet-maker produces furniture, the furniture dealer merely sells what is already produced. They both produce utilities, and neither of them can do more; the furniture dealer moves and re-arranges matter so as to make it more serviceable than it was before, the carpenter does nothing more. The sailor or the railway man who carries coal above ground produces it just as much as the miner who carries it underground. The dealer in fish helps to move on fish from where it was comparatively little use, and the fisherman does no more ... (Potter 1920, p.111).

The logic of Marshall's case, adopted here by Potter, has implications in political economy and in sociology alike. Even though the Webbs despised the social parasitism of aristocrats and ne'er-do-wells, they did not privilege the labour theory of value or accept its concomitant, narrow conception of productive labour. They did not identify the 'useful' class with those functions classified by Marxism as real, because productive labour. Theirs was a multi-class utopia, as distinct to the proletarian utopia imagined, for example, by Lenin in *State and Revolution* (Beilharz 1991, chap. 2; Polan 1984). Thus while the Webbs developed an elaborate and differentiated picture of the good society, for example in *A Socialist Constitution for the Commonwealth of Great Britain,* they agreed with that stream identified by Menger for whom socialism concerned rights to subsistence, whereas Marx somewhat ambiguously defended both the right of the labourer to the whole produce- for this is the logical consequences of the labour theory of value-and contested it, in *Critique of the Gotha Program,* where need replaces right.

Marxism and Political Economy

This correspondence is notable from the perspective of our own times, after the massive and bitter debates within Marxist scholarship of the seventies regarding the divisive issue of productive and unproductive labour. Leading figures such as Poulantzas and Erik Wright spilled gallons of ink fusing sociology and political economy in order to answer the question, who were the real workers? The premise, typically, was that only real proletarians were real people, those who both performed real, productive labour and those who would, in the last instance, be really revolutionary (Poulantzas 1975; E. Wright 1986; Beilharz 1987b). One later contributor to this debate, Carchedi, introduced into the discussion a forgotten theme from Marx's work, the idea that the productive labourer was not the individual but the class or the collective labourer (Carchedi 1977). This theme had been registered rather earlier, by A.D. Lindsay in his lamentably overlooked study of 1925, *Karl Marx's Capital*. Lindsay actually knew Marx better than later leading Marxists did. He indicated this fundamental ambiguity or shift in Marx's project, that the labour theory of value began, in Marx's hands, as a theory of individual right, but became one of collective responsibility (Lindsay 1931, pp.106-7). Although Lindsay did not refer to Menger, the logic of his argument was that Marx shifted from an earlier position, where labour had the right to the whole of its product, closer to the different sense that workers deserved a just wage, ie a wage deducted from the total social capital which, under socialism, would be the property of the working class as collective labourer.

Lindsay's interpretation of Marx is a radical reading, for he overlooks the logical consequence of the labour theory of value, that in each hour of labour performed by the worker but unremunerated consists a kind of legal theft or appropriation of labour by capital. Lindsay commences rather from the premise that socialism is, for Marx, essentially the democratisation of the collective labourer (Lindsay 1931, pp.105). The concept of the collective labourer, however, collides with that of the labour theory of value, as the latter is in its essence individualistic. The labour theory of value seeks to unravel from a complicated system of production and exchange the separate contribution of each separate individual, to discern what each severally creates and reward him or her accordingly. But if production is really social, then it ought be the case that the collective labourer produces value; the role of the individual is beyond rational calculation, and is rather a social fact (Lindsay 1931, p.106). In short, then, Lindsay proposes that Marx begins from the

Lockean premise in political economy that individual labours fertilise property - and radicalises his own theory by socialising it, but without ever finally breaking with the idea of labour as an individual value conferring individual right. A similar argument has been put by Heller in her discussion of Marx in *A Theory of History*. As Heller points out, the Marx of *Critique of the Gotha Program* protested against the primitive conception that the equivalent of the worker's work could be reimbursed to him or her in any society. The main question is not whether the equivalent is reimbursed, but rather the question of who disposes of the social wealth which does not flow back into the private consumption of the producers. If the disposal of wealth is in the hands of the associated producers themselves, the created wealth is no longer alienated, it is not capital, not private property so much as it is 'social wealth' (Heller 1982, p.272). Heller thus effectively reinforces Lindsay's point, that the logic of the collective labourer overrides that of the individualistic theory of surplus value, but textually it is held in tension within the earlier class analysis which remains a fundament of Marx's life-work. Meanwhile, the popular reception of Marx in the labour movement fails to pick up the latter thread at all.

Given that the concept of the collective labourer has exercised so little influence within the subsequent Marxist traditions, it is unsurprising that the Fabian alternative to the labour theory of value was also given such short shrift by communists throughout the twentieth century. For the Fabians had a broad, rather than narrow conception of social productivity or, better, social function-they understood that citizens under socialism have rights and duties, but did not subsume the figure of the citizen to that of the proletarian. They, too, may have favoured 'useful citizens' over parasites', but they did not simply draw their morality from the economic definition of what might constitute productive labour. This was the political premise beneath their sociological refusal of the proletarian utopia, whether Bolshevik or Syndicalist, and the premise of their multi-class conception of socialism (Webb and Webb 1912).

Certainly there were those who took the issue of citizenship more seriously than the Webbs, who did subsume citizenship not to class, but to function. Bernstein, for example, arguably took the citizenship principle more seriously than the Fabians (Bernstein 1965; Meyer 1977; Heiman and Meyer 1978). Yet ironically, Bernstein still persisted, as he revised Marxism, in viewing his position as Marxist. Bernstein may have fellow-travelled with the Fabian Society during his enforced English sojourn, but so did the more radical Korsch. All the while, though, Bernstein imagined that certain Marxian principles were self-evident. Thus Sidney Webb wrote to Bernstein, in 1895, in response to Bernstein's kindly Marxist counsel:

> all that I can say is that I am a worse heretic than you suppose. You are charitable enough to imagine that I err [on the labour theory of value] only through Ignorance - alas, it is more than that. Incredible as it may seem I have long since read the books suggested, and yet stick to my opinion (Webb 1895).

Bernstein, like Marx, was thus also ambiguous, if in a different way, for while he defended certain Marxian positions in political economy he also refused to derive ethics from economics or to privilege sociologically the idea of productivity. His was thus less a Fabian turn, in the strict sense, than a Kantian turn (Hirsch 1977; Bottomore and Goode 1978).

Fabianism: A Middle Class Sociology?

Whatever the limits of Fabianism, then, it avoided the perilous path of class ethics - proletariat good, bourgeoisie bad, which came to its critical apogee in Marxist thinkers such as Trotsky (Beilharz 1987a). The root of this problem analytically, however, is in Marx's work and not in the history of subsequent Marxism. For Marx's own project, commencing in *The Paris Manuscripts* as the critique of political economy, eventually became subsumed, by *Capital,* to political economy itself. This, of course, is part of a much broader modern trend towards the dominance of economy within thinking and within everyday life. Fabianism, by comparison, attacks parasitism in a sense continuous with Cobbett and Carlyle, opposing the functionless whether aristocrat or pauper, but refusing to differentiate firmly between working class and middle class in terms of putative distinctions between those who labour productively and those who do not.

My purpose here, however, has not been to replace Marxism with Fabianism, but rather to disinter Fabianism as a legitimate alternative to Marxism, both in terms of its political economy and its sociology. The Webbs in particular, achieved a sophisticated and balanced defence of socialism in terms of the so-called mixed economy. They envisaged, most notably in *A Constitution for the Socialist Commonwealth of Great Britain,* a complex and differentiated economy combining various property forms, private, public, state, local, municipal and co-operative (Webb and Webb 1920). Their views of parliament and the role of specialists leave something to be desired, for it is certainly true that the

Webbs' proclivity was to read politics as administration. Their political views suffered, but less than their views of political economy, at the expense of the dominant trends in social development enthused for by Saint Simon but increasingly horrific to those who still remain inspired by the classical conception of politics.

But if Marx opts at least partially for an interest-based, economistic politics through privileging the proletariat socially, do not the Fabians then merely commit a middle-class version of this sociological sin? Shaw was happy to rail against the useless rich, while making exceptions for those active and publicly oriented citizens such as Ruskin and the Webbs (and himself) who drew on capital or rent but remained committed to the conduct of public service (Shaw 1937, chap. 18). The Webbs, for their part, did at least to some small extent share Morris's hope that all work ought be good work, taking a clear distance from Carlyle's gospel of work. They knew full well that the middle class betrayed its purpose. As Sidney wrote in a paper entitled 'The Economic Function of the Middle Class' (1885), the middle class had been parasitic, had failed to live up to the mission which civilisation had ascribed it. The middle class had a function, to manage, invent, to follow the vocations; it saved, and it increased culture. Yet the middle classes were careless, presuming interest from capital or rent as a right while the working class and their children expired young, and lived without pleasure. Thus the middle class claim of right to interest without service ought be called by its name - it was simply robbery (Webb 1885, p.32). While the Webbs' sociology can be read as the utopia of professionals, it can also be viewed as a pluralistic, multi-class image of socialism which eschews the problems of syndicalism and Bolshevism alike (Perkin 1969, 1989). The very least that can be said is that Fabianism is a substantive tradition, one containing a number of significant thinkers and theories which, whatever their faults or anachronisms, ought be taken more seriously than it has been allowed to for a very long time. The end of communism's hegemony might thus serve less as a sense of loss than as a reminder of the local and enduring traditions which it first had to displace and which can now be regained.

Bibliography

ACTU, (1986), Executive Decision, ACTU Executive Meeting, 20 August, (mimeo), Melbourne.

ACTU, (1987), Decision of ACTU Executive Meeting, 7 March, Manual Handling (mimeo), Melbourne.

ACTU-VTHC Occupational Health and Safety Unit, (1984), 'ACTU Health and Safety Preferred Standard: Manual Handling', *Health and Safety Bulletin*, No. 40.

ACTU-VTHC Occupational Health and Safety Unit (1984), 'Women and Occupational Health', Discussion paper, *Health and Safety Bulletin*, No. 41, September.

Alexander, S., (1913), 'Introduction', in P. Reeves (ed.), *Round About a Pound a Week*, London: Virago.

Anonymous, (1919), 'Women in Industry', *New Statesman*, May 17, pp157-158.

Ashe, B. E., (1986), 'Manual Handling: A Brief Outline of the Issues Involved', *Journal of Occupational Health and Safety*, Vol.2, pp. 143-147.

Ayoub, M.M., (1992), 'Problems and Solutions in Manual Materials Handling: the State of the Art', *Ergonomics*. Vol. 35, pp.713-28.

Bacchi, C. L., (1990), *Same Difference: Feminism and Sexual Difference*, Allen & Unwin, Sydney.

Baer, J. A., (1978), *The Chains of Protection*, McGraw-Hill, Westport.

Baker, E. F., (1964), *Technology and Women at Work*, Columbia University Press, New York.

Barrett, B. and James, P., (1988), 'Safe Systems: Past, Present-and Future?', *Industrial Law Journal*, Vol. 17, pp.26-40.

Beals, Polly A., (1989), *Fabian Feminism: Gender, Politics and Culture in London, 1880-1930*, unpublished PhD thesis, New Brunswick: Rutgers The State University of New Jersey

Beilharz, P., 1992, (ed.), *Social Theory*, Sydney.

Beilharz, P., (1994), *Postmodern Socialism*, Melbourne.

Beilharz, P., (1994), *Transforming Labour: Labour Tradition and the Labour Decade in Australia*, Cambridge University Press, Cambridge

Bennett, L., (1984), 'Legal Intervention and the Female Workforce: The Australian Conciliation and Arbitration Court 1907-1921', *International Journal of the Sociology of Law*, Vol. 12, pp.37-58.

Berch, B., (1975), *Industrialisation and Working Women in the 19th Century: England, France and the United States*, unpublished PhD dissertation, University of Wisconsin, Madison.

Bishop, P., Cureton, K. and Collins, M., (1987), 'Sex Difference in Muscular Strength in Equally-Trained Men and Women', *Ergonomics, Vol.*30, pp. 675-87.

Black, N., (1989), *Social Feminism*, Ithaca, Cornell University Press.

Blagg, H. and Wilson, C., (1912), *Women and Prisons*, Fabian Tract No. 163, London, Fabian Society.

Braithwaite, John and Grabosky, Peter, (1985), *Occupational Health and Safety Enforcement in Australia*, Australian Institute of Criminology, Canberra.

Breen, N., (1988), 'Shedding Light on Women's Work and Wages: Consequences of Protective Legislation', PhD thesis, New School for Social Research, New York.

Britain, Ian, (1982), *Fabianism and Culture*, Cambridge University Press, Cambridge.

Brooks, A. (1988), 'Rethinking Occupational Health and Safety Legislation', *Journal of Industrial Relations, Vol. 30*, pp.347-362.

Buckland, D., (1985), 'A National Employer Perspective' in B. Creighton and N. Gunningham (eds), *The Industrial Relations of Occupational Health and Safety*, Croom Helm, Sydney, pp. 171-178.

Buckle, P. W., Stubbs, D. A., Randle, P. M., and Nicholson, A. S., (1992), 'Limitations in the application of Materials Handling Guidelines'. *Ergonomics*, Vol. 35, pp 95-154.

Bulley, A.A. and Whitlley, M., (1894), *Women's Work*, London, Methuen and Co.

Burvill, Chris, (1985), 'Women and Protective Legislation', *Refractory Girl,* Vol.28, pp. 27-9.

Business Regulation Review Unit (1987), *Review of Business Regulation, Safe Manual Handling*, Information Paper No.8, Commonwealth of Australia, AGPS, Canberra.

Caine, Barbara, (1982), 'Beatrice Webb and the "Women Question"', *History Workshop Journal*, no. 14, pp 23-43.

Caine, B., (1992), *Victorian Feminists,* Oxford University Press, Oxford.

'Candida', (1914a), 'Women as Law Makers', *New Statesman*, May 23, pp 204-206.

'Candida', (1914b), 'The Refusal of Maternity', *New Statesman*, June 20, pp 334-336.

'Candida', (1914c), 'The Right to Motherhood', *New Statesman*, June 27, pp 365-367.

Carson, W. G., (1989), 'Occupational Health and Safety: A Political Economy Perspective', *Labour and Industry,* Vol. 2 pp.301-16.

Castoriadis, C., (1987), *The Imaginary Institution of Society,* Cambridge University Press, Cambridge.

Celentano, E. J. and Noy, L., (1981), *Development of Occupational Physical Selection Standards for Canadian Forces Trades: Performance Considerations*, Department of National Defence, Canada.

Celentano, E. J., Nottrodt, J. W. and Saunders, P. L., (1984), 'The Relationship between Size, Strength and Task Demands', *Ergonomics,* Vol. 27, pp.481-488.

Chaffin, D. B., (1974), 'Human Strength Capability and Low-Back Pain', *Journal of Occupational Medicine* Vol. 16, pp. 248-54.

166 *The Webbs, Fabianism and Feminism*

Chaffin, D. B., Gary, D., Herrin and Monroe Keyserling, W., (1978), 'Pre-employment Strength Test. An Updated Position', *Journal of Occupational Medicine,* Vol.20, pp. 403-408.

Cole, G.D.H., (1920), *Guild Socialism Re-stated,* Longman, London.

Cole, M., (1945), *Beatrice Webb*, Longman, London.

Collette, C., (1989), *For Labour and for Women: The Women's League, 1906-1918,* Manchester University Press, Manchester.

Commission of the European Communities, (1987), 'Protective Legislation for Women in the Member States of the European Community', Communication COM(87) 105 final, Brussels, available from CEC, Yarralumla, ACT.

Confederation of Australian Industry (n.d.), *Manual Handling,* Position paper, Melbourne.

Connell, H. B., (1980), 'Special Protective Legislation and Equality of Employment Opportunity for Women in Australia', *International Labour Review,* Vol. 119, pp.199-121.

Coote, A., (1975), *Women Factory Workers. The Case Against Repealing the Protective Laws,* National Council for Civil Liberties, London.

Courtney, W.L., (1913), 'The Awakening of Women: New Types of Subordinate Women Brain Workers', Special Supplement, *New Statesman*, November 1, pp.xvii-xix.

Coussins, Jean, (1979), *The Shift Work Swindle*, National Council for Civil Liberties, London.

Coyle, Angela, (1980), 'The Protection Racket', *Feminist Review,* Vol. 4, pp 1-12.

Creighton, B. and Gunningham, N. (eds), (1985), *The Industrial Relations of Occupational Health and Safety,* Croom Helm, Sydney.

Creighton, W. B. (1979), *Working Women and the Law,* Mansell Publishing, London.

Crompton, K. C., (1985), 'An Employers' Peak Council View', in B. Creighton and N. Gunningham (eds), *The Industrial Relations of Occupational Health and Safety,* Croom Helm, Sydney, pp. 179-89.

Crowley, B.L., (1987), *The Self, The Individual and the Community,* Oxford University Press, Oxford.

Curthoys, A., (1988), *For and Against Feminism-A Personal Journey into Feminist Theory and History*, Allen & Unwin, Sydney.

Dawson, S., Willman, P., Clinton, A. and Bamford, M. (1988), *Safety at Work: the Limits of Self, Regulation,* Cambridge University Press, Cambridge.

Deakin, S., (1990), 'Equality Under a Market Order: The Employment Act 1989', *Industrial Law Journal, Vol.*19, pp.1-19.

Department of Industrial Relations, *(1990),International Labour Conference 76th Session 1989:Australian Delegation Report,* Australian Government Publishing Service, Canberra.

Drake, B., (1915), 'Women's Wages', *New Statesman*, October 9, p.13.

Draper, H. and Lipow, A., (1976), 'Marxist Women Versus Bourgeois Feminists', in R. Miliband and J. Saville (eds), *The Socialist Register 1976*, Merlin Press, London,

Eldred, C. A., (1975), *A Report of a Study of Women Training or Working in Outside Plant Craft Jobs in the Bell System*, Westat, Inc., Rockville, Marylands.

Emmett, E. A., (1992), 'Raising the Standard of Occupational Health and Safety in Australia', *Transactions of Mechanical Engineering*, Vol. 17, pp.75-9.

Employers Federation of New South Wales, (1987a), 'Employers Federation Submission re: Manual Handling', in *Employers' Review* Vol.59 n.5.

Employers Federation of New South Wales, (1987b), 'Manual Handling', *Employers' Review*, Vol. 59 n. 21.

Employers Federation of New South Wales, (1987c), 'National Occupational Health and Safety Commission Manual Handling', *Employers' Review* Vol. 59 n. 4, supplement.

Employers Federation of New South Wales, (1987d), 'Occupational Health and Safety Update', *Employers' Review*, Vol. 59 n 1).

Employers Federation of New South Wales, (1987e), 'Occupational Health and Safety Update', *Employers Review*, Vol. 59 n. 14.

Employers' Federation of New south Wales, (1987f), 'Occupational Health and Safety Update', *Employers' Review*, Vol. 59 n. 15.

Employers Federation of New South Wales, (1987g), 'Occupational Health and Safety Update', *Employers' Review*, Vol. 59 n. 16.

Employers Federation of New South Wales, (1987h), *Submission to the National Occupational Health and Safety Commission on Safe Manual Handling* , n. 17, March.

Executive Committee, Fabian Women's Group (1911), *Three Years Work of the Women's Group*, Fabian Society, London.

Executive Committee, Fabian Women's Group, minutes of meetings and sub-committee meetings 1908-1919.

Fabian News. London, 1906-1926.

Fabian Society, (1895), *Sweating: Its Cause and Remedy*, Fabian Tract no. 50, Fabian Society, London.

Fabian Women's Group, 1908 - 1919, minutes of Members' Meetings, Business Meetings and Public Meetings.

Fabian Women's Group, (1915), *The War; Women; and Unemployment*, Fabian Tract no. 178, London, Fabian Society.

Fawcett, M., (1913), 'The Awakening of Women: The Remedy of Political Emancipation', Special Supplement, *New Statesman*, November 1, pp. viii-x.

Fawcett, M.G., (1892), 'Mr. Sidney Webb's Article on Women's Wages', *Economic Journal*, Vol. 2, March.

Fawcett, M.G., (1889), 'The Appeal Against Female Suffrage: A Reply', *The Nineteenth Century*, 26, July.

Fawcett, M.G., (1904), Review of 'Women in the Printing Trades: A Sociological Study', *Economic Journal*, Vol.14, June.

Fawcett, M.G., (1913), 'The Remedy of Political Emancipation', in Webb, B. (ed.), 'Special Supplement on the Awakening of Women', *The New Statesman*, Vol. 2, November.

Fawcett, M.G., (1917), 'The Position of Women in Economic Life', in W.H. Dawson (ed.), *After-War problems*, London, Allen and Unwin.

Federated Miscellaneous Workers Union, (1987), Manual Handling Policy, Sydney, (mimeo).

Feitshans, I. L. (1992), 'The Law of Reproductive Health Protection and the work place after the Johnson Controls', *Health Values*, Vol. 16, pp.29-38.

Feurer, R., (1988), 'The Meaning of "Sisterhood": The British Women's Movement and Protective Legislation, 1870-1900'. *Victorian Studies*, Vol. 31, pp. 233-60.

Giddens, A., 1984, *The Constitution of Society*, Cambridge University Press, Cambridge.

Gilman, C.P., (1913), 'The Awakening of Women: The Arrested Development of Women', Special Supplement, *New Statesman*, November 1, pp. v-vi.

Goldin, C., (1988), 'Maximum Hours Legislation and Female Employment: A Reassessment'. *Journal of Political Economy*, Vol. 96, pp. 189-205.

Goldin, C., (1990), *Understanding the Gender Gap: An Economic History of American Women*, Oxford University Press, New York.

Greenburg, R.P., (1987), *Fabian Couples, Feminist Issues*, Garland Publishing, New York.

Gunningham, N., (1985), 'Workplace Safety and the Law', in B. Creighton and N. Gunningham (eds), *The Industrial Relations of Occupational Health and Safety*, Croom Helm, Sydney, pp. 18-53.

Hall, Philippa, (1989), 'Equal Employment Opportunity and Occupational Health-Interface or Barrier?', Paper prepared and delivered at Worksafe seminar, Melbourne, November.

Hamilton, Mary Agnes, (1932), *Sidney and Beatrice Webb. A Study in Contemporary Biography*, Sampson Low, Marston and Co., London.

Harrison, B., (1989), '"Some of Them Gets Lead Poisoned": Occupational Lead Exposure in Women, 1880-1914', *Social History of Medicine*, Vol. 2, pp 171-95.

Heather-Bigg, A. (1894), 'The Wife's Contribution to Family Income', *Economic Journal*, Vol. 4, March.

Heitlinger, A., (1979), *Women and State Socialism: Sex Inequality in the Soviet Union and Czechoslovakia*, Macmillan, London.

Hill, A. C., (1979), 'Protection of Women Workers and the Courts: A Legal Case History', *Feminist Studies* Vol. 5, pp.247-273.

Hirst, P. (ed.), (1989), *The Pluralist Theory of the State*, Routledge, London.

Holton, S.S., (1986), *Feminism and Democracy: Women's Suffrage and Reform Politics in Britain, 1900-1918*, Cambridge University Press, Cambridge.

Hopkins, A. and Parnel, N., (1984), 'Why Coal Mine Safety Regulations are Not Enforced', in Roman Tomasic (ed.), *Business Regulation in Australia*, CCH, Sydney.

Howie, A., (1988), *Manual Handling, Public Information Pamphlet*, Number 15, Committee for Economic Development of Australia.

Hutchins, B. L., and Harrison, A., (1966), *A History of Factory Legislation*, 3rd edition reprinted, Frank I Cass & Company Limited, London.

Hutchins, B.L., (1913), 'The Awakening of Women: The Capitalist *versus* the Home', Special Supplement, *New Statesman*, November 1, pp. xiii-xvi.

Hutchins, B.L., (1915), *Women in Modern Industry*, G. Bell and Sons, Ltd, London.

Hutchins, B.L. and Harrison, A., (1966), *A History of Factory Legislation*, 3rd edition reprinted, Frank Cass & Company Ltd, London.

International Labour Office, (1932), *Women's Work Under Labour Law: A Survey of Protective Legislation*, ILO, Geneva.

International Labour Office, (1934), 'Women's Work', in *Occupation and Health: Encyclopaedia of Hygiene, Pathology and Social Welfare*, Vol. 2, ILO, Geneva.

James, P., (1992), 'Reforming British Health and Safety Law: A Framework for Discussion', *Industrial Law Journal*, Vol. 21, pp.83-104.

Joint Committee, Fabian Women's Group and Fabian Research Department, minutes of meetings 1915-1917.

Kearney, R., (1988), *The Wake of Imagination*, London.

Kessler-Harris, A., (1982), *Out to Work: A History of Wage-Earning Women in the United States*, Oxford University Press, Oxford.

Kirkby, D., (1987), '"The Wage-Earning Woman and the State": The National Women's Trade Union League and Protective Labor Legislation, 1903-1923', *Labor History* Vol. 28, pp.54-74.

Klein, V., (1971), *The Feminine Character: History of an Ideology*, Routledge, London.

Landes, E. M., (1980), 'The Effect of State Maximum-Hours Laws on the Employment of Women in 1920', *Journal of Political Economy* Vol. 88, pp. 476-494.

Larsson, T., (1988), 'What does Experience Tell Us?', paper presented at the International Occupational Health and Safety Convention, Melbourne.

Lehrer, S., (1985), 'Protective Labor Legislation for Women', *Review of Radical Political Economics*, Vol. 17, pp.187-200.

Lemons, J. S., (1973), *The Woman Citizen: Social Feminism in the 1920s*, University of Illinois Press, Urbana.

Lewis, J. and Davies, C., (1991), 'Protective Legislation in Britain, 1870-1990: Equality, Difference and their Implications for Women', *Policy and Politics*, Vol. 19, pp. 13-25.

Lewis, Jane, (1983), 'Re-reading Beatrice Webb's Diary', *History Workshop Journal*, Issue 16, pp 143-146.

Lewis, C.E. and Lewis, M,A., (1977), 'The Potential Impact of Sexual Equality on Health', *New England Journal of Medicine,* Vol. 29, pp. 863-869.

M.A., (1914), *The Economic Foundations of the Women's Movement,* Fabian Tract No.175, Fabian Society, London.

MacKenzie, Norman and Jeanne (eds), (1984), *The Diary of Beatrice Webb: 'The Power to Alter* Things' (Vol. 3, 1905-1924). London: Virago in Association with the London School of Economics and Political Science

Magora, A., (1970), 'Investigation of the Relation Between Low-Back Pain and Occupation: Age, Sex, Community, Education and other Factors', *Industrial Medical Surgery,* Vol. 39, pp. 376-382.

Malker, B. and Zamore, K. (1987), 'Yrkesrelaterade belastningssjukdomar 1980-1983-en oversikt', *in Lakartidningen,* Vol. 84, pp. 376-382.

Mason, C., (1993), 'Anti-Discrimination Law and Occupational Health and Safety', in D. Blackmur, D. Fingleton and D. Akers, *Women's Occupational Health and Safety: The Unmet Needs,* School of Management, Human Resources and Industrial Relations, Queensland University of Technology, Brisbane.

McBriar, A.M., (1962), *Fabian Socialism and English Politics, 1884-1918,* Cambridge University Press, Cambridge.

McGregor, O.R.,(1955), 'The Social Position of Women in England, 1850-1914: A Bibliography', *The British Journal of Sociology,* Vol. 6, March.

Metcalfe, A.E., (1919), *"At Last": Conclusion of "Woman's Effort",* B.H. Blackwell, Oxford.

Milkman, R. (1980), 'Organising the Sexual Division of Labor: Historical Perspective of 'Women's Work' and the American Labor Movement', *Socialist Review,* January-February, pp. 95-144.

Miller, A., Treiman, R., Donald, J., Cain, P. S. and Roos, P. A., (1980), *Work, Jobs and Occupations: A Critical Review of the 'Dictionary of Occupational Titles',* National Academy Press, Washington DC.

Morgenstern, F., (1991), 'From the Particular to the General: Limitations to the Judicial Treatment of Social Policy Issues, *International Labour Review,* Vol. 130, pp. 559-567.

Morris, J., (1986), *Women Workers and the Sweated Trades: The Origins of Minimum Wage Legislation,* Gower Publishing Co. Ltd., London.

Muggridge, K. and Adam, R., (1967), *Beatrice Webb: A Life, 1858-1943,* Secker and Warburg, London.

Mullen, E., (1990), 'Influences on Health and Safety Practices in New Zealand Enterprises', in Griffin Gerard (ed.), *Current Research in Industrial Relations,* AIRAANZ, Melbourne.

Musil, R., (1995), *The Man Without Qualities,* Knopf, New York.

Nakanishi, T., (1983), 'Equality or Protection, Protective Legislation for Women in Japan', *International Labour Review,* Vol. 122, pp. 609-621.

National Council for Civil Liberties, Rights for Women Unit (1987), *Legislating for Change: NCCL's Response to the Equal Opportunities Commission's Consultative Document on Sex Discrimination Laws,* NCCL, London.

National Council for Civil Liberties, Rights for Women Unit, (1988), *Restriction or Protection? NCCL's Response to the Department of Employment's Consultative Document on the Restrictions on the Employment of Young People and the Removal of Sex Discrimination in Legislation*, NCCL, London.

National Council for Civil Liberties, Women's Rights Unit, (1986), *NCCL Briefing: Sex Discrimination Bill*, NCCL, London.

National Occupational Health and Safety Commission, (1987), *Safe Manual Handling: Discussion Paper and Draft Code of Practice,* Australian Government Publishing Service, Canberra.

National Occupational health and Safety Commission, (1990), *National Standard for Manual Handling and National Code of Practice for Manual Handling*, Australian Government Publishing Service, Canberra.

Neary, J., (1991), 'Women's Occupational Health and Safety-Development and Repercussions', Paper presented to Women, Management and Industrial Relations Conference, Sydney.

New South Wales Anti-Discrimination Board, (1984), *Protective Legislation at Work: A Case Study of the 'Weight Limit' on Manual Handling,* NSW Anti-Discrimination Board, Sydney.

New South Wales, Legislative Assembly, 1926, *Debates,* Vol. 107, pp. 636-678.

Nichols, T., (1986), 'Industrial Injuries in British Manufacturing in the 1980s-A Commentary on Wright's Article', *Sociological Review,* Vol. 34, pp. 290-306.

Nichols, T., (1990), 'Industrial Safety in Britain and the 1974 Health and Safety at Work Act: the Case of Manufacturing', *International Journal of the Sociology of Law,* Vol. 18, pp. 317-342.

Nielsen, R., (1980), 'Special Protective Legislation for Women in the Nordic Countries', *International Labour Review,* Vol. 119, pp. 39-49.

Nolan, B.E., (1988), *The Political Theory of Beatrice Webb*, AMS Press, New York.

O'Donnell, C., (1984), *The Basis of the Bargain: Gender, Schooling and Jobs*, George Allen & Unwin, Sydney.

O'Donnell, C. and Hall, P., (1988), *Getting Equal-Labour Market Regulation and Women's Work*, Allen & Unwin, Sydney.

Pease, E.R., (1963), *The History of the Fabian Society*, Frank Cass and Co. Ltd, London.

Potter, B., (1891), *The Co-operative Movement in Great Britain,* Swann Sonnenschein & Co. London.

Pugh, P. (1984), *Educate, Agitate, Organise: 100 Years of Fabian Socialism*, Methuen, London.

Pujol, M.A., (1992), *Feminism and Anti-feminism in Early Economic Thought*, Edward Elgar, Aldershot.

Quinlan, M. and Bohle, P., (1991), *Managing Occupational Health and Safety in Australia A Multidisciplinary Approach*, Macmillan, Melbourne.

Radice, Lisanne, (1984), *Beatrice and Sidney Webb: Fabian Socialists,* MacMillan, London.

Rathbone, E., (1917), 'The Remuneration of Women's Services', *Economic Journal,* Vol. 27.

Reeves, M.P., (1912), *Family Life on a Pound a Week,* Fabian Tract No. 162, Fabian Society, London.

Reeves, M.P., (1913), *Round About a Pound a Week,* Virago, London.

Reiss, E., (1934), *Rights and Duties of Englishwomen: A Study in Law and Public Opinion,* Sherratt and Hughes, Manchester.

Report of the Commonwealth and States of Australia Second Conference on Industrial Hygiene, 19 August 1924, Government Printery, Melbourne.

Review Committee to the Minister of Industrial Relations, (1990), *Review of Occupational Health and Safely,* AGPS, Canberra.

Romito, P. and Saurel-Cubizolies, M., (1992), 'Fair Law, Unfair Practices? Benefiting from Protective Legislation for Pregnant Workers in Italy and France', *Social Science and Medicine,* Vol.35, pp.1485-1495.

Rover, C., (1967), *Women's Suffrage and Party Politics in Britain, 1866-1914,* Routledge and Kegan Paul, London.

Royal Commission on Labour, (1894), Part 1, *British Parliamentary Papers,* (Cmd.-7421).

Rubinstein, D., (1986), *Before the Suffragettes: Women's Emancipation in the 1890's,* The Harvester Press, Sussex.

Rundell, J., (eds), (1992), *Between Totalitarianism and Postmodernity,* Boston.

Scutt, J. A., (1990), *Women and the Law: Commentary and Materials,* The Law Book Company Limited, Sydney.

Select Committee of the House of Lords on the Sweating System, (1887-88), *British Parliamentary Papers,* (Cmd. 5513).

Seymour-Jones, C., (1992), *Beatrice Webb: Woman of Conflict,* Allison and Busby, London.

Shop Distributive and Allied Employees Association, (1987), *Submission to Victorian Occupational Health and Safety Commission on Draft Regulations and Code of Practice for Manual Handling,* Melbourne.

Smart, W., (1895), *Studies in Economics,* MacMillan and Co, London.

Smith, E. (1915), *Wage-Earning Women and their Dependants,* Fabian Society, London.

Swedish Commission on Working Conditions, (1990), A *Survey of Job's Posing Special Risks to Health,* Ministry of Health, Stockholm.

Tawney, R.H., (nd), *Beatrice Webb, 1858-1943,* Geoffrey Cumberlege, London.

Thornton, M., (1990), *The Liberal Promise: Anti-Discrimination Legislation in Australia,* Oxford University Press, Melbourne.

Tombs, S., (1990), 'Industrial Injuries in British Manufacturing Industry', *Sociological Review,* Vol. 38, pp-324-343.

United States Department of Labor Women's Bureau, (1928), Bulletin of Women's Bureau, No.65, *The Effects of Labor Legislation on the*

Employment Opportunities of Women, United States Printing Office, Washington

War Cabinet Committee, (1919), 'Women in Industry', *British Parliamentary Papers*, (Cmd. 135).

Ward, J. S., (1978), 'Sex Discrimination is Essential in Industry', *Journal of Occupational Medicine,* Vol. 20, pp. 594-596.

Ward, Mrs H., (1901), 'Preface', in Webb, B. (ed.), *The Case for the Factory Acts*, Grant Richards, London.

Wardle, M. G. and Gloss, D. S., (1980), 'Women's Capacities to Perform Strenuous Work', *Women and Health* Vol. 5, Summer, pp. 5-15.

Webb (Potter), B., (1888a), 'Pages from a Work-Girl's Diary', *The Nineteenth Century*, Vol. 24 p.89.

Webb (Potter), B., (1888b), 'East London Labour', *The Nineteenth Century*, Vol. 24 p.138.

Webb (Potter), B., (1890), 'The Lords and the Sweating System', *The Nineteenth Century*, 27 (90).

Webb (Potter), B., (1902a), 'The Docks', in Booth, Charles (ed.), *Life and Labour of the People in London*, MacMillan and Co., London.

Webb (Potter), B., (1902b), 'The Tailoring Trade', in Booth, Charles (ed.), *Life and Labour of the People in London*, MacMillan and Co., London.

Webb (Potter), B., (1902c), 'The Jewish Community (East London)', in Booth, Charles (ed.), *Life and Labour of the People in London*, MacMillan and Co., London.

Webb, B., (1914b), 'Special Supplement on Women in Industry: Introduction'., *New Statesman*, February 21, pp.i-ii.

Webb, B., (1894), 'The Failure of the Labour Commission', *The Nineteenth Century*, Vol. 30, p.26.

Webb, B., (1896), *Women and the Factory Acts*, Fabian Tract No. 67, Fabian Society, London.

Webb, B., (1898), 'How to do Away with the Sweating System', in S. and B. Webb (eds.), *Problems of Modern Industry*, Longman's, London.

Webb, B., (1913), 'The Awakening of Women: Introduction', Special Supplement, *New Statesman*, November 1, pp. iii-iv.

Webb, B., (1914a), 'Voteless Women and Social Revolution', *New Statesman*, February 14, pp. 584-586.

Webb, B., (1914c), 'Motherhood and Citizenship', *New Statesman*, May 16, pp. 10-11.

Webb, B., (1914d), 'Personal Rights and the Woman's Movement', *New Statesman*, July 4, pp. 395-7; July 11, pp. 428-430; July 18, pp. 461-463; July 25, pp. 493-494; August 1, pp. 525-527.

Webb, B., (1915a), 'Special Supplement on English Teachers and their Professional Organisation', *New Statesman*, September 25, 1-22; October 2, 1-24.

Webb, B., (1915b), 'The "Pull" on Our Incomes', *New Statesman*, December 4, p. 204.

174 *The Webbs, Fabianism and Feminism*

Webb, B., (1918), 'Preface', in A.E. Metcalfe (ed.), *Woman: A Citizen*, Allen and Unwin, London.
Webb, B., (1919a), *The Wages of Men and Women: Should they be Equal?*, Fabian Society, London.
Webb, B., (1919b), 'The End of the Poor Law', in Various Women Writers (eds), *Women and the Labour Party*, Headley Bros. Ltd, London.
Webb, B., (1948), Drake, B. and Cole, M.I. (eds), *Our Partnership*, Longmans, Green and Co, London.
Webb, B., (1978), *The Letters of Sidney and Beatrice Webb, Vol. III 1912-1947*, Cambridge University Press, Cambridge.
Webb, B., (1978a), MacKenzie, N. (ed.), *The Letters of Sidney and Beatrice Webb, vol. I 1873-1892*, Cambridge University Press, Cambridge.
Webb, B., (1978b), (Mackenzie, N. (ed.)), *The Letters of Sidney and Beatrice Webb, vol. II 1892-1912*, Cambridge University Press, Cambridge.
Webb, B., (1978c), (MacKenzie, N. (ed.)), *The Letters of Sidney and Beatrice Webb, vol. III 1912-1947*, Cambridge: Cambridge University Press.
Webb, B., (1978d), *The Diary of Beatrice Webb (Microfiche), 1873-1943*, Chadwyck-Healey Ltd, Cambridge.
Webb, B., (1982), (MacKenzie, N. and J. (eds)), *The Diary of Beatrice Webb, vol. 1, 1873-1892*, Virago Press Ltd, Cambridge.
Webb, B., (1983), (Mackenzie, N. and J. (eds)), *The Diary of Beatrice Webb, vol. 2 1892-1905*, Virago Press, London.
Webb, B., (1984), (MacKenzie, N. and J. (eds)), *The Diary of Beatrice Webb, vol. 3, 1905-1924*, London: Virago.
Webb, B., (1985), (Mackenzie, N. and J. (eds)), *The Diary of Beatrice Webb, vol. 4, 1924-1943*, Virago, London.
Webb, B., (ed.) (1913), 'Special Supplement on the Awakening of Women', *The New Statesman*, Vol.2, November.
Webb, B. and Ward, Mrs. H. (eds) (1901), *The Case for the Factory Acts*, Grant Richards, London.
Webb, B., 1919, *The Wages of Men and Women: Should they be Equal?*, Fabian Society, London.
Webb, B., Hutchins, B. L. and the Fabian Society (eds) (1909), *Socialism and the National Minimum*, Fabian Society, London.
Webb, Beatrice, (1914a), 'Introduction', Special Supplement on Women in Industry, *The New Statesman*, February, n.21. pp. i-ii.
Webb, Beatrice, (1914b) 'Motherhood and Citizenship', Special Supplement on Motherhood and the State, *The New Statesman*, May 16. Pp. 10-11.
Webb, Beatrice, (1948) *Our Partnership* (edited by Barbara Drake and Margaret I. Cole). Longmans, Green and Co, London.
Webb, S., 'The Ethics of Existence', *Passfield Papers* VI, 4, p. 20.
Webb, S., 'The Economic Function of the Middle Class', *Passfield Papers*, VI, 20.
Webb, S., 'The Existence of Evil', Passfield Papers VI, 1, p. 35.
Webb, S., (1891), 'The Alleged Differences in the Wages Paid to Men and to Women for Similar Work', *Economic Journal*, Vol.1, December.

Webb, S. 1989, 'Historic', in G.B. Shaw, *Fabian Essays,* London, Walter Scott.

Webb, S., (1909), 'The Economic Aspects of Poor Law Reform', *English Review,* Vol.3.

Webb, S., (1912), 'The Economic Theory of a Legal Minimum Wage', *The Journal of Political Economy,* Vol. 20, p.10.

Webb, S., (1914), *The War and the Workers,* Fabian Tract No. 176, Fabian Society, London.

Webb, S., 1916, *Towards Social Democracy,* Fabian Society London.

Webb, S. and B., (1897), *Industrial Democracy,* Longman's, London.

Webb, S. and B., (1898), *Problems of Modern Industry,* Longman's, London.

Webb, S. and B., (1909), *The Break-Up of the Poor Law: Being Part One of the Poor Law Commission,* Longman's, London.

Webb, S. and B., (1910), *The State and the Doctor,* Longman's, London.

Webb, S. and B., (1911), *The History of Trade Unionism,* Longman's, London.

Webb, S. and B., (1911), *The Prevention of Destitution,* Longman's, London.

Webb, S. and B., (1923), *The Decay of Capitalist Civilisation,* Fabian Society, London.

Webb, S. and B., (1937), *Soviet Communism: A New Civilisation,* Victor Gollancz Ltd, London.

Webb, S. and Freeman, A., (1916), *When Peace Comes - The Way of Industrial Reconstruction,* Fabian Tract No. 181, Fabian Society, London.

Webb, S. and B., (1920), *A Constitution for the Socialist Commonwealth of Great Britain,* London,

Webbs, S. and B., (1912), *What Syndicalism Means: An Examination of the Origin and Motives of the Movement with an Analysis of its Proposals for the Control of Industry,* supplement to *The Crusade,* August 1912.

Wentworth, E., (1979), 'Protective Labour Legislation for Women and the (Victorian) Equal Opportunity Act, 1977', Research Project 730-413, November.

Wills, D., (1987), 'Safe Manual Handling-A New Regulatory Playground?', *Business Council Bulletin,* No. 34, May 1987, pp 8-19.

Wilson, G. K. and Sapiro, V., (1985), 'Occupational Safety and Health as a Women's Policy Issue', in V. Sapiro (ed.), *Women, Biology, and Public Policy,* Sage Publications, Beverly Hills, pp. 137-56.

Woolf, L., (1949), 'Political Thought and the Webbs', in M. Cole (ed.), *The Webbs and their Work,* F. Muller, London.

Woolfe, A. D., (1973), 'Robens Report-the Wrong Approach?' *Industrial Law Journal,* Vol. 2, pp. 88-95.

WorkCover Authority of New South Wales, (1992), *Back Injuries: Workers Compensation Statistics New South Wales 1990/91,* WorkCover Authority, Sydney.

Worksafe, (1986), *Safe Manual Handling: Discussion Paper and Draft, Code of Practice,* National Occupational Health and Safety Commission, AGPS, Canberra.

Worksafe, (1990), *National Approach to Occupational Health and Safety for Women Workers*, National Occupational Health and Safety Commission, AGPS, Canberra.

Worksafe, (1990), *National Standard for Manual Handling and National Code of Practice for Manual Handling*, National Occupational Health and Safety Commission, AGPS, Canberra.

Wright, A., (1979), *G.D.H. Cole and Socialist Democracy,* Oxford University Press, Oxford.

Wright, A., (1980) *Socialisms* Oxford University Press, Oxford.